MY MINDS AND I

MY

MINDS

AND

I

A DEVELOPMENT OF

SPIRITUAL PSYCHOLOGY

essential to

**PHYSICAL AND MENTAL
WELL-BEING**

CRANE

THE CHRISTOPHER PUBLISHING HOUSE
BOSTON, U.S.A.

DEDICATED TO

DR. ALBERT CLARKE WYCKOFF

Professor Emeritus of Spiritual Psychology

at the

Biblical Seminary in New York

For he has been a beacon in this stormy work

TABLE OF CONTENTS

LIST OF ILLUSTRATIONS

PREFACE

"My Minds and I", as a title, places emphasis upon a new and reassuring appreciation of the human brain. In an age bursting with startling advances, each must struggle for its place in the sun. The struggle in this case might properly begin with a scholarly review of the contributions of the last half century which have molded our beliefs. It would have to trace a drifting apart of worthy specialists, engrossed in their studies, and the efforts apparent in current literature to achieve harmony and correlation of their divergent trends. The controversies involved will become a matter of record in due course, however.

The plan adopted here, is rather to begin with first hand experience with disaster and follow the unfolding of the roles of the specific mental functions. In so doing, the ebb and flow of controversy over the dual roles of bodies influencing Self-determination, cannot be avoided. The evidence of research and of the experience which tests its validity, will develop in the process. The mental bodies which claim consideration in the duality problem are these:

The cerebral cortex, in its dazzling contributions to the rise and accomplishment of man, has rather blinded us to its limitations and shortcomings. Neurotic thinking habits which it acquires in these troubled times are the detrimental influences.

In a protected inner area of the brain, a mental body which is beyond the conscious range has been receiving growing recognition. Its heritage of drives and of advisory evaluating standards is of primary importance in currently evolving spiritual psychology.

Between these two is a small mental body which emerges in the light of various threads of evidence, as the seat of consciousness, of self. Here "I" at my command post may wisely contribute to mental harmony, or foolishly foster the subconscious thinking routines which breed internal conflict between the other two. Their proper appreciation permits greater assurance in constructive and creative thinking.

In the maturing tussles of personality and conscience, men ultimately face up to the problem of their higher responsibility. Is self alone enough, or is the mutual responsibility of man and God, which religion teaches, an essential reality? Can the intellectual integrity

13

of science heal the conflicting aspects of our current concepts? A quarter century ago a little hunch-backed wizard in the intangible field of electrical power, foresaw that it could be done. The flame which he fanned has been fed by so many in the intervening years that their findings are bearing results. It is none too soon, for the mental burden of our expanding wisdom is taking too heavy a toll.

Acknowledgments of contributing guidance in this report should be made to many men, for a project which seeks to coordinate new information from divergent fields requires much help. We are indebted to many friends, strangers and even unfriendly personalities for their contributions. Medical men, educators, men of religion and others have gone out of their way to furnish material or introductions or to consider and criticize portions of the undertaking. A number of acknowledgments are made in the course of reporting the undertaking. Among those who should be particularly recognized here are Dr. A. C. Wyckoff, Freeman Crampton, Dr. F. C. Symonds, the late Dr. John C. Schroeder, Dr. R. K. Compton, Dr. John B. Barker, W. P. Blake, Dr. Seward Hiltner, W. S. Saddler, Dr. F. R. Sanborn and Howard U. Herrick.

My sweet wife and son suffered with me through the years of increasing nervous fatigue. They helped, though not always approving, through the subseqeunt years of the project.

To all of these and many more, we extend grateful appreciation.

—E. V. Crane

FOREWORD

By Dr. Richard Kenneth Compton

"My Minds and I" is a valuable contribution to the field of human engineering. The author has drawn from science, medical research, philosophy, religion and personal experience; coordinating the material from these sources into a systemic order for understanding personality as a functioning whole.

The author has used the eclectic method of securing the scientific facts, theoretical hypotheses and spiritual truths which constitute the subject matter of his book. He develops the utility of intuition and inspiration in addition to reflective thought in the process of coordinating the materials from his multiple sources.

Any individual who makes a studious effort to understand himself, who seeks to develop a well-integrated personality and to acquire the resulting peace of mind, will find "My Minds and I" of inestimable value.

I feel justified in describing this work as a must in the library of all those who practice in human engineering; physicians, clergymen, educators, clinicians, psychologists, sociologists and personnel administrators, and those interested in the humanities for the purposes of their own thinking.

—R. K. Compton

My Minds and I

I

THE VALLEY OF THE SHADOW

Robbie's office was no different that evening in '44 than on an endless number of prior evenings. The little waiting room was full of people, some with sniffles, others looking tired or worried, some whom I had seen before. How a doctor could spend so much time patiently, with each one, when so many were waiting, was always hard for me to fathom. Waiting itself was very disturbing to me, such a waste of time, when the pressure was so great to get things done. Not enough time for anything!

When I went in, we checked over all the old routine, blood pressure abnormally low, digestion bad, nervous, tired, but still no signs of infection or ulcers. It would almost have seemed a relief to find something seriously wrong to blame it on.

The trouble had been building up gradually over a number of years under pressure of war time urgency until sedative pills were a regular diet, and that obviously wasn't good. The fact that many other men were in the same trouble was cold comfort. Robbie kidded me that I was getting older (46) and couldn't expect too much, but it was more serious than that. He had had me visit a variety of specialists for X-rays, blood counts, dietary studies and what-not. He brushed aside psycho-analysis for the facts were clear enough. This enumeration of one's ills is something to cut as short as possible and is only of interest insofar as it sheds light upon the nervous system and the undertaking of a major project.

That fateful evening Robbie wound up his review of the examinations made and the treatments given by saying, "I think we have tried everything we know how to do. I guess it is up to you."

It was months before the full impact of that statement was clear. Perhaps he should have said, "It is up to you and God" to imply that there was still some place to turn. Perhaps he meant it as a shock with the thought that shock might be desirable.

In any case, I had put my faith in him and had done everything he advised. Bringing work home at night had been discontinued.

Bed time and diets had been adjusted. A long rest was discouraged because Robbie said I would just take my worries away with me, in which, at that time, he was probably right. At any rate, the faith and confidence with respect to my health was left without support when Robbie "stepped out from under." It would have been very easy to give up at that point.

To turn to God for strength and help was hardly to be expected. The metropolitan atmosphere was not conducive to it. One went to church from time to time but one never discussed things religious. Even a quarter century back in the days at Yale, chapel was not "required" and was ill-attended. From one year's end to the next, there was no intimation that any force higher than man existed or could exist, and in the sheltered atmosphere of the faculty, there seemed no need to go farther. The Divinity School kept strictly to itself.

The point of view was rather summed up a little later by a young doctor of philosophy entrusted with large religious responsibility in the Council of Churches in New York. He was recently returned from specialization in the philosophical and psychological problems of religion and wrote me objecting to the idea that anything might exist in man above consciousness and referring to the "great *myths* of the Christian faith whose meaning is not altogether dependent on their literal truth in a scientific kind of sense." He had drawn from his advance work at Chicago Theological Seminary that "all theological truth is symbolic, analogical, and *mythological*."

An engineering professor lumped all things beyond the powers of man under the term metaphysics, and his derogatory tone clearly implied that no scientifically trained man would devote serious consideration to such a field. Great things were being accomplished technically. The atmosphere of the time and the place was thoroughly impregnated with the adequacy of man.

Yet there was I, abandoned as it were, by the trained specialists to whom I had turned in need. "Nothing wrong", physically, but yet worried, nervous, weakened by increasingly bad digestion and kept on the job only by ever-increasing resort to sedatives which masked but did not correct the trouble.

The question of whether to give up the job, which seemed to be getting me down, was settled shortly. I was ignominiously fired. Twenty-four years of successful engineering experience with one concern. I had written a sarcastic response to a caustic criticism which seemed unwarranted to me.

A cartoon appeared at about that time showing a man reporting to "the little woman" that he had been dismissed. His response to her query was: "The boss and I had indigestion the same day." The wry humor of it struck me. It was a sign of the times perhaps that such things were common enough to reach the comic strips.

The works manager who dismissed me was himself dismissed two months later, for such small comfort as there was in that. A procession of others followed him. Nervous tension was high in many places. Some men went to hospitals with nervous breakdowns. The production manager died of a heart attack on his way in one morning. So did one of the doctors, one who had advised me to take it easy. Fortunately, the war was to be over in a few months.

Weeks elapsed, unsatisfactory weeks filled with a variety of things, efforts to find a new connection without really wanting it, a few consulting jobs and a lecture or two, a try in search of a change of thought. We went to Skytop in January, a "Winter Wonderland" with plenty of snow and subzero cold. Young Ed was with us for several days between exams. We skated and had a try at skiing and walked in the snow. It was bleak and beautiful and the young honeymoon couples gave me something of the atmosphere of hope in spite of the service uniforms on most of the grooms.

One job prospect looked particularly attractive and I tried very hard to achieve it, making a number of trips south and west. Probably I was asking too much but that did not seem to be a problem. On the day of signing the contract, the price was cut sharply and I refused to accept. It was a great disappointment and when I phoned the news back to Eleanor, I could not help crying. Unseemly emotion at my age.

A few days later the lightning struck. Sharp pains in the right eye and across the top of the head. One doctor sent me to another and the verdict: "Acute glaucoma." All I had ever heard of glaucoma was blindness and it frightened me. I cried again and shivered with cold until they got me to the hospital and piled on blankets. The eye did not react to treatment and its capacity for vision practically disappeared. An operation would be necessary.

Eleanor arose to the necessities with a courage which I would not have believed her mild sweetness could muster. Wives have a way of doing that when it becomes necessary. She made all the decisions and arrangements. The prospect of expense in getting the best surgeon available did not stop her. I was moved to the Presbyterian Medical Center in uptown Manhattan even though that meant over three hours travel each day for her to be with me.

When the operation was over and found to be successful, I asked the surgeon, "What was it? Eye strain?" He was an international authority and should know. "No," he answered without hesitation, "Just nerves." I was still in the same old predicament. Weight and blood pressure down. Thoroughly discouraged, but no solution. What is it about nerves, nervous tensions and fatigues that can strike so hard? What does one do about them?

II

THE LIGHT

As April of '45 wore on, it must have been a discouraging month for the family. The prospects were certainly not clear and I must have been rather a depressing sight. Home from the hospital, I just sat in the living room with no particular desire to violate the doctor's injunction to be quiet. The black mask which covered my eyes had a small peep hole for the left one to see out when it chose.

One eye normally does most of the work and in my case it had been the right eye. Perhaps it was during the period of the mask that the left one decided it must take over and set out to adjust itself to the task.

Dr. Magary came to call shortly after the return from the hospital. It was the first time that an official pastoral call upon us had been in order. I was glad to see him for I hold him in highest regard. We passed the time of day and said the things which are appropriate but somehow never got down to the discovery of my lost confidence and the question of what might be done about it.

The fact remained that the "breadwinner" was still out of a job. Instead of an urge to get out and get one, there was just a glum conviction that it was no use. But something would have to be done and just sitting around the house and taking pills and vitamins didn't seem to be the answer. Such dregs of health as remained would only continue to dribble away. I had recited my troubles and symptoms over to myself until they would play off automatically, and the scare advertising of the drug vendors on the radio was a nightmare to me. What to do?

The idea of a "rest" still appealed to me even though I had done so little for months and had taken that expensive two weeks at Skytop in the Poconos. But it should be a long quiet rest. There was a fortunate possibility. Father had a house in the hills north of Saratoga. Summer after summer the family had gathered there but it had gradually been falling into disuse and should be disposed of.

I decided that three months there might be the answer for I had always loved the woods and open country. There would be grass to cut, wood to chop and repairs to make and we would be very much alone. For Eleanor, it would mean cooking to which she was not particularly accustomed, for we had always been fortunate enough to have a good cook. But she was game and the plans were made.

When the doctor made a final examination of the eye, pronounced me fit for travel, with precautions, we set out. The car was loaded with clothes for cold weather and warm. The trip was only a little way over two hundred miles but the orders were to make two days of it which turned out to be fortunate.

The first day it rained all the way. Eleanor drove and I tried to keep my eyes closed for the movement of the rain and the windshield wipers bothered them. We stopped for the night at the lovely old hotel at Red Hook. Father had hold me stories of his father stopping there. I had a bit of a scare for when I tried to nap before supper the left eye began to ache, though not as severely as the time of the attack in the right one. The long distance operator finally located Dr. Dunnington at his home. He was very nice about it and reassured me and prescribed a sedative which was all that was necessary.

Early the next afternoon we reached the house and began the homely task of airing out, making beds and laying in supplies. Mice had been into some things but generally it was in good order. There was enough dry wood in for the stove and fireplace for a few days.

Spring had come early that year and trees were out in full leaf. The grassy lane which led back to the house was blanketed with violets, both white and purple ones.

I began by sitting in a rocker on the porch and watching the birds. I noted down twenty-nine varieties while we were there. Then I began picking up the chores which needed doing, eventually even patching and painting the kitchen walls and ceiling.

Quite early we initiated the habit of walking the half mile over the hill to the village for mail and food. Greenfield Center is a quiet village with a general store and thirty or more houses scattered along the state road and one cross road. Returning one day, we surprised a doe browsing in the meadow below the house. She looked up and examined us critically for several minutes it seemed before bounding easily away into the woods.

Early in May, a freak turn of the weather precipitated a ten inch snow fall, after two months of early spring. The heavy snow on the fully leaved branches brought down many of them and much of the area was without power and phones for a couple of days. The little electric pump with which the water system had been modernized was not running of course. I donned two pairs of heavy wool sox in lieu of boots and tramped out to the well near the barns for drinking water. We were pleased that the barn area still boasted "open plumbing, openly arrived at," which was convenient in the emergency.

Our nearest neighbors, the Robinsons, had a place bordering ours to the south and west. Ralph had eight or ten cows at that time and had installed a milking machine for he was getting along in years and four sons had long since married and moved away. Obviously the power failure would give him a large task of milking by hand, so I conceived the noble idea of going over to give him a hand at it. I trudged over and found him at work. He grinned a bit at the idea but pointed out a pail and stool.

It was sort of a silly feeling but my efforts were so ill-rewarded that I soon gave up. Either the skill I thought I had at fifteen was now a lost art, or the Jersey was unwilling to favor a stranger. Ralph had a wonderful sense of humor and he glossed it over to save me embarrassment. The incident was probably good for some chuckles later.

As time moved along, my store of energy began to rebuild along with the wood pile. The sawing and chopping chore became more fun. Clearly I must be rested and yet the old sensations of discomfort at the stomach and at the throat continued to persist. The doctor in Brooklyn had told Eleanor confidentially one day that I was neurotic and she let it out. Neither of us knew at that time what the term meant but it sounded serious. Later I was to learn that these annoying sensations were the fatigue reports or complaints of nerve centers at the pancreas near the stomach and the thyroid at the throat, evidence of nervous hypertension.

But now that I was rested, why should they persist? Were they chronic now and what did that mean? I had yet to learn that a neurosis is just a fear or worry or other undesirable habit of thinking which is perpetuated by repetition until it becomes a habitual response like a nervous twitch. Hence, it returns again and again long after the need for it has disappeared. The continuance of the uncomfortable sensations were therefore disquieting. Worry begat worry. I recited my troubles to myself with appropriate self-sympathy and thereby established them the more firmly in my mind. What a vicious circle.

One evening late in May, Ralph's wife came over to call. We had known her for years, for her efforts had supplied many of our summer needs for eggs, butter and fresh garden things. This evening she sat very erect in a straight chair in the little living room, like a person with a mission. We conversed for a while about the health and activities of various members of our respective families, and then she came to the point. She knew of course, that I was up there in the hills trying to recuperate and she had gotten up her courage to try to help. She opened her purse and took out a little blue paper covered booklet which she handed to me.

"I got this at a Baptist convention in New York last winter," she said, "and I wish you would read it."

I promised to do so, and did, the next morning. It was a story of George Washington Carver, the negro scientist whose work with peanuts and their products and with other southern crops brought him national recognition. It traced his life, his struggle for an education and his devotion to his work, to the people about him, and to his students. The account was interspersed with little stories of his faith and of the love which he would lavish upon a sick plant. It told of his frequent resort to God in prayers for help in his work and in the solution of the problems for which he became so noted.

I fear that my materialistic scientific training at Yale had left me with something of the same incredulous realism as the young theologian who majored in psychology and philosophy at Chicago. To be sure I was an ordained elder in a large Brooklyn church, but I could not recall having ever asked God about my engineering problems. To borrow an expression from my young son, "it was hard to chew" for a hard boiled engineer, that a highly successful scientist could go to God in prayer for the solution of his problems, and get answers upon which he could and did act.

Yet the clarity and conviction with which the story was written was strangely appealing. Perhaps the seriousness of my need to find an answer for myself made it more impressive.

The man with the conviction was Glenn Clark, professor of English at Malcalaster College in St. Paul. He proved to be one of those enlightened educators who see more than a circumscribed routine in their responsibility. Now as it were, he set out to share his enlightenment with me.

The day I read Clark's remarkable account of Carver, I sent for a book which he had entitled, "How to Find Health Through Prayer." How could a man write under such a title in the light of the twentieth century higher education? But he had, and having found no other answer I read it. He used no confusing technical terms but drew simple word pictures which passed the tests of common sense and experience. We do suffer for our own selfish sins and to a lesser extent perhaps for those of relatives and community about us. We do magnify and dwell upon our envies and hates and fears until quite literally we do make ourselves sick. We do need to learn good housekeeping in our thinking and to find a source of standards and reassurance and peace of mind. One might almost be annoyed to be reminded that Christ had given us these answers so long ago. But somehow, the barriers melted away which seemed to have been interposed by the education and thinking of the times.

Two other books of Glenn Clark's were ordered and read in hungry haste. "The Soul's Sincere Desire" led one away from the selfish and self-centered to the "High Places" where one might check objectives for worthiness and responsibility. Then in, "I Will Lift Up Mine Eyes," the attitude and power of prayer were borne home to me.

Now that I would review these books to refresh my memory, they are not to be found. Those first copies and others which replaced them have been loaned and given to others who needed them and there should have been more. Other men also have poured their souls into similar efforts but these were the ones which came to me when I needed them. They were the leaven which stirred the revision of a lifetime's thinking. I have often wondered why that flash of inspiration urged Ralph's wife to bring that booklet to me at that time.

Brushing out accumulated dust and cobwebs takes time even in one's mind. Sorting out accumulations and deciding what to tear up and throw away requires an effort. I spent considerable time upon my knees as prescribed and had little difficulty in identifying errors of the past which bothered my conscience.

Any report, if it is to be of value, should be as precise and factual as it can be made. The feeling persists in me that this should be the most accurate report I have ever been called upon to write. At this point, memory brings up a line of an old hymn, "as the rank and file of Christianity, we remind ourselves that we do not ask a special vision or a prophet's ecstasy." Quite so, and yet perhaps when the need arises and is met, we are inclined not to give proper acknowledgments.

Most of us have heard the old prescription for the solution of problems, "let's sleep on it." Few people who have problems to solve have not had the experience of awakening early to realize that their thoughts have clarified and a solution is taking shape.

The morning of July the sixth, was one of those, and the outstanding one for me. I awakened at about four with the first rays of the midsummer sun streaming into the bedroom. There was distinctly a new feeling of enthusiasm and confidence. I arose from my prayers with the conviction that the past was forgiven and behind me, the future was new and fresh and all things were possible. I dressed quietly and slipped out for a walk to think out the meaning of it.

Over the hill I walked, toward the rising sun and the little grave-yard on the next hill. The dew was fresh on the roadside flowers and the birds were singing their best, a time when God does seem to possess the world. Instead of stopping to rest at the village store, I turned along the slumbering street past garden flowers and a church, deserted in the combination of two small protestant flocks. Past the parson's house, he now served four churches, traveling west and north, about a twenty-five mile circuit for his four sermons. On up the state road and soon out into open country again, towards King's Station, the mail stop for Porter's Corners. A few cars of early workers were passing now and and one man almost insisted that I ride with him. Toward home again by a backroad. Five miles before breakfast seemed inconceivable, even if I had been much younger. But the exhilaration, the joy of being born again, starting afresh, and the concentration of thoughts and new plans lent a buoyance and an obliviousness to time. This morning writing of it, as many times since it happened, I have felt that exhilaration and surge of confidence.

One thing which had bothered my literal and material interpre-tation of the things of religion was the idea of miracles. Now it began to seem possible that the relationships of mind and body and soul might actually work together in a restorative manner. The "mir-acles" of the shrines of Saint Ann de Beaupré and of Lourdes in France had troubled me but now perhaps I could follow them. It is suffi-ciently miraculous that broken bones will knit and damaged joints will mend, but a complex attitude of mind, a sick unhealthy attitude (neurotic, said my doctor) favors the accident or other cause and then enlarges upon and emphasizes the debility until courage and confidence wane and the future is black indeed. Then a place which reminds one of God, a prayer, an example, a person whose assured faith is somehow contagious, a combination of circumstances pene-trate the gloom and give new and more potent meaning to the things Christ taught us. The lame miraculously hang up their canes and crutches and find that their will to walk is restored to them. The depressed and discouraged business man or engineer puts behind him his mental crutch, be it self-sympathy, sedatives or liquor, and sub-stitutes new enthusiasm for thoughts of suicide or collapse. In the twenty-third psalm we are reminded that God "restoreth my soul."

Yes, the restoration of confidence and courage and hope, of faith itself, *is* quite a miraculous experience.

We may charge off the circumstances which lead up to it as mere coincidence if we will. Many a young psychologist of this age would have us do so in his enthusiasm for the all encompassing competence of his new "science." And yet, we had just entertained at dinner three young people, seniors, of Syracuse University, who evidenced that confusion of thinking. They were guests of the local parson on a summer Christian study mission. Conversation at the table clearly indicated that they were in a dilemma whether to discard the teachings of religion or those of psychology, or to somehow resolve the apparent conflict. One of the girls impulsively confided the decision of her roommate at school who was majoring in psychology: "I've decided that it is foolish to go on living. I'm going to commit suicide."

I had never sunk to consideration of suicide though I was far from certain of survival after the doctor said there was nothing more he could do for me. The gray-gloom of New York's weekday Godless-ness was no help. But then Mrs. Robinson's faith brought me in touch with Glenn Clark's books. A chapter in one of them caught the attention of my desire for understanding, call it scientific or what you will. I had done quite a bit of reading along technical lines, and at the same time quite a bit of reading in philosophy, psychology and what-not, a vague groping for the behavior of the mind in this business of living.

In one of his books, Clark devoted part of a chapter to evidence which showed a tie between areas and functions of our nervous system on the one hand and the functions of character, the spiritual responsibilities, on the other. It was logical and acceptable in the light of my own experience. It gave the clue. Medical research, psychology, philosophy, religion were *not* in conflict. Erroneous interpretation here and there might give that impression, but there is a basic unity and it can be shown. If conflict in the minds of technically trained youngsters is to be cleared up, it must be done.

What could I contribute? Many other men must be working on such a problem and why should I? We hear of the "call" to preaching, to doctoring, to invention, research or art, and here it was face to face. I knew then that I had to do something about it and I wanted to. I've argued with that urge and excused the inadequacy of my progress for seven years at this writing but still it persists.

Was I competent to tackle it? It looked more like a searching and unifying project for a university, but if so, someone must "spark" it.

I was literate after a fashion, two degrees, but not a doctorate. I had done successful technical research in my unappealing speciality, cold flow of metals. I had taught, lectured and written, even a book. Engineers often have to do coordinating tasks in which they must seek pertinent data in many fields and I was no exception. But even these arguments left it a task which appeared almost impossible. At least I had one advantage. Surviving an experience with severe nervous fatigue gave me a first hand familiarity which was to prove valuable.

A plan took shape that morning. A friend had suggested that I join his research and consulting organization. That should provide a living and still permit freedom enough for study and writing. Perhaps the work could become a thesis at Columbia or Yale. But in the meantime, I must try to live it, to work it out in experience and to straighten out my thinking.

Years before when our son was little, I had converted the old carpenter shop near the barn to a sleeping quarters and sitting room apart from the family. Its old hand hewn timbers were still exposed. One could lie in bed and see light between the shingles but the roof didn't leak enough to bother about. The windows I had put in gave plenty of light.

It was utterly quiet but for the birds and bees, an ideal spot to write and then stretch out to rest and reflect. In fact it was here that an important step in thinking impressed itself upon me: Clearly one must consciously gather together the bits of facts and evidence which one would organize into a report. But having done so, continued conscious effort falls desolately short of putting the loose ends together into a satisfactory unity. Discouraged, I lay down to rest. Soon it became apparent that in those periods of relaxation, the more completely conscious effort was relaxed, the more effectively did organization take place and the resultant conception flash into the mind. The observation was useful enough of itself but later proved to be a checking point of considerable value to my understanding of my mind's behavior.

Letters were interspersed with project notes. The last couple of weeks at Greenfield flew by. The first consulting job was lined up. Underwood was designing a new typewriter and my experience in metal working should be useful. The association with the research and consulting organization was also assured. Correspondence was started with Columbia concerning study there. I was looking forward with real enthusiasm to getting back on the job!

What had wrought the change? William Brown, Professor of the Department of Mental Philosophy of Oxford wrote, "I have become more convinced than ever that religion is the most important thing in life and that it is essential to mental health." He might properly add that mental health is in turn essential in many respects to physical health. Spiritual, mental and physical health are closely allied. But how?

III

SEEK AND YE SHALL FIND

Christ's injunction to all of us to straighten out our own thinking has assumed a convincingly personal aspect. The first effort to summarize what I had learned so far, was put into a paper under that title in the fall of 1945. Dr. Magary examined it and permitted me to present it before the Session of our church:

The engineering habit, born of necessity, of coordinating available technical data and reasoning thence; with faith in the inviolability of the universal laws, points some interesting paths in mental usages.

Electrical, mechanical, chemical and electronic equivalents of elements of the body and mind, daily become more obvious. We are probably in a position to engineer a fairly complete man, less the capacity to grow and to rebuild. But with chemical functions, partial mentality and substitute materials, he would fill a large building, for our engineering is definitely crude in its imitations of God's creations.

The signal receiving system of the five senses, together with the translating, recording and responding portions of the conscious are fairly well explored. Subconscious control of certain functions, kept separated from the conscious, to keep them foolproof, is recognizable as good engineering practice. Electrical transmission characteristics of the interconnecting nerve system have been explored to some extent, as by encephalograms and cardiograms.

Analysis of the endocrine gland system progresses slowly. Apparently, however, the electrical transmission lines of the nervous system terminating at the ductless glands, send forth hormone messengers, which in electro-chemical terms, may be presumed to be ionized molecules. Combining data from medicine, psychology and philosophy with observations and experiences, this endocrine system becomes identified with what has been called the superconscious, a circuit which is beyond and, for many purposes, above the conscious level. In the case of the gonads, a definite two-way transmission of sex messages between mind and glands is obvious. A question and answer relationship in matters of courage and temper indicates the electrochemical advisory service of the adrenal glands. Fatigue signals are recognizable from the pancreas, the thyroid, the pituitary and possibly the thymus, aiding in checking their electro-mental functions.

The pancreas, at the solar plexus, acting electrically as a filter, functions selectively in digestive processes, and also clearly discriminates against our fears and worries in the mental circuit. When some visual or audio signal, received and transmitted to the (wire recorder) section of the brain stimulates a worry response, malstored amongst the useful habit and action sequences, the pancreas advises against it. If proper mental hygiene does not point out that fears are rubbish of the mind to be swept out, the pancreas expresses fatigue in feelings often misassociated with the stomach. If not relieved with rest and cleansing, it fails also in its overseeing of digestion, with the resultant sequence of diarrhea, ulcers and collapse.

The thyroid, suggests electrically a circuit breaker or shock absorber in the endocrine circuit. Its swelling under nervous tension and panic, and under prolonged perceptual study is a source of worry if not understood. Its medical function of initiating electrolytic combative measures through the bloodstream, against disease and infection, is presumably retarded by overexertion in the superconscious circuit.

The headaches which follow much effort to picture or visualize a new mechanism or design, appear to confirm the identity of the pituitary with the mind's eye, the imagination. Electrically it suggests the cathode tube of television in the mind's circuit. Its signals are faster than word signals, as light is faster than sound. We see a solution in a "flash", but require some time to crystallize it in words. One of its sections is also associated with the emotions.

In creative thinking, those who must reach solutions of greater or lesser import, beyond computation, record or experience, find that the answer does not come in conscious effort. It may take recognizable form at three or four the next morning or days later. Many "dreamed up" solutions have proven remarkably pat. That one cannot "sit in" consciously on this higher process of thought tends to vindicate the term superconscious.

The pineal gland is one which may temporarily elude us. The temptation, electrically, is to associate its function with radio. God seems to have anticipated man in every other invention, and there is evidence here too. Electrodes outside the skull cavity pick up encephalograms of frequency and potential variations within it. Mental telephony or telepathy is experienced more often than chance or association can discount. Inspiration is attested by too many, and in too many ways. Again the function is in the range above the conscious. We receive through the conscious "senses" and translate out of our education a wide variety of signals, although some, such as Chinese and Morse code, are beyond many of us. Certainly an "idea" comes and we recognize its presence before we clearly grasp it. To the Christian, and the Hindu, this inaudible receiving function in the circuit above the conscious offers an explanation of conscience, satisfaction and inspiration. Obviously, our training and practices must be such that we are attuned to it. So also we must be trained and practiced for the conscious reception of Braille or blinker code or French, if they are to have meaning for us.

The coordination of the glands of the endocrine group adds up to health and happiness, or contrariwise, for the individual. As an electrical circuit, seven functions are coordinated with each other and with the receiving, sending and storage facilities of the conscious circuit, as well, it is obvious, as with the secondary control functions of the subconscious. Like any electrical mechanism, it may be overloaded and damaged. Mentally the superconscious, the judgment perhaps corresponds with the governing board, the general staff, the faculty committee. Its functioning may be warped to uselessness by mental disease, such as egotism or self pity, or by careless or willful disregard of the council of its component members. On the other hand, its capacity for teamwork under a good coach or for fine orchestration under capable leadership is tremendous. The Christian will point out that the Divine guidance, sought through appropriate prayer, which the engineer would hope to receive at the pineal, is its priceless component.

The electrical details and relationships of atoms of the several elements, and hence of all matter; the indestructibility of the energy represented thereby; and the constant disintegration and re-integration, which so far as our groping knowledge goes, applies to all things, animal, vegetable or mineral, throughout the universe; may carry conviction, to the Christian cognizant of such things, of the indestructibility of the Soul.

It is conceivable that the electrical charges energizing the subconscious, the conscious and the superconscious circuits of the individual, may constitute that "spark of life." Their departure, necessarily leaving the body inanimate, may resemble that neutralization which releases the neutron from the atom to some postulated rebirth.

This effort to set down a few convictions, has turned out to be, not a thesis, but a creed, another creed, differing a little from many others before it, and foredoomed to be superceded as comprehension and language permit its clarification. It began years ago, with negative thinking, destructive criticism characteristic of youth, an uneasy dissatisfaction with the religious education of the time and the place. It continued, under some innate urge to try to answer why or whether instruction in Christianity should not be kept clearly abreast of our unfolding understanding of God's Creation. It had some fruition in one of those not uncommon miracles of restoration of faith and health. It seems to mature constructively now in the urge to find a spot, a Christian University perhaps, where it may be developed further, and turned to useful ends.

*   *   *

The paper was well enough received to encourage me to send it to Yale Scientific Magazine. There it was published in the October issue of 1946 under the title of "Mental Engineering", but that ended the encouragement for a time.

In September of 1945, I went to Columbia University in New York to enroll for a year of resident work to gather material for the project. Eleanor had agreed that we could get along for the year and knew how much I wanted to do it.

Surely at Columbia there would be ideal access both to informed men and to literature and reports of current research which would support a coordinating thesis. I asked permission to work under the departments of Medicine, Psychology, Philosophy and Religion and outlined a plan with what I felt was proper appreciation of its problems and limitations.

There were difficulties. Transcripts of my record at engineering and graduate schools twenty odd years before, had to be obtained. Interviews were necessary with the deans of Engineering, Medicine, and Religion although the last one never could be arranged. It was difficult to judge what might be behind the words of apparent encouragement, but it seemed to be the old conviction that the gulf between religion and science was too great to be bridged.

Finally the decision was handed down. "The authority could not be arranged" for work under those departments. Aside from personal disappointment, there was the unsettling thought that such conflict could exist between old established branches of learning in our universities.

Three years later that same Dean of Religion expressed his feelings in a letter which I have kept. A mutual friend had submitted my proposal for research to demonstrate that science can support religion and that the processes of the higher mental circuit are literally those which religion refers to as the spiritual. He wrote back expressing his opposition to such a project as follows:

Sept. 1st, 1948.

Dear Dr. S.————,

Thank you for letting me look over this interesting parable—comparing processes of thought to those of electricity. I am, however, too ignorant in both the psychological and electrical realms to judge the aptness of the comparisons.

So long as a comparison of this sort is treated as a simile or analogy, it is interesting and may be clarifying. But our mental organism is not a mechanism, and a process of thought and an electric current belong in different realms, although not necessarily unrelated. Our Lord found analogies between the physical and the spiritual in His parables, and we may do the same. But parables are not scientific demonstrations, but poetic comparisons. They are none the less valuable; but the two types of thinking *must not be identified*. A psychologist may find this comparison fruitful, and it is interesting to have an engineer employing his technical knowledge to illuminate mental processes.

I am gratefully returning your material.

Sincerely yours,

My effort *was* certainly to come up with a "scientific demonstration" which might dissipate the conflict in the minds of scientifically trained youngsters and of men like myself. It seemed a crying need of the times. Nor did Christ's parables appear to me to be mere "Poetic comparisons." There was vital meat and meaning in them which coincides well with our current state of knowledge.

Rebuffed by the university, I went back to the normal processes of seeking out the information needed to fill in the gaps in the project, and to discussing the findings with those in a position to help. The libraries in New York are well equipped with text books and the periodic reports of research of the various technical societies. The dictionary was especially valuable, for each of the specialized branches seemed to be competing with the others in the establishment of its own private language. I could not complain, however, for engineering is equally guilty.

At about that time I was told of the research and educational efforts of the Mental Hygiene Society and the National Association for Mental Health. The work was started through the urge to help, of a man who had recovered from an even more serious siege of nervous fatigue than my own. Surely here the findings of my experience would receive sympathetic attention and be put to some useful service.

Dr. Stevenson, the executive secretary gave me a courteous reception and examined the resumé I had prepared. I seem to recall that he was the son of a minister. Abstractly he thought well of religion but apparently not in connection with mental hygiene. The association of character responsibilities with endocrine nervous centers he felt was pretty well demonstrated and borne out by experience, but publication of it to those who might be needing the explanation of their troubles should await "proof", probably a long wait. Three years later, Dr. Symonds gave a copy of my manuscript to the president, for comment but neither comment nor acknowledgement could be obtained.

The battle lines were forming. Strong differences of position were appearing. This was developed further in a conversation last year with a psychiatrist, a member of our local Mental Hygiene Society. A major portion of his problems were with people disturbed to the point of hospitalization by the "guilt complex" conflict raging within their minds. A textbook on psychology sees this as a conflict between the behavior of the person and the moral code which they have acquired, presumably in their religious training.

The Christian might recognize conscience in action and prescribe prayer for forgiveness, and some psychiatrists do. But inadequacies of training and practice may make this difficult. At any rate a position is taken in psychology that the morality itself is wrong and that morality rather than the patient's behavior is at the root of the trouble. The psychiatrist with whom I was talking therefore ended his remarks against religion in mental hygiene by stating flatly, that: "It (religion) is dangerous!"

It might not be right or universal but that was a point of view. The great Dr. Freud of Vienna, whose acute observations contributed so much to the analysis of mental troubles, was a bitter atheist and his unbelief became thoroughly implanted in the teachings of the new psychology along with his worthy work. Perhaps he was not wholly to blame, for at the same time there was rampant the materialistic trend in philosophy in which man's all-encompasing wisdoms would brush aside ideas of any power above man as mere superstition.

It has been the attributing of such thinking to the broad field of "science" that has brought bitter remarks about science from the pulpit. Quite clearly the anti-religious front in psychology has had strong influence upon the thinking and position of the medical profession as it has in political concept. Must one now choose between the background and teaching of religion and the ostensibly antagonistic position of psychology or compromise on an undignified and unsatisfactory straddle?

Leading schools of religion seem to have adopted such a straddle. Whether it is the lack of maturing practical experience in faculty inbreeding, or the attrition of Freudian materialism, they are spiritually weak. Accumulated data tends to show that materialisticly slanted educational policies have contributed to the production of several generations weakened in their spiritual fortitude and their resistence to mental stress.

Many men abandon agnostic materialism for faith as they grow older. Young psychologists had assured me this was the workings of a fear complex but when I experienced it myself it was quite the contrary. The fears and worries which had destroyed my digestion were replaced by courage and confidence. With restored health and faith I went on to heavier responsibilities, enjoying a feeling of greater security than I had known before.

Then there must be something wrong with the way in which we have put together our newly acquired beliefs with the older wisdom of Christianity. There must be some adequate answer to the confusing conflict between the presumably worthy men charged with educating us. The experiences so far were disturbing to me, but the conviction that a sound unity in physical, mental and spiritual well being can be adequately shown, was stronger than ever. I could not help but feel that it just had to be done.

IV

THE UNITY AND THE POWER AND THE GLORY

Like many other men I had retreated from the city when my mind was troubled, and in the refreshing beauty of the woods and the hills I had found God.

This is referring back to June and July of 1945. Under the hand hewn rafters of the old carpenter shop I was reaching feverishly for words to try to express the picture with which my mind was filled. Possibly the word "vision" may actually apply, as it was used in translation of the simpler Hebrew and Greek to describe the rather sudden burst of understanding, the visualization, yet to be expressed in words by the men of those times.

Be that as it may, the first thing I tried to bring out was that the basis for our morality and mental health might be described as the laws of human behavior and that such laws were part and parcel with the laws of nature and the laws of science.

That may seem obvious, but it had not been so to me nor to men of my generation as I knew them. The cold laws of science were fresh and precise, backed by laboratory demonstrations which were easy to follow. The laws of nature seemed to be falling into a similar category, from one's glimpses of biology, zoology and botany. But the things we learned in Sunday School and at home seemed a bit fuddy-duddy and out of step with the "higher education" at college.

Now clearly, that isn't so. But how could such a fact be expressed so that other fellows could appreciate it. First we must see something of the human structure and its workings, how ideas are interrelated with nature's mechanisms. In so doing, we will have to try to avoid the specialized vocabularies of research. We are all interested in how we think and how we should govern our thinking. But such valuable discussions as the Hixon Symposium on "Cerebral Mechanisms in Behavior" held at the California Institute of Technology, must assume a specialization which is impractical for most men in other fields.

The difficult thing, perhaps, is to see how an electrical system can observe and comprehend and store such things as facts and figures, laws and sentiments; how it can draw them out, examine and compare, select and choose; and finally how it can issue the instructions and carry out the decisions so arrived at. Yet why should that be so difficult? Suppose instead of looking at man, we look at the things mere men have designed and built. Men accomplish such things through ingenious application of the laws of science. The resultant devices are much easier to look into and check than man himself. For present purposes it is not even necessary to examine the pertinent laws and the means of their application.

Engineers have had to learn the laws of mechanics, of electricity, of chemistry, etc., so far as they are known, and to learn that these laws may not be violated if one would succeed. That our "inventions" work, may be taken as sufficient evidence that the laws of science have been complied with. Then let us merely pick out a few devices and remind ourselves of what they do, to help us picture the equivalent processes in men and in the lower forms of life.

As youngsters we shouted across from one cliff to another and waited for the echo to come back to us. The physics teacher explained later the simple laws which relate the speed of sound in air to the time required for the echo to be reflected back to us. Under the same law, and endless centuries ago, Nature taught blind flying bats to time the echo of their high pitched squeaks and to know that when the echo came back too quickly, they were too near an obstacle. Another law having to do with frequency or pitch or length of the sound waves required that the bat use for this purpose a fast wave of 50,000 cycles per second. That is in the (supersonic) range above the human capacity for hearing which is limited to 18,000 cycles per second, or less. Not until the second world war did engineers apply such wave principles to directional and distance detection devices (for submarine warfare).

Even more remarkable to us was the discovery that in a similar manner still faster electrical (radar) waves could be directed beyond the range of vision, echoed back from an objective and not only timed for distance, but made to draw a pattern of the object on the fluorescent screen of a viewing tube. Thus a Jap battleship concealed in the black of night at a distance of ten miles was sunk on the first salvo of radar controlled naval guns. At the same time pilots were enabled by radar to "see" their targets through heavy clouds. Later proximity fuses were equipped with miniature wave sending and echo receiving devices to explode the projectile on which they were carried as it passed near to a flying plane. The success of the device reflected the clever application of many of the laws of science or of Nature, some of which have not yet been stated for text book purposes.

Can such scientific principles properly be called laws of Nature? Restricted research information now released, discloses that Nature had applied them successfullly in the distant past and in the dim depths of the ocean. The electric eel came in for war-time investigation, and it is found that he utilizes radar principles in his electrical (nervous) system. He broadcasts at high radar frequencies from nerve pits near the tail and receives at nerve pits at the sides and top of the head. He times, plots and analyzes the returning pulsations to determine direction, distance, size and shape of his neighbor. If he judges it to be an enemy or prey, he attacks and employs direct current stored within himself at pressures as high as 20,000 volts to electrocute the unfortunate adversary. To the electrical engineer this poses nice problems of insulation and electrode design. Nature does not violate the laws of science, for the eel's short broadcast range of about a hundred feet is compatible with its frequency which is up in the neighborhood of 100,000,000,000 cycles per second.

If man has a perceptive capacity of a similar sort he knows little of its use. Yet recognition of the possibility is not entirely out of order as we shall see.

In another field we contemplate with engineering pride, a new era in lighting, fluorescent or "cold" light. I. T. Sanderson punctures that pride, pointing out with what skill Nature has anticipated our invention. Fireflies signalling back and forth, deep sea fish with fluorescent headlights or rows of floodlights, luminous bacteria which light the surface of the water, luminous centipedes and worms, glow in a variety of colors. He states that these and certain plants store organic substances, which, when brought in contact with oxygen in air, water or blood, chemically causes waves of energy in the visible band to be given off. He comments relative to the variety of mechanical actions by which plants and animals accomplish these lighting phenomena, upon the durability of Nature's equivalents of switches, bulbs and wiring.

Engineers of the Sperry Gyroscope Company, in trying to improve their remarkable gyroscopic flight-control instruments, report their discovery that Nature had solved one of their problems some fifty million years ago. In working on an artificial horizon for airplanes, an equilibrium indicator, they found just back of a fly's wing, a similar flight instrument consisting of a tiny ball on the end of a hair-like rod, which vibrates 150 to 210 times per second in a plane in fixed relationship to the insect's fuselage. Its principles were substantially the same as those of the device which they had engineered, even to the frequency. The deviations in the line of flight were registered electrically through nerves at the base of the rod to guide the maintenance of flying equilibrium. Without the instrument, the insect's flight became erratic. Nature's tiny device was just what was needed in aeronautics.

Pointing out in these examples, the prior practice in Nature should in no way detract from man's less skillful efforts to duplicate the principles for and apply the laws to his own advantage. It may even lend weight to the advisability of Dr. Carver's method of going to God in prayer when he was so successfully seeking such answers. It also bears out the observation that a scientist makes his discoveries through his faith in the fundamental logic and perfection of the System. Certainly as the basic laws are uncovered by men widely separated in space and time, there unfolds an interrelated pattern which is basically simple in spite of the infinite variety of permutations and combinations. It becomes apparent too, that while the "discoveries" are new to us, the laws of the universe, whether known or unknown on this speck of a planet, remain the same through the ages.

*   *   *

The human body and its nervous system are replete with chemical, mechanical and electrical devices which cannot help but be of interest to all of us, whether or not we have gone beyond high school physics. We have all heard of atomic energy though we may not have delved into the infinitesmally small negatively and positively charged particles which are combined in so many different ways to form all matter, and all the chemically complex components of the body. We may not have heard that one of these tiny charges, positive or negative depending upon the individual, rides pick-a-back on each healthy red corpuscle in your bloodstream to keep it from clogging with its neighbors in the tiny passage ways of the skin. Groups of such minute electrical charges, as messengers, gallop along selected nerves to stimulate a group of muscles into just the amount of movement we may wish.

The electrical forces which thus energize a man are remarkably delicate and sensitive, far more so than in man's commercial devices. To study them medical men use highly sensitive electrocardiographs when recording the accomplishments of the heart, and the electroencephalograph, a modified radio receiver to study changes of electrical voltage and frequency in the brain.

Many youngsters have enjoyed the body's capacity to store static electricity, somewhat as the eel does. They scuff along a rug on a cold day and then cause a small spark as they touch some unsuspecting person. They have also observed how contact with the body improves the radio reception of small sets under favorable conditions.

You have probably seen charts of the body showing the nerves branching all over and through it like the limbs and branches of a tree. This electrical messenger service might be compared in complexity with those of the telephone system in a good sized city. The nerves are enclosed in branching tubular sheathes filled with fluids which chemically supply the needed energy. They are not metal wires or coaxial cables, but for the understanding of most of us, the nerves do convey and direct messages along selected routes for both sending and receiving purposes.

The telephone receiver and the microphone both receive sound waves out of the air and change them to electrical waves which are promptly dispatched along a conductor to a destination. Similarly the ear receives sound waves through the air to the ear drum, and changes them into electrical waves to travel back along nerves to the brain area. Consciously responding, we return messages along other nerves to a group of muscles whose movements we combine to produce suitable sound waves. So also the unintelligible electrical fluctuations approaching us over the telephone line are changed back to sound waves in the form of understandable words at our ear piece. Be it acknowledged that God's workmanship is infinitely superior to our engineering and manufacturing, for the human sound equipment is more compact, more durable and works on a far smaller expenditure of electrical energy than anything man does commercially.

The eye receives light waves registering colors, shapes distances, position, movements. . . . It changes the whole observation into electrical waves suitable for transmission back along the bundles of nerves to the brain for interpretation and storage or appropriate action. The engineers efforts to accomplish similar ends with the electric eye, the telephoto services by which newspapers transmit their pictures and the television camera are all crude by comparison, though still remarkable.

At some of our universities electrical "brains" have now been installed to perform the lengthy computations of astronomy, etc. Where necessary these machines can "remember"or hold numbers for future use. They are large adaptions of adding machines, comptometers and other business machines in common use. Some such machines exercise powers of association and selection similar to those of the brain though they do it awkwardly as they shuffle through masses of punched data cards. But for the mathematical duties only of a brain they are still cumbersome for they occupy the space of a good sized room. Specialists on the mechanisms of the mind point out that (providing it is honestly directed) the brain tends to check and cross check, and to average out its errors, whereas the machine duplicates or multiplies any error introduced by the failure of any one of its many parts.

For comparison with the brain's storage facility, which is memory, men have designed devices of many sorts combining electrical, mechanical and chemical principles. The primary substitute for memory began with writing and printing, books and libraries which are now being compacted to tiny microfilm records for storage. Nature's approach may be better compared with talking picture film and with wire-recorder tape. Some electro-chemical modification of the complex molecular structure of the brain cell may set up the code pattern from which the thing to be remembered may be reconstructed. The scientific understanding of this is not yet clear, but we need only a general idea of the process for our present purposes.

The prospect of building a synthetic man or a robot might tempt us for a moment, after noting the foregoing comparisons. If we are willing to accept the proportions of a large plane or ship, to give space enough for our devices, we might imitate a considerable portion of the mechanical, electrical and chemical procedures of man. We would undoubtedly forego any consideration of reproduction, growth or even the maintenance functions of repairing normal wear and tear. We might of course put a crew of men aboard but that would reduce the whole idea to the ridiculous.

It may clarify the picture of the problems ahead, however to compare ourselves with the monster. Let us accept the short-comings of such a monster as a submarine and grant it a crew even though crewless devices are built for some purposes. Our submarine does get around pretty well, digests its supplies and even rebuilds minor injury (through the efforts of the crew). Like a man, it "lives," within itself receiving its information on what goes on about it through hearing, seeing and feeling devices.

That is an important point, for most of us have so taken for granted our "five senses" that we fail to distinguish some of the vital relative values. Threatened loss of the sense of sight or hearing, the prospect of living in darkness and quiet, cut off from our surroundings, help to bring home the point.

Quite literally "we" do live at some quiet, dark and potentially peaceful spot within our brain. The rest of our structure provides the support, the mobility and the information to that area, and in accordance with its instructions. Thus if, we choose to open our eyes, a view of what is going on around us may be received, interpreted as to meaning, and delivered to our command post for whatever utility it may be. Some of these reports especially the visual ones may be so vivid and absorbing that we may miss other sensed impressions and "extra-sensory" perceptions from rusty or undeveloped services.

In the monster we have chosen, the synthetic nervous system is a mass of pipes, wires and gadgets of all sorts. "We", the captain at the command post down inside, must decide what to do from information arriving over that system. Lights and dials tell of the physical readiness and worthiness of the ship. Poor visibility may be obscuring the periscope. Listening devices may sound a warning. Radar and radio bring in signals to be interpreted and decoded.

The charts and code books, the drilled capabilities of the crew, the training of the officers, all contribute background of instruction and experience, a consensus of opinion must be reached, a plan of action determined or selected and orders issued over the intercommunication system for the execution of the plan. If everything has been fully observed and correctly done, the results will hinge upon how well judgement was exercised. At the same time, if rules were violated or orders disobeyed, disaster or court-martial may be anticipated.

The "synthetic man" thus has simulated a typical functioning of the circuit of the human mind. There is suggested in the sketch something of the relationship of training and of responsibility to higher authority and to the rules or laws, a responsibility which is common to mankind.

Higher authority, over mankind; God. In youth, our curiosity leads us to question many things which we do not understand. It is part of learning. Later, "feeling our oats" and knowing all the answers we may try the materialistic position. "It can't be, because you can't prove it, to me." In education, laboratory experiments and demonstrations back up the textbooks, where possible. Such demonstrations constitute experience. To know that God *is,* some of us have to await serious trouble, and then learn through experience.

Thomas A. Edison, who contributed so much to modern lighting, came to believe firmly in God. In discussion of the problem with a friend of my father's, he said, "Show me the scientist who says there is no God and I will show you a man who is not a scientist."

Edison, through his faith in the teachings, and the laws of science, was a highly successful scientist. What are these "laws"? They constitute our best effort to state governing principles, the basis of the System as we find it. One hardly need emphasize that these "laws," or rather the principles, which they represent, are nothing new. Apples fell down long before Newton set up the law of gravity. Only man's effort to express the law may be "new" (and perhaps inadequate).

The unity of the laws of science and of nature has been indicated in the examples cited in this chapter. The power of the laws lies in the observation that we cannot violate them with any degree of success. The glory of the System reflected in the laws is not the glory of man.

The laws of human behavior are a guide to judgment, to decision, to success and happiness. They are the manual of the captain at the command post in our synthetic man, and are equally essential to us all. We have been learning of them over a period somewhat longer than our acquaintance with the laws of science. Yet a unity, a common background of the laws is observable. The power, the inviolability of the laws of human behavior, like those of science and of nature should become apparent as we ramble amongst the problems and furnishings of the mind. Inseparable therefrom will be the implication of personal responsibility and of higher Authority.

V

MINNEWASKA

"High in the Shawaugunk Mountains of Ulster Country are a group of lakes, famous for their limpid beauty and the sheer magnificence of their natural setting." That accurate description is in the words of Geologist Myers who goes on to explain the character of the rocky cliffs and their glacial origin way back in the Pleistocene Age.

It was that natural beauty and magnificence which took us there for vacation amongst rhodadendrons and later blueberries in 1946. One enjoys and profits spiritually by such relaxations, and besides I had a problem to think out. My first manuscript had been quite soundly rejected, and rightly so, I must admit. In it I tried to describe the mind above the conscious, and aside from its controversial nature, the paper was too heavy, hard reading, and not adequately clear.

I have thought often since of Glenn Clark's recommendation in "The Soul's Sincere Desire" to repair to the high places when problems need a solution. He was urging the humble attitude of prayer and the power of God's guidance, inadmissable as that may seem in the modern technical curriculum.

It was not at all inadmissable in the wild beauty of the woods and rocks. The two old frame hotels, on cliffs high above the lake, were run by Quakers, and the people who came there appreciated the atmosphere which prevailed. Each morning after breakfast there was a short non-sectarian religious service, and it was well attended.

Clark referred back to the practice of Christ and of Moses and others of their time. Their practice of going up into the mountains when they had a problem to work out, was in order to be alone, alone except for God's presence with them. Moses struggled on the mountain at Harab with the problem of leaving his safe retreat and going back to Egypt to lead his people out of slavery, an assignment for which he did not feel capable.

After the completion of that escape he again went up into the mountains, Mt. Sinai, to ask guidance in the governing of his restless people. His early training at the Egyptian court and his familiarity with the moral code contained in part in the Egyptian "Book of the

Dead" may properly have supplied some ground work for his thinking. The inspiration of Divine guidance which he acknowledged, should be borne out by the rightness and historical significance of the laws which Moses gave to his people. In spite of the difficulties of time and repeated translation, his ancient interpretation is still a basic contribution to our concept of the laws of human behavior.

In those ancient days and unnumbered times since, the hills have been a temple where men might meet with God.

Even I, in my little way, could not but feel that, somehow God *is* with us, and that His presence is easier to sense amongst the woods and the clouds. The problem which "had me stopped," was how to check and how to show clearly the relationship which I could see existing between; (1) the laws which Religion endeavors to teach us, and (2) the character responsibilities of a portion of the human mental equipment, and (3) the mental and physical well-being of the individual.

The doubts which assailed me were all fairly obvious. Wasn't it too much to undertake? Wasn't it too soon to try, and wouldn't someone else do it better? So what? The "snake-pit" stories of the wrecked personalities in our mental hospitals rather haunted me. But for each mind wrecked, how many were there who need not crack *if* current confusions of thinking could be dispelled. The first effort had been utterly inadequate.

Psychosomatic. That is a key word and one to which we cannot help but give some attention. In the overlapping of modern fields of specialization many words have been given different shades of meaning by different specialists. This one is no exception and in some instances the shaded meanings are so far from the original as to contrast like black and white.

In one sense, the surgeon-general has said that half the hospital cases in the U. S. are psychosomatic, and others have indicated that milder cases in the general populace may be in a similar proportion. In this sense, the reference is to mentally induced physical disorders, the upset bodily functions of people whose thinking is not well kept. It is a rather negative shading, through the dark glasses of the medical profession's essential interest in the things which are wrong with humanity.

Literally the meaning of the word, from the original Greek, is a combination of psyche, which means soul, and soma which means body. Soul and body.

The positive meaning is the opposite to the negative view of the psychiatrists and psychologists and that is not in any way critical of the worthy object of those professions. Their urge is to diagnose and to find cures for people whose twisted thinking upset the normal functioning of their bodies.

On the positive side it may be discerned in Christ's teaching that a function of religion is to maintain a clear and healthy functioning of the mind for the benefit of the whole individual. The meaning of the word is reflected in the title of the Department of Religion and Health of the Federal Council of Churches. Soul and body in the right functioning sense as opposed to the mal-functioning.

Technically both the negative and positive aspects of the word focus on a nervous system or a portion of the whole electrical control which has been called the autonomic (self-governing) system. Elements of this system are responsible, as we will see, for many aspects of physical health. They are also sensitive to ill chosen habits of thinking which we know as complexes, neurosis and such. By the same token a proper point of view, good mental health, is accompanied by proper functioning of the controls and by good physical health. "Psychosomatic" soul and body, whether for better or for worse, it covers a subject of interest to most of us.

My work at the libraries during the first winter had shown that it was not an easy subject to search out of current literature. Pertinent material was hidden away in a wide variety of books and periodicals. The texts which had gathered material of the generation preceding were largely biased to either the negative or the positive point of view and often only to a minor subdivision of one or the other.

A book which I had brought along and was studying at the time was Physiological Psychology by Professor C. T. Morgan, Chairman of the Department of Psychology at Johns Hopkins University. It was dated 1943 and presented in a studiously thorough and clearly evaluated form, data upon the structure and functioning of the human nervous system, supported by experimental work on animals. Morgan makes a strong effort to appraise normal functions but he still represents, quite properly, the point of view of the medical profession, with a primary interest in the malfunctioning mentality. He follows the conventional approach of psychology to mental processes in that he recognizes no instinctive motive higher than our desire for pleasure and our concern with pain, anxiety and fear. Morgan's clear study provided good clues but he did not go on to link mortality and behavior with character and its higher responsibilities. We must find the way to do that if we are to show wherein religion is essential to health and to happiness.

Another textbook was positively discouraging, for it took an op-

posing point of view; religion was wrong. The proponent wrote with
authority for he was a Professor of Psychology and his book was
edited by a college president to lend futher weight. It was described
as, an objective approach to mental hygiene, which was just what I
sought. It was required reading in my son's studies at Yale.

The book presents well the psychological approach to mental ailment with case history support for conventional interrelation of such
trouble with shortcomings of childhood training and with the emotional reactions and the habits of thinking of the patients.

I found in the first chapter, the author's statement of psychological
position with regard to religion and the law which it states. It should
be considered because it represents a major premise, a basic concept
which has had a wide influence on thinking in psychiatry, and medicine and even upon general academic thinking and policy. It's origin
seems to be largely in the materialistic era.

Man, in facing the problems of living assumes an attitude, a point
of view characterizing himself as an individual, in his solution of those
problems and in arriving at his choice of a course of action. Whether
his decision is right or wrong in the eyes of the Theologian or in the
eyes of the Psychiatrist is again a matter of the attitude of that individual as influenced by his background. The author states this point
of view for psychology as follows: *

"Up to the present . . . (man's) . . . . . attitude toward adjustive
difficulties has been a moralistic one.

"In the evolution of theological concepts (from sufferers possessed
by demons) . . . . . the maladjusted are sinners who suffer from the
effect of wrongdoing. . . .

"Many unfortunate individuals believe, because of training that has
engendered an unenlightened theological attitude, that their difficulties are sins. . . .

"The sin-conscious attitude is especially common and harmful in
adolescents' adjustive struggles, particularly in those dealing with
parental control and sex.

"Even . . where primitive theological interpretation has been abandoned, an equivalent moralistic attitude exists equally detrimental. . . ."

*   *   *

So the battle lines are drawn. The student must achieve his own
point of view by making his choice:

1.   Psychology which he learns in the halls of higher education, is

* "The Psychology of Adjustment", L. F. Shaffer; Houghton Mifflin Co., Boston,
1936.

right, and the religion which he may or may not have been taught at an earlier age, is wrong, or,

2. Religion, with a long and potent history, is right and psychology is wrong, or,

3. Perhaps this conflict is more apparent than real and he may eventually be able to resolve it for himself, assuming that the preoccupations and responsibilities of living permit.

I was in the position of a student and was endeavoring to learn. This was a new experience though, for in the scientific and engineering subjects there might be expansion and clarification of theory, but my texts did not take fundamentally opposed positions. I had no choice but to take the third alternative. My thoughts noted on parts of the book, differed with those of its author. Yet he had presented well a position held by many men. What seemed to me to be unsound conclusions in this material could easily trace to difficulties of observation and to positions taken by such pioneers as Freud whose useful work was strongly tinged by conflict with morality and society. Nevertheless there was a wealth of worthwhile observation of human problems of thinking in it and in the other similar sources.

As a student I felt that I might have some advantage both in years of living and in personally experiencing things in which the authors were theorizing, but certainly my differences of opinion must be regarded with caution. It seemed obvious when a theory was quite opposed to the facts, as I had observed them, but then the observation must be examined for bias. It did become clear so far as the apparent conflicts were concerned, that neither the theologians nor the psychologists had done too good a job of trying to understand what the other one was talking about.

If the behaviorists have drawn some faulty conclusions in the efforts to reason from external cause to external effect without adequate understanding of internal influences and processes of the thought, that does not condemn the whole effort. If volunteer teachers in Sunday Schools have not given all of their pupils adequate fundamentals to cope with problems of behavior that also is understandable. But there are some points of agreement to be observed and of disagreement to be resolved.

It may be agreed that a person's physical health is favorably or adversely affected by their habits of thinking.

Agreed also that one's training, experience and contacts with other people, for better or for worse, contribute to establishment of those habits of thinking. Sources of trouble which are planted in this manner may be hard to discover from the outside.

It is also readily agreed that much adverse mental (and resultant physical) health stems from disturbing controversy raging unseen in the mind of the person, *and* that *one* of contending factors therein, is basing its case upon the moral code or the law. Whether the accompanying mental discomfort is called frustration in the terms of the psychologist, or conscience in the terms of the theologian, the difficulty may build up to serious proportions if proper cleansing and healing treatment is not undertaken.

It is at this point of diagnostic analysis and consequent treatment of this rather common ailment that the extremists of the opposing camps register their disagreement.

The Christian psychiatrist (there are quite a few) seeks to diagnose the disturbance and then asks the sufferer to kneel with his pastor and ask God for forgiveness of his sins and for strength to combat them.

The Freudian psychiatrist, agreeing with the diagnosis that the moral code and the idea of sin is the evil root of the patient's trouble, seeks to implant the counter-thought that the law is wrong, and the patient's disturbing past may be condoned in his or her mind.

Perhaps we may suspect that the latter doctor will share with Freud (and possibly with the frustrated patient) an antipathy to any personal responsibility to the higher authority represented in God.

I cannot help but observe now, in the light of hindsight, the extent to which the atheist's resentment of responsibility to God resembles the self-centered child's resentment of parental restraint. It is just such a maladjusted habit of thinking or neurosis as many which disturb peace of mind, mental health.

But there I have gone beyond the period of our 1946 visit to Minnewaska. And while this biographical departure is under fire, let me add another, for it was not until 1948 that a book and a short article appeared, both bearing on the problem with which I was struggling.

Not very far from Minnewaska is Orangeburg and its Rockford State Hospital for the mentally disturbed and distraught. On its staff, Dr. Hiram K. Johnson, M. D. was also trying to find the firm ground in the jumble of conflicting points of view. In the April 1948 issue of Psychiatric Quarterly, he expressed his dissatisfaction with weak points of psychological thinking. Under the title, "Psychoanalysis-Critique," he presents a well documented consideration of problems in the diagnosis and treatment of the mentally ill. He undertakes to show that anti-moralistic and anti-idealistic fundementals of Freud are false.

Dr. Johnson senses as the other part of the problem, the inadequacy or utter absence of religious presentation in higher education. He observes: "An obvious explanation of the rise of the Freudian psychology stems from the fact that with the dying out of religious life in our western civilization, the resulting vacuum should call for some kind of secular priesthood. And it is precisely in our respectable, upper economic brackets, where, as always the religious impulse is at its lowest ebb, that the psychoanalyst has established himself . . . making quite dogmatic pronouncements as to good adjustments and bad adjustments and, if a Freudian, preaching the gospel of heterosexual grace."

The evolution of education reaches a point at times where some portions require a revamping and housecleaning. Dr. Johnson was one of those who recognized that such a need existed. Other men undertook studies of the evidence, seeking a solution, even as I felt that I was doing in my small way. One of them was making progress on the positive side.

Dr. Ernest M. Ligon, was teaching at Union College about sixty miles from Minnewaska. He had sought his answers through arts courses, philosophy, theology and a major in psychology and then developed them farther in the Union College Character Research Project. He had gone through Freudian "free" associations to which Johnson applied the descriptive title, "systemized nastiness," and came out with the conviction that the sound basis for thinking and living lay in development of strong character, and the foundation for that in turn was best found in Christ's teachings. He presented his approach and his conclusions in the book, "A Greater Generation." In it he foresaw great possibilities as others have, in a general understanding of mental and spiritual behavior and maintenance.

There are many more, but these three text books by Morgan, Shaffer and Ligon scan three major aspects of our problem:—Morgan, brain, body functions, nerve linkage and usage; Shaffer, mental problems and maladjustments; Ligon, mind, character and the laws of behavior. The differences of opinion on relative validity of laws, relative ideals, and relative responsibility merely emphasize the need for clarification. Essential relativity of the positive psychosomatic, the healthy soul-body relationship is set up. The problem of demonstration must be solved by careful assembly of data from the many sources. Could one man hope to do it?

VI

MIND ABOVE THE CONSCIOUS

Leaf through the files with me to June of 1950 to get a proper introduction for this portion of the discussion and then we will go back to the chronological sequence of events.

Eleanor and I were then living in the pleasant village of Mount Gilead, Ohio. I had been asked to come there as a Chief Engineer of the Hydraulic Press Manufacturing Company as the former chief was going to try his hand at other responsibilities. Be it said that I had pointed out that mine was largely a mechanical press background and had urged that they bring up a man from their own organization. However, it proved a very pleasant association filled with problems which were interesting to solve. The company had started making cider presses for the farmers and had grown from that to the construction of presses for the production of many metal and plastic articles. During 1949 we undertook the designing and building of presses of 18,000 tons capacity for finish-forming large steel pipe for oil lines. The problems involved were serious enough, but now still larger presses are needed.

It was the height of autumn when we had arrived in 1948, and the big trees along the main street were a blaze of color. We joined the Presbyterian church and received a most friendly welcome. There was an active man's bible class and I enjoyed participating in its discussion. One of the class' responsibilities was for a member to give a few words of encouragement each year to those of the Sunday School who were graduating from the town's high school. It was necessarily a small group but I was flattered, as older men are, to be asked to give the address. There were twelve minutes allotted for the talk and I undertook to compress into that time a description of one's mental and spiritual functions which I hoped the boys and girls might find useful.

White graduation robes and caps were worn in Mount Gilead and they looked quite appropriate to the fresh sweetness of the youngsters that June morning. The eyes of the assembled adults beamed approvingly upon them, as always during such affairs. I tried clumsily to catch the intent of that beaming approval in opening the remarks to the graduates:

"You are the new graduates. You are now, progressively, 'ON YOUR OWN' to a greater and greater extent. Do you realize that with these new honors, you are becoming the embodiment of our hopes, you are being sent forth to carry the banner into the next generation.

How have we equipped you for your adventures? In school, you have acquired valuable information, useful procedures, skills of the mind. This growing heritage of mankind, which has accumulated, thanks to language and writing, is a proud distinction of the human race. It equips us to use the wonderful mind God has given us.

Let us examine that mind for a moment and recognize in it THREE interesting operating levels. The conscious facility is the street level or business floor where the mind brings things in from the world about us (through the five conscious receiving senses) and then consciously sends things out again by word and deed. The president's office is there where YOU make your decisions and give your orders.

The subconscious is the next interesting level, the basement storage area where we put away the things which we have learned, to bring them out again as we need them, the information, the skills, and habits of thinking. It is an interesting warehouse which we will find needs a conscious housecleaning at times, for some of the dusty habits we store there may not be good ones to have around.

But the third level is the most interesting, for it includes the private offices upstairs, occupied by the board of directors. Actually, it is a second complete nervous system which controls all the functions of the body and mind which we cannot consciously control. Let me tip you off to something your teachers may not have pointed out. The responsibility for organizing your thoughts is in this system, beyond your conscious range. If you have a hard theme or report or some creative work to get underway, try getting all your working material together and well in mind. Then close your eyes and relax conscious effort to let the ideas get together. There is a wise old expression, "let's sleep on it," which many men have found takes proper advantage of this organizing capacity.

In experimenting with this higher mind, you will note that the idea which flashes into your mind is not yet expressed in words. Words are just tools of the conscious and are different for different peoples. The language of the higher mind, we have come to recognize in feelings, emotions, sense impressions, conscience, satisfaction, intuition, inspiration, the flash of an idea. It takes time to express that idea in words after we have recognized it.

As we study this mind-above-the conscious, we find that it controls the physical functions of growth, and heart action, and digestion and nervous energy. But more important than those things and its organizing of thought we are beginning to see that it is in truth, our spiritual function, our source of courage, of hope, of faith and of loving service. Its duties are those which ancient prophets envisioned in their references to the heart (of the mind).

The church has equipped you with teachings of Jesus and the prophets to help you to understand its language and to utilize its guidance. It has endeavored to teach you to distinguish the call of right and duty from the conflicting temptation of selfish greed or envy or laziness. It is interesting that these and other possible temptations become dangerous to us as we permit them to become "habits" in our thinking, bad habits which become stronger with practice.

The reason for saying that religion is essential to your mental balance is that it provides you with means of distinguishing bad habits from good ones, and gives you the courage and determination to seek them out before they do you serious harm. Alcoholism, chronic bad temper, envy, hatred and long practiced fears, and worries, are such bad habits of mind. Those habitual disturbances which the doctors call neurotic and psychologists describe as complexes, all trace back to selfish and self-centered bad habits which religion calls sins. The medical profession is finding that more and more of our mature physical difficulties trace back to such bad mental housekeeping. One modern writer points out that we must learn to cleanse ourselves in several ways. We bathe ourselves externally. We drink lots of water to wash out our digestive system. We exercise to stimulate a cleansing circulation throughout the bloodstream. We breathe deeply of fresh air to cleanse the lungs and we must also practice mental and spiritual hygiene to keep healthy minds.

But we must do more than just keep ourselves strong. The obligation of the law of survival of the fit which Christ expressed in the Parables of the Salt and the Candle must unselfishly satisfy our instinctive urge to service if we are to gain satisfaction and "peace of mind." Many of the problems we meet in life would seem insursurmountable if it were not for that confidence which is in fact, FAITH. Do not ever forget that it is always your privilege to turn to God for inspiration and guidance which comes to you through the wordless language of your higher circuit. If you care to ask how the "sixth sense" can work, just think of radio and television. The nervous system is a marvelously intricate and delicate electrical system which interprets and records the heat waves, light waves and

sound waves which the conscious senses receive. Now there is growing evidence that electrical wave reception is also a function of the
mind, but of the higher circuit. As yet our knowledge of its attunement and interpretation is limited, but many of us have found that
sincere and unselfish prayer is answered.

YOU ARE increasingly "on your own" but you need never be
wholly alone. Glenn Clark gives us the parable of the apple in which
he points out that one rotten apple will turn a whole basketful bad.
Then asks, will one bad man turn a whole community bad? No. Not
likely. Then what was wrong with the apples? Look at one of the
good ones. Where is it defective? Look at the stem. That is it. It is
disconnected from the health-giving tree. Then what of man? He
who is disassociated from God is distinctly in peril.

Good luck on your way! And if you cherish the good things
which are yours, the "luck" will be good. Keep spiritually clean and
strong. Keep your prayers honest and unselfish. Keep God with you
always.

May we give you a prayer to take with you:

*Father, help us please to appreciate the marvelous unity and power
and glory of Thy System throughout the Universe.*
*Help us to know the unity and the power of Thy laws in Nature,
in Science and in human behavior.*
*Help us to honor and to fulfill the responsibility which we have,
each of us, to Thee and to Thy laws and to Thy people everywhere.
Help us to appreciate this accompanying privilege of coming before Thee in the temple of our minds to ask Thy forgiveness for
our selfish sins and shortcomings, to ask Thine aid in cleansing and
rebuilding ourselves physically, mentally and spiritually, and to
ask each day Thy guidance and Thine inspiration as we undertake our chosen services to Thee and to Thy people.*

*   *   *

The prayer had been formulating gradually during those morning sessions on my knees which Glenn Clark had persuaded me
were so necessary.

Recognition of the three operating levels of the mind which I
endeavored to picture to the young people, is a most important
point in our appreciation of the problems and the maintenance of
mental well being. It is also a point which plunges us again into
interesting and enlightening controversy.

As I am thrown this way and that among the strong personalities
who have expressed their position on the subject, this problem looms

up as one which must be resolved. Without sorting out the responsibilities and accomplishments of the minds' departments, we cannot avoid confusion of relative values in the age-old considerations of conflict versus calm, self-determination and Divine Guidance and finally of man-supreme versus Man's responsibility to higher authority, to God. Those battlegrounds have lost none of their interest and should just whet the appetite of our courage.

How many levels of mentality? Be we of one mind or of two or more? Swedenborg in his philosophic writings, found many levels. Brain specialists picture a thought which is gathering force or meeting erosive resistance as it progresses from layer to layer of brain cells. They resent the suggestion of three major levels as over simplification. Certainly in the marvelous complexity of the human mind, an extensive departmentalization does seem necessary to explain all that goes on.

My generation had to be satisfied in starting out with just two divisions, the marvelous conscious, pride of the materialist and a catch-all subconscious which took in everything else. It was not until I had been wading about through the problem for some time that the seriousness of the confusion and controversy began to dawn upon me. That is one of the reasons for gathering (in later chapters) a variety of notes and observations on common place conscious and subconscious activities and the nervous system through which they operate.

Two nervous systems have been mentioned and it is probably time to distinguish them. Of course they work closely together, as a unit in the well-balanced individual, and yet each has many elements and functions. Each includes storage areas, judiciary areas, communications networks for receiving and sending its messages internally and externally of itself, and finally the group of organs, muscles and mechanisms which it utilizes and commands.

The "voluntary" nervous system is the one with which we have a feeling of familiarity, for it is the one which I, as captain of my ship, use to get my reports, arrive at my decisions and give my orders to the muscles of body or throat which are to carry them out. It includes the five conscious receiving senses (sight, taste, touch, hearing and smell) the outer brain areas (cerebral cortex) which man has developed beyond other animals, and the branching nerve connections to the muscles which move us about and give us speech. It is the conscious system. Subordinate to it are those responsibilities which are properly called subconscious and which may be controlled by it when and if it wills. Thus we will see later that the subconsciously stored skills, practiced routines and habits may, and often do function without conscious supervision. In a sub-subordinate class are reflex actions operating from neurons or command posts remote from the brain but still consciously controllable at will.

The second nervous system came as a surprise to me when I first read of it, and continues to amaze me as evidence of its activities accumulate. Named the autonomic system, meaning self-governing, it controls bodily (and mental) functions and services which are out of the control of the voluntary system. I have wondered at times whether an unintended implication in the name might not actually be correct, whether the responsibility of the system might not include the governing of self as it resides at the conscious command post in the voluntary system. It seems more reasonable at present however, that mental services of the autonomic circuit are primarily advisory to conscious decision, but do tend to take over command when the conscious facility becomes too seriously confused or fatigued.

The autonomic system brain areas are centrally located and appear to include those referred to as the thalamus, hypo-thalamus, midbrain and others. Its organisms include the ductless glands of the endocrine system (pituitary, thyroid, adrenal, sex, etc.) which dispense hormones and genes for a variety of remarkable and vital services. The muscles which it controls are primarily the "smooth" muscles, heart, eyes, digestive tract, bloodvessels, rectum, etc., although it does exercise a control parallel to that of the voluntary circuit, over facial muscles and others. Two major communication networks of nerves serving the autonomic circuit cover balancing or complimentary functions (Morgan described them as antagonistic). The Sympathetic group generally have to do with mobilizing and expending of our reserves while the Parasympathetic nerve group channels the replenishing and conserving requirements. Other nerves bring in reports from the external receiving senses and disperse orders to some of the "outer" muscles, duplicating or paralleling certain voluntary nerve groups. The bloodstream also serves the autonomic system as a communication network, for through it travel the hormones which, as electro-chemical messengers and task forces, take care of many interesting needs, as we will see later.

Controversy rears its ugly head in evaluating the relative levels of the autonomic and voluntary systems. Those who place the voluntary system and the conscious "self" at the higher level, would seem to be influenced by three points:

1. There is a rather basic assumption in psychology that; because prototypes of the human autonomic system are recognizable in forms

of life which are lower and more primitive than man, therefore it must be of a lower order than the voluntary system which has developed to its highest state in man.

2. The truly remarkable rate of man's cerebral (voluntary) developments and his material accomplishment resulting therefrom.

3. A rather general academic acceptance of the material concept that there is nothing higher than man (or than man's conscious thinking.)

As I read the current evidence however it seems reasonably certain that the mental responsibilities of the autonomic system are of a higher order than those of the voluntary circuit, remarkable as it is. May we not keep an open mind on that alternative until that evidence is considered in later chapters.

Regarding point one above, some creatures developed special long legs for hopping, others developed wings for flying and teeth for fighting. Man developed a material thinking capacity which made it possible for him to make substitutes for long legs and attached wings, and fighting teeth. But all of these creatures possessed endocrine-autonomic systems which, as we can now see, were charged with responsibility for their digestion, their reproduction and other family relationships, for life and probably even for survival itself. Certainly those are vital responsibilities.

Regarding point two, man's remarkable development and accomplishment trace in some large part to the (accidental, perhaps) invention of language and then of writing which permitted him to take advantage cumulatively of the experience of generations before him and of others of his own generation. The means of conveying more and more complex ideas made it possible to build more and more complex mechanisms and concepts. The same adaption of elemental brain cells which went along with this process might have happened in an ape or giant rat under similar circumstances.

With respect to point three, the high regard for man's accomplishment which sometimes leads him to place himself above all else, may seem to be a pardonable pride in academic eyes. At the same time, it is just such egomania which often biases and warps men's judgment to a point of uselessness when they are in responsible positions.

Let us grant that the laws of human behavior may still be imperfectly interpreted and inadequately taught, but when a professor of psychology permitted himself to follow Dr. Freud's warped condemnation of them as moralistic and detrimental, he lays himself open to a question of bias in the rest of his work and influence. On the other hand a real problem does exist in finding how best to calm, cleanse and rebalance the fevered minds of those whose behavior (both mental and physical) conflicts more or less violently with some potent force within the mind, whatever we name it.

Whether this potent force resides in the autonomic mental responsibility, the superconscious some have called it, we shall have to see. Perhaps we should visualize it as a "Dutch Uncle," chiding the wayward conscious "self" for its headstrong misbehaviors. No matter how stable our own peace of mind may be, we are still interested in a better understanding of disturbing mental influences, aggravations, conflicts, frustrations, attacks of conscience, whatever we call them.

There are many surprising activities and responsibilities yet to be identified and considered in both the voluntary and the autonomic systems. Many levels or subdivisions of each may be useful to the specialists, but for our purposes here let us be satisfied with just three broad general levels as they were outlined to the graduates:

1. Our remarkable conscious facility which brings the material upon which it may base its decisions from three sources. The first of these is at its own level and deals with our environment, that is to say, with the reports from the outside brought in by the conscious receiving senses.

2. A subconscious facility devoted to the storing and furnishing when required, of our learned routines, our practised skills, our habits of action and our habits of thinking. This is a reasonably identifiable brain area, and its mental responsibility is the one which calls for mental hygiene and attention to the laws of human behavior.

3. The third source of information to aid in conscious decision, be it lower, equal or higher, is the autonomic system. Morgan identifies among its provinces, the advisory reporting of "internal environment," a current statement of our health and assets, the state of our energy and courage. Others go on to include here the seat of logic and conceptive thought, of the creative urge, of emotions and sense impressions, etc. The exploration of this remarkable portion of our equipment becomes a major part of our project. Keep in mind as we proceed, the question whether the Christian may see in the autonomic system those mental responsibilities which have to do with character, and even the spiritual values which characterize the soul.

For the moment it is necessary only to agree on considering the *three* broad levels of mental activity.

VII

RESEARCH AND INTEGRITY

The "project" which has been unfolding is merely one of under-standing my own thinking facility and its responsibilities, if any. "Merely." Why should one gradually build up to the writing of a book for such a purpose in this day and age? Or is *a* book enough? If we take it seriously, can any one man hope to present a fair, unbiased and adequate coordination of current data, or should he limit his thoughts strictly to himself and leave the whole project to some research institution?

Obviously correct. The project should be outlined with all the conviction we can muster, and turned over to research. Among the men with whom I discussed that solution, four stood out in their genuine effort to help. Dr. Roswell P. Barnes of the Federal Council of Churches; Dr. F. C. Symonds of the Board of National Missions (of the Presbyterian Church); Dr. Willard C. Rappleye, Dean of Columbia University's College of Physicians and Surgeons and Dean Edgar S. Furniss, Provost of the Yale Graduate School. As I page through the correspondence of 1948 and '49 it is clear that others helped with their advice on proposals and their recommendations but these men went out of their way to make arrangements and to obtain me interviews.

The first proposal boiled down to half a dozen closely typed pages with a couple of charts. It was duplicated a dozen times or more and modified and reworked at other times for submission to different people and agencies.

Some agency of government research seemed like a possibility. At about that time David E. Lilienthal, then head of the Atomic Energy Commission, expressed his regard for the better things of life in a radio address. I appealed to him for suggestions, submitting the proposal. He referred it to the Director of the Division of Biology and Medicine of A.E.C. His response of June 29, 1948 said:

"The ideas which you propose are unique and interesting, and we have gone over them with great care. However the National Research Council and the Social Science Research Council are presently undertaking a comprehensive study of this general field which we feel will go far toward resolving the problems that have been raised. Accordingly, I would advise that you *await* the results of these studies before initiating your program."

Whether this courteous response was intended as encouragement or as a polite brush-off, I tried to follow up with both of the agencies mentioned without much success. On a trip to Washington I went to the magnificent home of the National Research Council in the Academy of Science Building on Constitution Avenue to find out more about it. (My first contact with the Academy had been several years earlier on an invitation to Los Alamos which I muffed in the obscuring secrecy). Dr. Philip Owen, had the active responsibility under Dr. Weed for the Council's work in Endocrinology. That seemed to be just where the "project" would fit in, because of the psychosomatic relationship of endocrine hormone distribution and autonomic mental functions. Dr. Owen was free to admit that he had given no particular thought to the positive interweaving of physical, mental and spiritual values in this work. But to the proposal that the council might undertake research to clarify the association of autonomic functions and the moral laws, he was quite specific. The council's project could cover research subdivisions or specialties, but *not* an overall coordinating project. Dr. Owen did confirm for me the recognition of the tie between brain areas and endocrine gland centers in the autonomic circuit.

Dean Rappleye of the College of Physicians and Surgeons, Columbia University suggested that I take the matter up with Dr. N. D. C. Lewis, professor of Psychiatry and director of the New York State Psychiatric Institute. I submitted a research proposal and requested an interview.

This was in September of 1948, shortly after the attacks in the public press upon the unsatisfactory conditions in the mental hospitals of some states. The attacks undoubtedly helped in stimulating public support, but they must also have added to the woes of the distracted men who were trying to run the institutions.

Dr. Lewis wrote back a courteous note regretting that, regardless of his "interest in these important matters, the administration of a research hospital and the duties of a heavy university teaching load" combined to limit his activities.

My first reaction to this particular disappointment was to wonder that the administration of a *research* hospital did not allow time for discussion of a research proposal which he seemed to allow was important. I should probably recall however, that I was asking a difficult reversal of thinking, especially with respect to the Freudian point of view which he was undoubtedly teaching.

The recommendation that I try the Rockefeller Foundation seemed more hopeful. The Rockefellers were strong Presbyterians and the new president of the Foundation, Chester I. Barnard, had stated in a recent press interview that the Foundation was "considering an entry into the fields of ethics, morals, philosophies and religions", because, "there can be no solution to the problems of civilization that does not take into account the ideals and spiritual aspirations of man." Furthermore, the man who made the statement was a business man and probably an engineer, not "conditioned" to the more debatable concepts of psychology.

It was January of 1950 before it was possible to meet and talk with him. We seemed to see eye to eye during the discussion. The next day however, and presumably after consulting with the medical and technical specialists of his staff he regretted that the project was "not one that we ourselves could foster, and it is not within the framework of our present undertakings . . . If it were to receive more extended consideration than we have been warranted to give it under the circumstances, it would have to be presented by a competent group of the highest standing in the various fields affected and sponsored by an institution oustanding."(Of course, that was exactly why I had hoped that the Foundation with its experts would undertake it.) He finished the letter:

"I should myself wonder whether neurological science had as yet developed to the point where the proposed inquiry could be fruitfully carried out." That is a crucial question.

The neurological experts do give us most of the material we will need for the structural explanation, but the electrical engineering problems are still something of a no-man's-land. I stooped to wonder whether his stumbling block might be the position of the psychological materialists that the idea of any power higher than man is pure myth and superstition and no mere industrialist or engineer should be recognized to the contrary. Such unworthy thoughts must not bias our approach to the problem however.

* * *

The secretary of the Bolligen Foundation, which supports some of the Yale projects, wrote on November 9, 1948:

"I may say that I read all of the material which you gave me with much interest. I appreciate the amount of thought which you have given to this undertaking and the interesting nature of your approach to the problems involved. I do think that to carry such a project through would require a very substantial amount of work over a considerable period of time. The Trustees do not feel that, in view of existing commitments, the Foundation can take on the support of an additional project of this scope." The man who wrote the letter, appealed to me, and I felt that he meant what he said.

* * *

My final appeal of this sort was to the half-billion Dollar Ford Foundation. Its secretary, Burt J. Craig is the sort of man for whom one can establish an extremely high regard on short acquaintance and Chairman Henry Ford II has gone on record for his belief in our Christian ideology.

Mr. Craig devoted considerable time to my discussion of the urgent need for a project of this sort and to the outline of the material available which I felt was adequate to carry it through. He gave me the report of their directors outlining the purposes of the Foundation in behalf of all humanity. To quote only one of these:

"The Ford Foundation will support scientific activities designed to increase knowledge of factors which influence or determine human conduct, and to extend such knowledge for the maximum benefit of individual and of society."

In the opinion of both Craig and myself, the project was definitely within the scope of the Foundation. However, when the requirements had been complied with and a proposal had been submitted to an associate director whom I had known distantly thirty-five years ago on the Yale campus, the word came back with "regret that we cannot support your research proposal on Human Engineering." It softened the refusal by going on to say:

"I am sure you will understand that because of the many demands upon our resources, we must limit ourselves to those activities which most closely fit the initial emphasis of our program. It goes without saying that this decision in no way reflects upon the merit of your project."

The letter closed with best wishes for the success of the project. Well, perhaps it was best that way. Perhaps the job could only be done by an oldster, providing he had adequate experience and could muster the necessary intellectual honesty.

It was easy to find excuses why I should not do it myself for the normal demands on an engineering executive keep one under considerable pressure all of the time. So I did make one more try, to turn it over to research. Chester Barnard had rejected the project for Rockefeller Foundation but had said it should be sponsored by an outstanding institution. I would try once more to stir up some interest at my Alma Mater, even though it was there that I was sent away to find a research foundation.

The proposal for a research program at Yale was prepared with appropriate recognition of the spiritual background of Yale's inception and of the opportunity for authoritative collaboration of all of the sciences and the School of Religion. As the neural systems are electrical and the intangibility of mental and spiritual functioning trace to electrical rather than physical sequences, the plea cited the prediction of an outstanding scientist who had made great advances despite the limitations of intangibility. Electrical wizard Charles P. Steinmetz foresaw a quarter of a century ago that; *men will open their laboratories to a study of spiritual power and when they do mankind will make more progress in a generation than it has ever made.* The gathering research material to justify his insight, identifies the spiritual laws and functions with specific mental bodies and with health and balanced thinking. The first writing of the proposal cited much of the evidence.

The Yale Scientific Monthly was the obvious medium through which to submit such a proposal. The president of the Yale Engineering Association which sponsored the Monthly, read the proposal with care and felt strongly enough about it to recommend it personally to the editorial staff. They rejected it however on the ground that there was too much technical detail. The next vacation period went into rewriting it without the supporting data but emphasizing a series of propositions to be demonstrated. These unavoidably underlined the shortcomings of theoretical assumptions in current psychology. I had gone to Yale department heads to check my material and on that occasion found only one adamant materialist. When the board again declined to present the project it was on the ground that editorial policy limited them to "scientific material" and "your subject must, of necessity involve pure speculation."

President Seymore of Yale had spoken at about that time with pride of Yale's "outstanding schools of Medicine and of Religion." Yet when one endeavors to put a finger upon the misconceptions to eliminate the conflict which must not be permitted to exist in a community of the two, adequately scientific data is brushed off as speculation. The great research centers politely turn aside a proposal to gather the evidence which might straighten the matter out. What is wrong?

A Harvard professor writing on the endocrine glands of the

autonomic system felt that the glands affected the mind and opined that the major use of the mind was for rationalization.

By that I understood him to mean that most men's thinking goes little beyond the excusing or alibing to themselves of their own short-comings as they compare themselves with the apparent behavior and accomplishment of those whom they may select about them.

It is a common habit of the sophisticated to look down upon other mentalities; or perhaps that is just a warped impression. But there is an interesting point to be considered:

Intellectual honesty has its place in the well balanced mind. The professor suspected that most men are not sufficiently honest in their private thinking to recognize their faults for what they are. We would prefer to think that we honestly and intelligently recognize our own faults even though we may still pamper a few weaknesses. Regardless of what caustic remark the shades of Diogenes may have to make about the "honest man," the matter of intellectual integrity, fair play and honor is vital, both to the concepts of mental hygiene and to resolution of the controversies which plague our project.

In those writings, upon which other men may have to place reliance, we set down, (1) What we believe to be true, or (2) what we think other people think we should be thinking as too many have done, or (3) what we want other people to think regardless of how false we may know it to be. In the last category the Communists have given us a monumental exhibition of dishonor and some of our own commerical and political propagandists have also fallen a long way from the precepts which glow through the preamble of our constitution.

The declining Behavorist school of psychologists argue for external observation of cause and effect in the subject's reactions, skipping over the internal reactions which they seek to discover. The theory is that introspection, observation of one's own reactions, is too prejudiced, too warped, literally too dishonest to have any value. This theory has justification among the maladjusted, the neurotic by reason of habitual wrong thinking, those with whom the clinical psychologist is dealing. Yet intentionally or otherwise that same investigator resorts to the condemned introspection in writing down his conclusions of what went on between the clinical subject's stimulation and reaction.

Research people are inclined to accept on faith the integrity of the prior reports upon which their own work may be based. It also is likely to be true that their own reports will be factual, honestly set down. Most of them are young people and inclined to be idealistic. It is when we get to the stage of analytical coordination of test results and of observations that ill founded conclusions may be influenced by inadequate integrity on the part of the author in coloring his work or in accepting conflicting material without adequately testing it. It would also appear to require a certain amount of courage to stand by convictions rather than to compromise with a commonly accepted fallacy. In any case you who read what this project sets forth, will judge whether I have succeeded in being honest in gathering and reporting its data.

In one of the letters to the National Research Council I questioned the assumption that "the conscious or voluntary system was of a higher order than the autonomic system in man" and asked what relative research there might be underway. Dr. Lewis Weed of the Council referred my letter to Dr. Harold G. Wolff, M.D. of the society of the New York Hospital. He wrote me a thoughtful letter analyzing participation of the two circuits in man's behavior. He recognized participation of both circuits and emphasized the importance of conscious decision, to health and survival. He closed by saying, "There is *no* centralized research in this field, but throughout the country interested persons are pursuing *one or another aspect* of these biologic reactions."

The coordinating project is not yet under way (1949) and the efforts to interest a research foundation or university were unsuccessful. There seems to be only one obvious alternative. Let us proceed therefore to seek the evidence together, for such conclusions as we may reach.

VIII

MINNEWASKA AGAIN, AND PRAYER

That is a proper title, for the two went together. Prayer was a recognized and valued privilege of many if not most of the people who went to Minnewaska, and they were worthy folk of substantial responsibility in their various activities. Then why should I even take time to make such an observation? It would seem self-evident to most of the people with whom I associate. Yet the experience in behalf of the project might lead me to believe that many men whose responsibilities would presuppose high intelligence, were convinced that the idea of prayer was naive, mere superstition or as best "pure speculation".

In spite of the rebuffs, the proposition was so clear and so urgent in my own mind now that there was no turning back. Therefore the return to Minnewaska and its attitude of reverence was refreshing and reassuring. The winter had been a busy one with engineering research and design work which was under pressure as always. As I recall it, one of the problems that year was the development of the machining of new alloys at elevated temperatures. The mental engineering project was an extracurricular activity.

We took three weeks for our vacation and I brought along paints and sketches. I planned to undertake an illustrative effort to portray the three levels of mentality and the presence there of the Divine influence. It was something of a reaction to a repulsivly Freudian illustration of the mind's operation prepared for "Life" by Artzybasheff.

It should not be supposed from this that I am an artist. A few efforts at oil painting in the early forties were prompted by an effort to divert my mind from the drumming insistence of business problems. The pictures were not too atrocious, possibly by reason of some engineering sense of perspective and relative values. Be that is it may, my efforts in the open doorway of our little balcony initiated friendships with a couple of vacationing artists who paused to kibitz and advise. One of them was in charge of the art work of a large advertising organization, but had taken time from that work to paint a picture of the Christ. His conception portrayed a fine strong face, glowing with the character so evident in Christ's teachings.

Each morning at nine, as was the custom, the guests gathered in the large parlor of the hotel for a hymn, a short discourse and a prayer before we scattered to enjoy the beauties of that wild country. The ministers whom the Smiley's invited were of many denominations and from different parts of the country. Presbyterian Harold de Windt dwelt often upon the close relationship of mental and spiritual hygiene to good health and peace of mind. The Reverend Keipfer related stirring experiences of the nearness of faith and courage in the wartimes. Dr. Stauffer revealed a deep insight into the better side of human character but had little to say of his own fine work for Helen Keller's John Milton Society in its activities for the blind. Incidentally I still treasure a letter of approval and encouragement from him.

Neither they nor I had any question of the efficacy of prayer in view of our own experience. Yet we all realized that the materialistic point of view among educators, and unwittingly, the ever-questioning approach of training in the sciences both added to the difficulties of young people in resolving their own position.

Perhaps it will help if we try to list their honest questions and then see how far we can go in answering them:

1. How can prayer work? That is to say, could there be a human "radio" system which we might utilize in prayer? The biology textbooks make no mention of it and logicians have argued flatly that such a function could not exist.

2. Why don't I hear answers to my prayers?

3. If there is reason to suspect a radio sixth sense, where is it and how can it function?

4. Knowing what we do of radio, what would be the problems of range and tuning in a human system?

5. How can God take care of us all and all our little prayers? (Perhaps this should be the question to end all further discussion).

Parents have often had to answer a curious "Why" with "Daddy knows best," but the questions are fair enough, so let us explore the material we have available for answering them.

Question one, how can prayer work? The current youth of the world accepts radio, television and walkie-talkie sets as normal services and no longer marvels at transmission without wires over greater or lesser distances. But to suggest that the human system has such equipment built into it raises many questions. Why didn't I know it was there? Why can't I use it? Or can I? Will it work as short range as well as long range? Do other people use it? How can it work?

Having such questions very much in mind, I fell into a discussion of them one evening with a radio engineer. He was with the Federal Radio and Telephone Company, a division of I. T. & T. and we met that night in 1945 in a Pullman car enroute from New York to Pittsburgh. We had some time on our hands and the subject seemed to appeal to him as it did to me.

We reviewed the technical comparison of the telephone with the similar human capacity for receiving sound waves (at the ear) changing them into electrical waves for transmission (over nerves) and sending out other (spoken) sound waves. We discussed the language and circuit reasons for believing that a similar radio wave receiving and sending function might exist in the autonomic circuit. We reviewed the comparable but extremely small currents, amperages, and voltages, of the human system.

"But", he argued, "such minute voltages and amperages would not have any sending range."

"Wait a minute," I countered, "you are thinking in terms of the power requirements of commercial sending and receiving sets. But they are gross, clumsy, inefficient things by comparison with what we are talking about. The human system is infinitely more delicate and more sensitive, far better engineered than anything man has built."

He was silent for a moment and then he said, "I think you are right, and perhaps I can illustrate it."

He then told briefly of his two year training in telephone and radar communications services for the Signal Corps. By one of those coincidences his "orders" arrived just before he was to be married. The wedding plans were unceremoniously cancelled for an indefinite period. Without having an opportunity to see his bride-to-be, he was sent down to Florida and put on a plane to fly to Africa. There he participated in the invasion of World War II and went on up through the subsequent invasions of Sicily and Italy.

Three months later there came an unexpected opportunity for a leave. He caught the next plane back, but of course he was not permitted to send any advance word of his return. The A.T.C. plane landed in Florida in the early evening and he rushed at once to a phone and put in a long distance call to his fiancée. The operator put through the connection but he heard no word of greeting. It did sound as if someone was there, possibly crying.

He said, "Honey are you there?"

"Yes," she sobbed, "I have been waiting all day for you to call and was afraid that you were not going to."

We both sat, choked up emotionally for a moment or two. He had not been able to send a commercial telegram to tell her of his return, but somehow the message went through and she sensed its meaning.

Women in wartime are not always so fortunate. A girl of my own generation, and one for whom I have the highest regard, saw her lover off to France in World War I. Some time later she was sharply concerned emotionally for him. Two weeks later came the official telegram from Washington, telling of his death, at that time, and she had sensed it.

In the fall of 1946 I was discussing the spiritual aspects of mental processes and this matter of prayer, with the Young Peoples' Group of our church in Brooklyn. As the meeting closed two of the young men came up to talk to me and one related an experience of his own in the second war. He participated in the invasion of France on D-Day. As they charged up the beach he was hit and wounded. He was taken soon to a field hospital and later to a base hospital. About a week after the injury he received a letter from his mother and in it she asked what had happened to him at that particular time and day.

A business man in Alabama told me of seeing a man approaching him from across the yard of the plant carrying a telegram. While the man was still some distance away he sensed and knew that the message the man bore, told of the death in action of his own son. It did.

What is this means of intercommunication, both long and short range? Most older people seem to have had some experience with it. The term mental telepathy has been applied. An earlier appellation, the sixth sense, may also prove to be a partially acceptable description. Materialistic theorists have tried to explain it away as pure coincidence or autosuggestion. Both explanations undoubtedly apply in some instances but I am sure my wife and I have arrived simultaneously at the same idea, where one has thought of and the other has spoken of it far more often than it can be shrugged off in such a manner. Extrasensory perception is the name applied to it in scientifically conducted tests at Duke University. Dr. Rhine's experiments use cards and symbols to be visualized by a distant receiver. It certainly lacked the emotional urgency of the instances I have cited. Even so, his test subjects demonstrated a perceptive capacity which is beyond the ordinary range of the conscious receiving capacity. The results have been better than the laws of chance would permit us to disregard.

On another train trip westbound out of Washington, D. C. I met a young man whose foreign appearance and fresh complexion attracted me. He was a well-educated chap teaching in Heidleberg and travelling in this country on a teachers exchange arrangement. Our discussion rambled to the efforts of psychological theorists to laugh off the sixth sense, whatever we may wish to call it. That reminded my companion of an experience which was so pertinent that I begged his leave to make notes of it and to have his name and address which he printed neatly for me.

Gert was born and brought up in Estonia and the family property there was extensively wooded. One winter weekend when he was eleven years old he brought a group of friends home and they were allowed to take horses and skis and go out into the woods. On this occasion when they were ready to return at night it was discovered that one boy was missing. The youngsters looked for him without success and eventually returned home where Gert's father promptly set about organizing search parties.

As the evening wore on without report of him, the boys were sent to bed. Gert told me that he must have been asleep a very short time, when in a dream he saw the lost boy sitting at a point in the woods which he recognized. It was so vivid that he wakened at once and went to his mother about it.

She said, "Oh, that is just a dream. You go back to bed."

He wouldn't have it so, for the impression was too firm in his mind, and he went to his father. The reaction of his father was like his mother's. "Why I have twenty men out there searching for him. Now you go back to bed."

But Gert still insisted, and nothing would do but that he get dressed and his father go with him to the point he visualized in the dream. They found his very frightened friend and brought him home safely.

In most of these incidents there has been an element of urgency which tends to increase the nervous tension, quite literally to raise the voltage of the sender's nervous system. There is also an element of attunement, a community of interest between sender and receiver, mother and son, a man and the girl who became his wife. In Gert's story, it was himself whom the boy knew and would think of in his panic, and the message got across.

Naturalists have reported some similar sending and receiving capacity among animals. One such published report told of a mother fox lying at the mouth of the den while the cubs played about. Then one of them wandered too far away. The mother stood up and pointed. There was no sound, but the cub turned around, looked rather sheepish and ambled back.

Have you not had the experience of looking at the back of a person across a crowded car or room, then having them somehow sense that they were being watched, turn around and return the gaze? A cat and bird will often react to your gaze in the same way, although it is not always possible to gain their attention.

Most of the instances related have dealt with messages which do not seem to have been voluntarily initiated. That relates them to the involuntary facial expressions and sounds which are so expressive and have similar meanings in most lands and times. These means of communicating such things as concern, distress, warning, affection and so on and are usually initiated by autonomic (thalamic) reactions.

But may ideas be transmitted between minds by conscious initiation (as in prayer)? It is told of John Burroughs, the naturalist, that he used some such communication means when he wished to summon his sister to visit him. He didn't write her but thought about it, and shortly she came.

My own sister tells of an instance related to the sale of their Brooklyn house, when she wished to reach her husband. She knew that he was not at his office that day and that he was not in the habit of calling her during the day. So she sat down and repeated, "Now Charlie, you call me up. Charlie, you call me up." Shortly the phone rang and it was he on the line. The urgency was not great, but there was the attunement of man and wife, and the idea got across.

A humorous experience of my own is dated March 16, 1946 in my notes and happened one morning on a crowded subway car of the Brighton line in Brooklyn. I found a place to stand near the middle of the car. As my eyes wandered idly from advertisements which I should have known by heart, to newspaper headlines, to people, my attention settled on two who were sitting nearby but facing away from me. The seat was built for two but the girl certainly didn't have her share of it and looked as if she might fall off. The bewhiskered old fellow beside her appeared to be asleep and was not sitting anywhere near the side of the car as he should have been. To see whether it would work, I concentrated upon him and repeated in my mind, "Wake up and move over to give the girl more room." It took me two or three stops, several minutes and many repetitions to gain his attention, but then he awakened, removed a package which I had not seen, from the seat beside him and placed it in his lap. He moved over and the girl moved over to a more comfortable position. Was it coincidence? I think not, for almost immediately the old buzzard looked around and singled his tormentor out of the crowd for a rather reproachful look and turned away. The girl also looked at me, apparently appreciatively, and then went back to her reading.

That incident satisfied me, in my own mind, that a consciously initiated message *can* go through such transformation and transmission and retranslation as is necessary to be intelligible in the mind of another person. That doesn't mean that we know all about it and can do it at will, though perhaps we do affect other people's thinking far more than we realize. There seem to be a variety of factors involving range, power control, attunement, acceptibility of the message and attention or confusion of the receiver's mind, all of which enter into the success of the transmission.

The incidents which I have related are not fiction. They are screened and related as carefully and as accurately as I know how.

And yet there are those who will wave them aside. My notes record a pertinent conversation with a practicing psychiatrist on the evening of May 17, 1951. It was after an adult Mental Hygiene class at one of our high schools and he was one of those on the discussion panel. He was apparently thoroughly indoctrinated with the Freudian habits of thinking.

Of such incidents as we have been considering he said, firmly "It is all coincidence."

On the subject of the sensing of meanings not expressed in words, he was equally obdurate, "One can't think except in language."

Of human receptions and transmission of radio type waves, he said, "I can't conceive that it is possible. There is no receptor."

I had pointed out the evidence to the contrary, briefly, to be sure, for the conversation was held over a cup of coffee and it was getting late. All I could conclude with was, "Doctor, how can you say such things?"

I have quoted since to myself that there are none so blind as those who will not see. But perhaps the trouble was with myself. I had not gone far enough back into his preconceived notions and knowledge, to establish a starting point and build a clear presentation. The things which he found it difficult to believe are those which we should examine with particular care.

* * *

The second question, "Why can't I *hear* the answers to my prayers"? has occured to many people. The word "hear" is the clue, for we realize at once that the things we hear are messages received at the ear, messages which came to us as sound waves through the air.

The sense of hearing is part of the conscious nervous system and is quite easy to check and follow consciously. It has been relatively easy to explore and much is known about it. The sound waves which it receives are changed at the ear to electrical waves and carried to identified brain areas for interpretation of the sounds. There, we store our understanding of the screech of brakes, the clap of thunder and the word sounds of the languages we may have learned.

Quite clearly the answers to prayer and the messages which come to us over considerable distances, do not come in on sound waves, which have a very short range. If they did, they would be easily recognized as such and we would truly hear them. Then literally we do *not* "hear" them although we do sense their reception. This just confirms the more or less obvious observation that the messages are not received in the conscious or voluntary circuit and are not expressed, as received, in the language which we learn and store in the brain areas of that circuit even though we may soon express them in that language.

We must turn therefore to the autonomic or involuntary circuit, and my psychiatrist friend to the contrary notwithstanding, we must recognize another language or means of expression. The word "involuntary" is our clue, for this circuit is beyond voluntary control although there are certain common functions of expression where the nerve specialists find that some facial and other muscles have actuating nerve connections from both circuits.

Thus a smile may be consciously ordered or forced, or it may be quite involuntary, an expression of the "inner environment" and emotions which are an autonomic evaluation. I recall that when my dear father had a stroke, the left side of his face and mouth drooped sadly for some time by reason of the failure of the voluntary nerves on that side. But when an involuntary smile brightened his face the muscles on both sides responded. The smile was initiated from a different and unaffected brain area.

In the same category we may recognize the involuntary but meaningful facial expressions of pleasures, pain, rage, attention, confusion, fear, misery, confidence and so on. Similarly a laugh, a scream, a sigh, a chuckle or a groan may spring involuntarily from our throats. In these and many more we recognize at once that the involuntary circuit has quite adequate means of expression. Furthermore it is language which is quite independent of race or antiquity.

It has a rather general and universal aspect to it. Can this means of expression be at the root of our radio intercommunication?

When we think of radio, we think of audible and recognizable words, but here on second thought, we have an instrument which receives something we cannot hear, radio waves, meaningless pulsations, and changes them at a loudspeaker into something we can "hear" and which we comprehend. To be sure if it were attuned to a foreign station, the language used might be one which the interpretation brain cells of our hearing system had not been educated to understand. It would be all Greek or Chinese to us. Thus if we are to apply conscious thought to messages arriving over our personal radio system we must sense their meaning and then express them in the language we have learned.

I recalled vaguely a biblical story having to do with the confusion of languages which I associated with the Tower of Babel. Upon investigation there proved to be two stories. The first, in the early dawn period in which men's imagination conceived and their ingenuity built the tower. Up to that period, they had gotten along with a (semi-instinctive) common language but thereafter they spread apart and developed many languages. Much later the eleven apostles in their early preaching, observed that devout men of many tongues understood their sermons each in his own tongue. Undoubtedly in those days the tongues around the Mediterranean Sea had not yet become greatly differentiated. Facial expression and gesture of an instinctive and universal order were supplemented by the relatively rudimentary language of the times and their heartfelt message got across.

Personally, I have often risen from prayer with an idea formulating in mind which answered all or some part of the problem before me. At other times, to be sure, the answer did not come for some time, or did not come at all. Whether that might be due to my formulation of the question or to some elements, of selfishness or unworthiness in it is open to question. At other times, even though I had not formulated the need in prayer, I have felt that I was talking or writing "above my head" expressing the point I wished to make, better than I have ever formulated the thought. One recalls that God promised several times to put the necessary words into the mouths of His servants.

Moses was one of those who received such a promise when he was hesitant about tackling the assignment to rescue his people from Egypt. It used to bother me considerably to read Bible passages stating that "God spoke to Moses and said - - - - - - -." My young and scientific curiosity couldn't conceive how such a conversation could take place then, but apparently could not in our current age. Gradually the explanations have become apparent.

Even with our present versatile language it is difficult enough to convey a thought so that it cannot be misunderstood. The reports of Moses' time have been translated and retranslated to a point where the meaning of words is readily lost. Moses recognized the high order of the demands made upon him and understood what was meant. Perhaps it was easier in those days to recognize and interpret autonomic communications. One's conscious mind wasn't so taken up with "book l'arnin'" and conflicting confusion. We are inclined to "dress up" our stories and reports to make them impressive and perhaps the ancient reporters and their translators were no exception. The unvarnished truth is always hard to get at. Perhaps conversation with God is not as mysterious as it has been made to seem. Perhaps our attention really has been diverted from one of our remarkable assets by the interest in our conscious development.

The involuntary and instinctive facial and vocal expressions which have been described are generally grouped as emotional and associated with certain centers of the autonomic circuit called the thalamus and pituitary posterior, which will be discussed later. Other portions of these interesting centers are assigned the responsibility for logic, the organisation or growth of thought. From or through these sources comes the idea which "flashes in our (conscious) mind" to reward our best thinking efforts (and our prayers). We will often note that this wordless idea is of such complexity as to make us hesitate and search for words to adequately describe it.

Here we have an idea, a message which comes *to* the conscious and *from* the other circuit. It is something which we comprehend or sense in all its intricate meaning, but it takes an appreciable effort for us to translate it into the language which we may happen to use for conscious expression and for (sound wave) conversation.

My psychiatrist friend who said, "One can't think except in language," was just uninformed for back in World War II scientific research led the president of Brown University at Providence, to announce that *much* of our thinking is not expressed in language (although they did not undertake to distinguish conscious expression from autonomic). You and I may observe that this is so and the universtiy demonstrated it by a series of tests. Thus it is pointed out that a young mother does not need to resort to language to understand the instinctive expressions of need of her baby. A musician senses the rhythm and harmony of music without resorting in his mind to the mystifying symbols of the printed score. A good mechanic or service man senses his problem but would be slowed down materially if he was required to express his diagnosis in words, before proceeding with the work to be done.

We have noted that people do have experiences which bear out the idea of a radio sixth sense and that the universal language of the autonomic offers a medium of expression for it which is inaudible but comprehensible.

*   *   *

The third Question:—Where is this radio sixth sense and how can it function?

Its location we do not know yet, precisely that is, and those who wish to do so may stop right there. But while much of our knowledge of mind and body is still inconclusive in some respects, there is a working basis of evidence which is highly revealing, and may be quite convincing to you as it has been to me.

First, we must recall something of what is meant by wave transmission without really getting into a review of our college courses. We have all watched the visible waves in motion as ripples spread from the point where a stone is dropped in still water. Dropping the stone initiated a wave movement along the surface of the water. But not all waves are visible. The dropping of the stone also initiated sound waves, a similarly progressive disturbance in air which carried the sound of the splash to the ear, and the light wave disturbances which reported the movement of the falling stone and its splash to the eyes.

The various invisible wave transmissions travel at different speeds. Thus a flash of lightning, a spark traveling between a cloud and the earth, initiates a light wave which, we observe, reaches the eyes much more quickly than the sound wave reaches the ear. It also initiates a radio wave disturbance which reverberates as static in your set and travels roughly midway between the speed of sound and the speed of light.

A deep bass voice sounds a low note which travels relatively slowly with a long wave length and a low "frequency" measured in cycles or wave per second. A soprano note has a shorter wave length and travels faster with a higher frequency. Dogs and bats can hear (supersonic) notes having frequencies higher than those to which the human ear is attuned.

Table one compares an interesting group of natural, com-

CYCLES PER SECOND

20
10_____

        COSMIC RAYS   EXPERIMENTAL X-RAYS

19   GAMMA RAYS   DIAGNOSTIC X-RAYS
10_____   COMMERCIAL X-RAYS

18
10_____

17
10_____

16
10_____

15   ULTRA-VIOLET COMMERCIAL PROC-
10_____   ESSES

     LIGHT WAVES RECEIVED   ELECTRICAL LIGHTING
14   BY MAN'S EYES   MOVIES, TELEVISION PROJECTION
10_____

     HEAT WAVES
13   SKIN HEAT RECEPTORS,   RADIANT HEAT, COMMERCIAL
10_____   MAN, ET AL

12
10_____   ODOR WAVES (RADAR-LIKE)
     HUMAN NASAL RECEPTORS

11
10_____   RADAR, ELECTRIC EEL, CERTAIN
     DEEP SEA FISH SEND AND RECEIVE.

10   RADAR, COMMERCIAL
10_____

MEGACYCLES PER SECOND

1000_____   RELAY TRANSMISSION FOR RADIO
                                AND TELEVISION.
100_____   TELEVISION
10_____

                              WALKIE-TALKIE FIELD RADIO
1_____

KILOCYCLES PER SECOND

1000_____

100_____   160 ⎤
                            ⎥ RADIO BROADCASTING
             55 ⎦

     SUPERSONIC WAVES
10_____   BATS
     DOGS
1_____   SOUND WAVES, RECEIVED   SOUND WAVES, COMMERCIAL, TELE-
     AND SENT BY MAN   PHONE, MICROPHONE, LOUDSPEAK-
     EAR AND THROAT   ERS

CYCLES PER SECOND

1000_____
100_____   25, 50, 60 CYCLE ELECTRIC POWER
10_____   LONG WAVE, ROUND THE WORLD
                                RADIO

     "BRAIN WAVES" IN MAN, FIG. 1
     FREQUENCIES RECOGNIZABLE WITH
1_____   EQUIPMENT NOW USED.

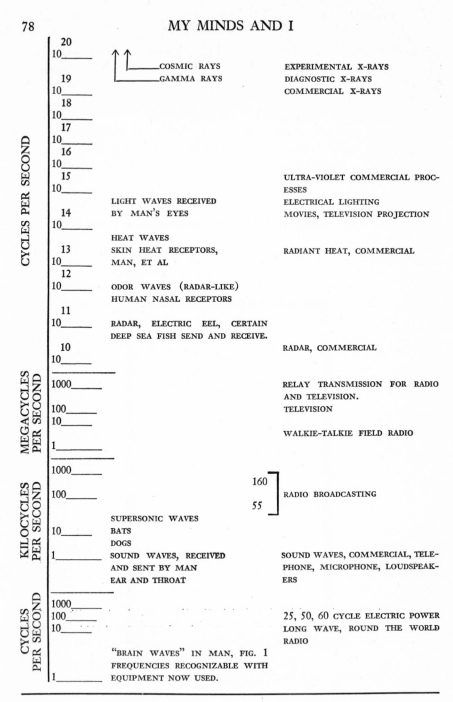

TABLE NO. 1 TABULATION OF NATURAL AND
COMMERCIAL WAVE FREQUENCIES

mercial and human frequencies. The range taken is limited to those which interest us here. Such tabulations or wave length spectrums may be and have been extended in both directions to include all sorts of natural, astronomical and physical rhythms and periodocities to help us to visualize the system and unity of the cosmos. One such "Spectrum" offered rather apologetically in January 1946, in "Electronics Industries", extended from the 200 million year period of rotation of the Milky Way Galaxy of which our earth is a member, down to the very short, fast frequencies of X-rays but did not include the still faster cosmic rays which are constantly arriving at earth from outer space.

Medical research has taken considerable interest in the recording and interpretation of what are termed brain waves. An instrument known as an electroencephalograph is used to amplify and record changes of electrical voltage and frequency within the brain area.

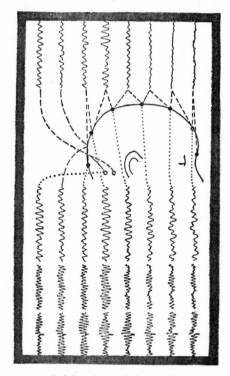

Figure 1. Brain waves recorded by (encephalagraph) receivers at points indicated on the outside of the scalp. They detect variations of overall voltage and apparent frequency in the electrical activity of billions of neurons under varying conditions of nervous tension or of rehabilitating activity. Illustration by courtesy of Massachusetts General Hospital and Life Magazine.

The instrument is a highly sensitive radio receiver equipped with a single or multiple pen recording device to make an ink record such as Figure 1, of the changes which it finds. Its pick-up points or electrodes are made to adhere to the scalp at various points for better reception. The insulation provided in the outer protective layer of the brain and the skull, together with the rough differentiation of reception from different areas combine to show that the reports are received by a radiation effect rather than by conduction through the bloodstream or through the mass of individually insulated nerve fibers in a particular skin area.

Transmission of a message over a telephone line would yield curves or squiggles rather similar to those in Figure 1, although the telephone requires much more power. It uses a rather slow wave carrier current and the different frequencies and strengths of sound waves entering the mouthpiece cause changes in the electrical current which alter the shape and characteristics of the carrier wave.

The relatively large areas of the brain which are checked at each electrode position of the encephalograph, must necessarily combine complex groups of thought activities and therefore represent composite electrical effects. Even so, rather different patterns are found for different brain areas and for different times of day and different conditions of mental urgency.

Investigators thus far seem to agree upon three general frequency ranges having roughly distinguishable characteristics. Slow waves of about ½ to 5 per second appear in infancy and are dominant in deep sleep. A medium frequency of about 6 to 13 waves per second (Morgan says 8 to 12 per second) appears in youth and is dominant in most people during waking hours. This range has been called the alpha rhythm. There is also a higher frequency range of around 14 to as high as 60 waves per second which is found with the slow waves of infancy and also occurs in most adults in periods of drifting off to sleep, dreaming and reawakening. This has been termed the delta rhythm.

The subordinate routines of autonomic control which function around the clock and regardless of age may be associated with the first or very slow groups. The relatively protected position of the autonomic brain areas may make it more difficult to pick up these signals when the outer areas are more active.

The medium range or alpha rhythm appears at present to be concerned with conscious level functioning by reason both of occurrence during waking periods and of tests which tend to confirm this assumption, as I read Morgan.

The higher or delta range he reports, is indentified with certain emotional reactions which would therefore indicate autonomic participation. Higher voltage of the delta waves during sleep may offer some confirmation of autonomic organization of thought during nonconscious periods. The expression, "Let's sleep on it", sums up the situation.

The sagacity of that ancient observation has been borne home to many engineers and professionals. How often have you gone to sleep, troubled by an unsolved problem, and awakened early with a solution to it?

The Chief Tool Engineer, for a large manufacturing concern in Hartford related a typical story to me in August 1945. He was recounting his troubles with an automatic machine of novel design which just wouldn't work. All available talent had been struggling to solve the difficulty for days, and management's patience was wearing thin. Then one morning as he was awakening he found that the solution had taken shape in his mind for he visualized the machine running. He saw clearly the working mechanism at the point where the trouble had been experienced. He arose quickly and sketched the mechanism as he saw it in the dream. That day the parts were made up and tried. The machine worked like a charm. Such things have happened often enough so that the trade has a name for it; "dreamed up solutions."

But to return to brain waves and their frequencies, it is interesting to observe that the instrument currently in use might receive and amplify waves of far higher frequency than those discussed but its pen mechanism would not be fast enough to record them. Instruments might be assembled from existing commercial research units using light beam recording to properly search the field. Quite possibly such work is already under way but at present we cannot prove whether or not higher frequency waves are present in the brain's functioning.

If we examine Table 1, we will observe that sound waves and light waves both have frequency ranges above those which have been identified thus far in nervous system research, yet both are received and distinguished by specialized nerve tips in the ear and in the eye. Between sound and light waves are the ranges of radio waves and of radar waves such as those employed by the electric eel and by certain fish which have been brought up of recent years from the dark depths of the ocean. *Time* for April 9, 1951 reports on one named Gymnarchus niloticus, investigated by Zoology Professor H. W. Lissman, of Cambridge, England.

Human radio functions have had some research recognition. Dr. Robert T. Lustig of Grand Rapids, a specialist in electro-biology was sent to Germany in 1946, heading a five man team to check progress there for the U. S. Government. Upon his return one of four major items to which he gave prominence, was the discovery that certain parts of the body are controlled by impulses, that do not travel over nerve trunks but over human "radio waves". He credited this to Dr. B. Rajewsky, accomplished fifty-two year old director of the Kaiser Wilhelm Institute in Frankfurt on the Main. "While the theories are complicated," Dr. Lustig said, "They explain many mysteries in inter-ralationships in body mechanisms."

"The impulses," he explained, "come from tissues, mostly from the brain, and strike a response with certain distant (nerve) tissues in the same way that a radio sending station need not be wired to a receiver. Dr. Rajewsky determined (that certain) human (nerve) cells are miniature oscillators, (like radio tubes.)

An individual neuron or nerve unit in the human body consists of three major elements each of which may be modified in a wide variety of ways to serve special functions. These include the receiving end or dendrite and its connecting nerve fiber running whatever distance may be required to the cell body itself and a sending system of axons or actuators with nerve fibers connected from the cell body. These neuron units may serve in the receiving system with their dendrites either in the body's outer surface, or in the actuating system with their axons attached to the muscles which they are to call into operation; or the neurons may serve an intermediate function in the chain of command as storage centers, coordinators, etc. As such they receive their messages from the axons of other cells and relay them in turn to the dendrite of still other cells.

The receiving elements of different neurons are engineered in many different designs to suit the functions they are to perform, and nature provides a lavish supply of them in order not to miss anything. The little receivers of the sense of touch are distributed throughout the skin to report an itch or the attack of a marauding mosquito. Scattered among them are the heat wave receivers or temperature recorders. A multitude of light wave receivers line the retina of the eye. Another group arranged to detect the different pitch or frequencies of sound waves are strategically placed in the ear. Taste, smell, pain, internal conditions, supply centers, etc. all have their specialized receiving dendrites and the neurons which evaluate their reports and forward appropriate electrical messages.

I was surprised to run across a report that investigators at Yale were convinced that the sense of smell is an electric wave reception. They placed the wave frequency range of odors at around a million million cycles per second. Accordingly the receptors' dendrites in the nasal passages would be attuned to frequencies more or less between those of the eye and the ear (and above the radio and radar range).

In view of the enormous number and great variety of receptor terminals and the admitted difficulties of identification, it is certainly not intellectually honest to say, as my psychiatrist friend tried to, that "there is no receptor" for a radio function.

Actually we may expect to find several; an extremely short range signal system for the bodily remote controls in which Dr. Rajewsky is interested; message transmission in a frequency band between hearing and smell; and something of a television function to account for the "dreamed up solution" and Dr. Rhine's extrasensory perception of shapes in the band around ten to a hundred million cycles per second. All of them are intermediate bands between those which we know now that we *do* receive.

Where is the receptor? Actually it will be a group of dendrites. These may be distributed throughout the skin or localized in one area. There is some suggestion that the pineal gland, which has characteristics of a receptor might be the seat of one or more groups, an internal third eye which scans the wave transmissions which we know exist between sound and heat.

These radio and television receptor dendrites and the neurons to which they are attached are almost certainly part of the autonomic circuit and not in the conscious or voluntary circuit. We can say this for two reasons. First because we can consciously check and sense the location of the five conscious receiving groups. And second because the messages which the conscious area receives from these centers are expressed, not in consciously learned languages but in the emotional and sensed impressions, of the autonomic mental activities.

At present, we can only say that we have not yet identified such reception centers or areas, and must add with equal candor that we have not yet developed instrumentation or technique equal to the task. Personally I believe that it can and will be done within the century, and that clarification of our point of view and development of our thinking procedures will be part of the technique.

Such identification of the neuron receptors assigned to the intermediate frequency bands of human radio and television should be of value and may help to silence or at least divert cynical controversy. But in the meantime, we may recall that men conversed over the sound waves before they understood the neurology of the ear and throat and men prayed before they thought to invent radio or to recognize its anticipation in nature.

*　　*　　*

In question four we permitted our youthful curiosity to ask our mature wisdom, such as it is, about the wave lengths or frequencies, the ranges and the tuning of our mental radio system.

From the tabulation and discussion of transmission waves and their frequencies we may note that there is no distinction in the waves whether they are to be received by man or by some scientific or commercial device made by man. The same sound waves may be received by ear and by telephone or microphone. Man has found certain bands or ranges of frequency suitable for radio, radar and television transmission and it is probably a safe assumption that any natural equivalent of these, like the electric eel's radar will fall into the same general bands.

To be sure, in man's development of commercial radio, he found it necessary to start with sound waves, in whatever language may be used, and to convert them into some unintelligible jargon of electrical waves for radio transmission. He then reconverts them to sound waves at the receiver's loudspeaker.

In the mental radio system this conversion and reconversion may not be necessary although a similar sequence is followed in the conscious reception of light waves and sound waves and the conversion of their messages for electrical transmission over the nerve system. If we have correctly observed the functioning of mental radio, it takes the message in the universally sensed code or language of the autonomic circuit, which is already an electrical transmission and transmits it in that form to the receptor neurons of the recipient's mind.

On second thought however, we should probably go one step further at each end and recognize the conversion to and from the individuals' conscious area and language. That is, I consciously frame some thought in English for transmission to my wife's mind. It must undergo some conversion into the language of my autonomic circuit and thence, if I succeed in gaining her attention, to hers. There she must sense its meaning and reconvert to words to make some remark about it to me as she so often does.

A story may be pertinent as to the universality of this language of the sensed impressions. The wife of a lawyer friend of mine is herself a lawyer who gives freely of her time for charitable legal work. I believe it was the summer of 1946 that she and her little daughter took a kitten with her when they opened up their summer home in Great Barrington. A few days later it was discovered to her daughter's distress that the kitten was missing. As she helped her daughter search for it, a thought flashed into her mind of the home of a friend a ways down the hill toward the village. It was getting late however and she dismissed the thought. The next morning came, and again there was no kitten to be found, and again the thought came to mind of the acquaintance down the hill. She decided to stop there on her way to market and a little later she did.

"Hello. Have you seen anything of our lost kitten?"

"Why yes. There is a kitten up in that tree."

The lost was found.

Certainly it could be dismissed as coincidence, if you prefer to do so, but on the other hand there are the same characteristics of urgency and attunement which have been found in other instances. The urgency was there for the lost kitten in the tree was scared. The attunement was there for the kitten had been separated from its own mother for some time and would naturally think of the one who fed it, and took care of it, when it was in need of help. Such a message of distress should be easy to convey and to sense. Apparently the message did get through twice before action was taken on it.

The matter of attunement involves selection of, or tuning to a frequency common to both sender and receiver, and also gaining the attention of the receiver.

In the instances of the longer range transmissions we seem to have observed something of a community of interest between sender and receiver. Affection and interdependence may enter into the attunement of husband and wife, mother and son, young man and sweetheart, the kitten and the one who took care of it.

The sender's success in gaining the attention of the receiver may be a matter of urgency as in screaming or shouting, or it may be a matter of persistence. The telephone jangles a noisy bell to gain attention. A radio operator may have to persist a seemingly endless time with his SOS before he gains the attention of a potential rescue ship.

At the bridge table, or a social tea it becomes almost a matter of social violence for a mere man to break into the dear ladies' conversation. Such things merely indicate that for any intercommunication between two people, first the two must be in attunement to the extent of being willing to talk to each other, and second the sender must gain the attention of the receiver.

In my humorous experience with the old codger in the subway and in my sister's effort to reach her husband a certain amount of persistence was required. We may note there the need to catch an instant when the receiver's attention was not concentrated on some thought or action and possibly further persistence required to convince them that we mean what we are saying.

In the overseas experience it might be suspected that the women were sitting waiting at their instruments as it were, that their minds were quite steadily upon their loved ones in the danger zones. Be it said at the same time that such a practice is not one to encourage except in the presence of strong faith. Otherwise fear-filled ramblings of the imagination may conjur up detrimental false alarms. Not a few women have literally worried themselves sick through inadequate faith, for that is the way of psychosomatic disruption of health as we shall see.

At the highest level many men have demonstrated attunement with God to an outstanding degree. From Christ and the prophets of old on down through Martin Luther, Knox, Calvin, and all, to many current occupants of our pulpits; the evidence of inspiration has been and is strong. But it is not limited to those called directly to God's service. Among scientists, Steinmetz, Carver, Edison, Einstein, Sinnott, Condon and many others have expressed their personal acknowledgement of God's guidance. Many doctors whom I have met, have risen above Freudian malconditioning to a warm and radiant faith which they are free to express. And even you and I can sense the answers to our worthy prayers, for it is the privilege of all men.

*   *   *

Question five. How can God take care of us all, and all of our little prayers? Well obviously I don't really know. Probably no mere man can actually know. But you and I have asked ourselves that question many times.

That being the case, it must be admitted as a live question to which answers may be sought. How would you organize the handling of such a voluminous service if you were in God's place? How are the observable overall controls organized in Nature and in the human body?

We marvel in our readings, at the balancing forces which keep the planets, the stars, and the galaxies in their periodic orbits, and at the systematic disintegration and reintegration of their life cycles as we begin to understand them. It is easier perhaps to follow the brief life cycles of the amoeba or the fruit fly in the studies which have been published upon them. We marvel also at the interlocking food supply services and the checks and balances upon pestilence and oversupply, balances which we succeed in disturbing from time to time.

So also in the human body there are marvelous checks and balances. There are destructive forces, acids, enzymes, bacteria which participate in digestion and the removal of undesirable elements and by-products, and the fighting of disease and infection. There are also the constructive forces which build and rebuild and which store reserves to be dispensed as required. Over all of these are the controls exercised through nerves and hormones from involuntary and instinctive autonomic brain centers which have the responsibility for our positive health. To be sure, again, we may consciously, though perhaps not intentionally disturb these controls, for of such are psychosomatic disorders.

The humble attitude of prayer is in itself a spiritually healthy thing. In the repetition there of prayers which we have memorized, we remind ourselves of the rules and regulations for living, the spiritual values which should be kept in mind. This is a form of private spiritual hygiene or calisthenics under the general supervision of the Higher Authority but not really requiring specific attention. It is like the routine paper work of a large organization which saves the management trouble, and accomplishes the purpose, so long as it is conscientiously attended to. It is like the instinctive provisions of migration, reproduction and self-preservation which take care of many requirements automatically without specific supervision. Such repetitious prayer keeps the conscious self reminded of its unselfish position and righteous point of view, both essential to Christian behavior.

As we proceed from behavior to accomplishment there arise the prayers, expressed or felt, for guidance and inspiration. Here again, "the Lord helps them who help themselves". We have been provided with the facility in the autonomic circuit for the organization of thought. We must help ourselves consciously by gathering the basic material from which the solution may be evolved. Even so we may not achieve the answer if our mental attitude, our point of view is not satisfactory. It may be so self-centered, so biased, distracted or confused that we cannot or do not sense the answer, the idea which flashes into our mind. On the other hand the attitude of humble faith and confidence appears to facilitate the process. And at times the answers to problems framed in prayer seem to come from beyond ourselves for we recognize no precedent for their formulation within our own thought experience.

In matters of physical health and of peace of mind, which presupposes mental health, the approach of prayer may be expected to establish the liaison between conscious and autonomic efforts which can clarify and cleanse and restore. It opens the way to help ourselves which is often all that is necessary.

At times however, as in my experience related in the first chapter, we have sunk too deeply in the rut on our own bad habits of thinking to help ourselves out or to be helped by our ordinary medical and spiritual advisers.

A few months ago our beloved John Barker was preaching on the subject of angels and the guidance and assistance which they rendered in biblical times. It troubled me some for there should not be any difference between those times and these. Then the light began to dawn. A short time later a rabbi explained to me that the word "angel" meant "messenger of God."

My mind went back to my own experience. What or who had inspired the reticent wife of the farmer in Greenfield to ask me to read the booklet which introduced me to George Washington Carver's faith and to the writings of Glenn Clark. They were the leaven which restored my health and changed my outlook on life.

Her fleeting and unsought mission bore results which merit my endless though unexpressed gratitude. My need for restoration of faith was great, but at the time I didn't know it, nor could she. Surely she qualified as a messenger of God, an angel.

Now as I look back on life, it seems easy to recognize a number of people who were God's messengers. Voluntarily or involuntarily they performed acts or delivered messages which savored of inspiration and benefited the lives of others when most needed. I can even identify occasions where I, a most ordinary mortal, may have performed a similar service.

How can such things happen? We have examined the means by which minds may communicate with other minds at a level out of the conscious range. Is there any reason to assume that minds cannot involuntarily render assistance. This suggests many possibilities of unexpressed influence within both the family and the community. Deeper influences of environment may be present than we have visualized. God seems to organize the essential services through the normal media which are at hand.

How should I visualize God, the Higher Authority to whom I feel that I am responsible in my own small way? It has been said that we are created in His image. Physically? or spiritually? I believe that we will find in the autonomic circuit, the spiritual, the character responsibilities which we hold to be Godly. We esteem in man those qualities which we attribute to God.

It has been pointed out that things unseen are the real and the permanent values. The thoughts and character of a man's inner mental and spiritual self are more real than the things he may say, or the outward show he may put on.

The word "actor" describes one who has learned to voluntarily imitate the involuntary emotional expressions of the autonomic circuit. The latter are real values which we often conceal or suppress. We describe them variously as tragic, sympathetic, affectionate, etc. Compared with these the visible show is often a hollow and passing mockery.

The human body as we see it and all the furnishings and things about us are very complex arrangements of electrons and protons, energy spaced and arranged in the stabilized form of matter. All of it may be broken down again, largely or completely, into energy, invisible, powerful, indestructible energy.

Electrical devices and the human mind and higher circuit are powered by energy, positive and negative charges in motion or ionizing a modification of form. A thought or message in motion is energy in action. A thought in storage requires an energy shift in the complex molecular structure of a neuron.

Then the mental store, the heritage, the character and the nervous activity of the man are static or dynamic energy. And his influence upon others and God's influence upon him involves the same invisible and indestructible energy. Perhaps then, I may go so far in my own effort to understand, as to conceive God as the summation of all energy, all powerful, omnipresent, unseen, permanent and universal. From there I may go on to visualize the creation of our heritage of character in His image, the fine and worthy qualities which we sense and hold in high regard.

At the same time, it probably serves an acceptable purpose to picture Him, physically in my mind's eye, as a forceful and friendly patriarch to whom I may turn respectfully in my times of need.

INTERLUDE

We have some hard work ahead of us so let's stop and consider the plan of action for a moment. Back in July of 1945 I sensed an obligation and have been struggling to fulfill it.

Confused combinations of eary misconceptions in scientific efforts to understand the human mind have combined with materialistic influences and theological inadequacies to place our educators in a difficult position. They must endeavor to teach our young people to use their minds in a scientific manner to cope with the complexities which our rapid material progress presents. But it has been difficult to correlate the vital principles of religion in an overall unity, and even our great research foundations have shown reticence about undertaking the task.

Regardless of how fool-hardy it may seem for an individual to try to spark so explosive a project we are in the midst of the effort.

The next ten chapters study elements of the human system step by step. First conscious and subconscious activities, then spiritual, emotional and instinctive responsibilities of the "involuntary" system are considered. The essential information had to be drawn from many different sources. The presentation will undoubtedly be done over and much better as time progresses.

You will probably not find these chapters easy reading although my son, Ed, paid me the compliment of enthusing about them. The comparatively few technical names of organs and systems are identified in illustrative charts.

In opposition, one of my loyal critics was severe with me for including these chapters in the book. He felt that delving into our inner privacy should be relegated to a separate volume and we should proceed to the conclusions reached and then go on to develop their application for mental and spiritual health.

The matter of application leads us on to an almost infinite variety of fields and approaches. One of these would be to chart the workings of the mind in an effort to understand how we learn for the purposes of education. Fig. 2 anticipates discussion in succeeding chapters to chart the process of learning. It will help us to examine our own thinking as we note our sources of "input" wisdom and examine our evaluations of the evidence which is to be considered.

The critic had a point however in his desire to by-pass the controversial considerations and the pondering of evidence. Why not skip over to page 222. Read Chapters XIX and XX discussing the field of mental and spiritual hygiene, and the tribulations of ill-governed and unbalanced thinking. Then read Chapters XXI and XXII the conclusions concerning the duties and privileges of our minds, and their balanced usage.

Perhaps the statement of the conclusions will be as far as you want to go.

If you do wish to return and evaluate the material from which those conclusions were drawn, advance reading of them may be helpful. The chapters on the elements of the system beyond the conscious will probably require slow reading. While the data is still inadequate in some places, the influences of voluntary thinking and instinctive wisdom, drives and evaluations upon mental and physical well-being were fascinating to me and I hope will prove equally so to you.

PHASE I OF L E A R N I N G   (PARTICIPATION OF MENTAL BODIES)

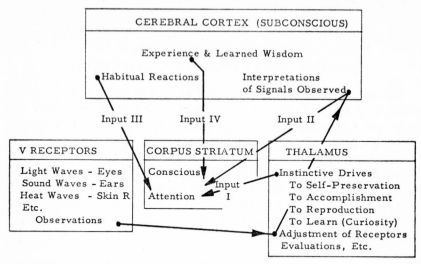

PHASE II OF L E A R N I N G

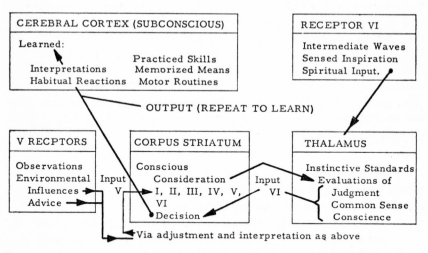

Figure 2. The Learning Process—Phase I, focusing of conscious attention (under influence of drives) and bringing together pertinent material. Phase II, consideration of input material, evaluation thereof, and decision upon a resultant which is to be stored as "learned" for future use. The different mental bodies, their locations and functions are to be examined in succeeding chapters.

IX
BIGWIN AND CONSCIOUS THINKING

Eleanor and I have just arrived at the Bigwin Inn, a well appointed vacation spot on a Canadian lake. The two weeks planned here will fly by but I want to soak up some relaxation to go back refreshed to the design problems of the big forging presses.

The mornings are assigned to writing but the rest of the day we devote to the scenery and the activities. Yesterday we climbed to the highest part of the island and up the tower. That gave us a wide view of Lake of Bays and its wooded islands and the steep shores. From such a height the waters of the lake were a smooth and glassy blue. Truly, "He leadeth me beside the still waters"—for refreshment of mind, for thinking.

Bigwin is not like Minnewaska. It is more modern, more worldly, more showy but it falls short of the rugged magnificence of scenery and it lacks the human acknowledgement of God's presence which the Quaker Smileys maintained in their brief daily religious services. Perhaps that makes it a fitting place to consider man's conscious facility for thought, that accomplished and worldly sphere of activity wherein we seem inclined for a time to feel that *we* reign supreme. The matters of Higher Authority and personal responsibility need not be considered however, until we come again to problems of mental balance and its maintenance.

*   *   *

The conscious, (the voluntary, the command post), the activity which distinguishes me, myself, to the rest of the world. What do we know and what can we observe about it?

1. Can we properly separate it out of our complex system as a single entity, a unit which can be examined as such?
2. What does it include and where is it?
3. How does it function?
4. What are its activities?

Forgive me for setting up the problem again in a series of questions. So much material comes to hand that it seems a proper way to try to avoid confusion.

"Voluntary" was one of words used to describe this major function and responsibility. The things I control voluntarily; the things I decide to do for whatever reason; the actions, the expressions, the conversation, the physical and mental operations which I order and carry out, (whether or not I have given adequate thought to the decisions), these distinguish the functioning of the voluntary nervous system.

The word "conscious" is also applied to description of the voluntary functions and system. It is in contradistinction to; (a) non- conscious or *in*voluntary autonomic responsibilities, (b) the unconscious state, when the conscious system is inactivated by sleep or anesthetics or damage and (c) the subconscious which will require consideration by itself.

Before by-passing it however, we may note that the subconsciously used areas and nerve tracks are distinctly part of and incorporated in the conscious system. The prefix "sub" properly indicates that the subconscious activity is subordinate to the conscious system and controllable by it at will. The two must be distinguished because we do have subconscious operation apart from and simultaneous with conscious operation.

Consciously it is only possible to carry out one operation at a time. Some of us flatter ourselves that we are different in that respect, but a little impartial observation will prove otherwise. Involuntary operations and subconscious procedures may be and often are in action at the same time as some single conscious consideration or operation:

A woman may knit (as has been noted) with her fingers pursuing a practiced and subconsciously controlled repetitive movement. At the same time she can carry on a consciously directed conversation. But if the routine falters and she drops a stitch, she must stop the conversation and devote conscious attention to picking up the stitch.

I follow the long practiced (subconscious) routine of washing and shaving each morning and at the same time devote my conscious effort to planning my day or solving some design problem. Then sheepishly I discover that I am lifting the razor to shave but have omitted the detail of first applying the shaving cream. "Absent minded" we call it, for the "conscious mind" was engaged elsewhere leaving the established routine to the subconscious (which may falter or be diverted).

Of an evening, I sit comfortably and peruse the newspaper, *and* listen to a news broadcast. Ah, two conscious efforts at once! But it doesn't work for I get interested in the paper and discover that the newscast is over and I haven't heard a word of it. Furthermore while

I was concentrating on the article, my wife asked me a question and I hadn't the faintest idea what it was about. The autonomic nerve connections to my ear had registered a mild warning so that I stopped reading and asked her what it was she said. My conscious attention could be swung from one thing to another rather quickly but it does not grasp or function on more than one at a time.

As I sit here concentrating upon the formation of the next phrase, I am a bit annoyed by diversions, because my fingers persist in subconsciously reacting to pursue a minor itch or discomfort which I would consciously prefer to ignore.

We may whistle while we work or carry on an animated conversation while we drive a car or feed a punch press, but when something goes awry with the subconscious routine, it may be too late to get conscious attention back on the job. Many deaths and accidents trace directly to the misconception that a "genius like I," can pay conscious attention to two things at once.

The command post was the third descriptive title given to this unit of mental operation. The thought was developed earlier that here "I" hold full sway as captain of my ship. Here I receive my reports of what is going on within and without, determine what supplies I must take on, decide upon my purpose and my course and give the orders to carry out what I will. I may lose limbs, eyes or other appurtenances and yet find a useful way to carry out my purpose. But if this vital unit of thinking equipment is destroyed or rendered inoperable, then the world will see me as a useless hulk.

Just to remind ourselves of the trite and obvious, the passerby may see us as a figure or a face, well groomed, and attractive or otherwise. But the things which count are what we do and accomplish, how do we conduct ourselves and discharge our responsibilities. How well have we learned to utilize our remarkable conscious facility and the services upon which it may call?

*   *   *

2. What does the conscious or voluntary system include and where is it located?

Being a nervous system, it is comprised of neurons, nerve cells, great numbers of them, specialized for many purposes with groupings and interconnections to suit those purposes, yet in certain essentials acting as a unit. That is to say, the conscious unit (of several billion neurons) can concentrate its undivided attention upon only one thing at a time, an activity, a consideration, a weighing of decision.

This unit system comprises four major groupings, each of which will require further division:—(a) *The Receiving senses,* in which groups of neurons with specially devised receiving terminals pick-up the various pressures, pains, wave movements, chemical reactions etc., which carry the information we seek. (b) *The storgage areas,* the major portion of neurons, which store the information we are to keep and use. Here again there is a great deal of departmentalization, grouping of information by sources and by (motor) uses. We will compare these warehouse groups with business office files for information, correspondence, etc., although their indexing seems to be much more efficient. (c) *The operational system,* a spreading network of neurons and their sending nerve fibers; to convey the instructions and bring into desired action the muscles of throat or body which are to carry out the action decided upon. (d) *The organizational system,* the intermediate neurons which provide the pathways and mediate the harmonious combination of subsidiary associations and compilations into ultimate decision, ready for delivery to the operational network, (c).

The neuron, the multi-shaped building block of which all this system is composed, is a thing of intriguing interest. It is a trained and retrainable living thing, requiring nourishment, expending energy and subject to fatigue and even death within the living host. The aspect of its healthy life rather than its fatigue and death is one which we would emphasize. It is the aspect vital to those kindred professional and business people whose energy-consuming mental efforts tend to be carried on in an unhealthy atmosphere of frenzied pressure, and to those worried and distraught people whose inadequate mental housekeeping has led them into fatiguing conflict and confusion.

The variously specialized neurons have much in common with the many other cells of which the body is comprised. Like that simplest form of life, the single celled amoeba, each has an outer permeable membrane through which it draws its needed nutriment and expels its waste products. The cell maintains through its membrane an equilibrium condition with respect to temperature, pressure and electrical energy (the positive and negative charges known as ions.) Each cell contains much water which acts both as a solvent for chemicals and an electrolytic fluid for electrochemical reactions. Its structural members are largely compounds of carbon, hydrogen and oxygen. Phosphorous, nitrogen and sulphur play important parts as do mineral salts of calcium, potassium and magnesium. Other elements also have vital places, but oxygen is thought to be the most essential to refreshment of fatigue.

The whole nervous system operates in a bath of cerebrospinal fluid which serves to supply the necessary nutriments for rebuilding and refreshment, and to carry away the waste products. Enclosure of this liquid is provided by the brain envelope, the spinal column and a branching system of tubes, which enclose the nerve fibers. The refreshing water and chemicals are brought into this system by bloodstream arteries at the midbrain. The waste products are removed by veins at the lower rear portion of the brain.

Each nerve cell or neuron, is distinguished from other body cells for it extends one thread-like receiving fiber out to a terminal receiver which picks up the information it seeks. It also extends other fibers to make connections with the receivers of other neurons which should be influenced by the digested message or signal which it passes on to them. The great numbers of neurons which are reporting, intercommunicating and counteracting permit the observation of fine shadings of color or meaning or influence and carry out a delicate weighing, intermingling and counterbalancing of many neuron influences or thought forces as their message progresses.

The primary *receiving* groups (a) of the conscious system may now be recognized as not five but *six receiving senses*. The obvious five are the senses of sight, hearing, taste, touch and smell. The sixth sense of the conscious is that group of internal receiving neurons which make contact with the autonomic system. They permit us to sense its reports of internal environment such as appetite and nervous tension, the emotional evaluations, conceptive ideas, instinctive drives, inspiration, etc. The name ramii has been given to the comparatively limited group of interconnecting fibers furnishing the communications between the two nervous systems. What we may know of the sixth sense services to the conscious system will develop when we consider the autonomic system and its various centers.

Sight, the visual receiving sense, begins with the focusing of approaching light waves through the lens and upon the retina of the back of the eyeball. There are three successive layers or groups of neurons in this area alone. The first layer possesses two types of specialized receiving tips described as rods and cones which are directed toward the lens. These are electrochemical light-sensitive receivers which convert the color combination, light intensity and the duration which registers movement into electrical form for transmission. Under these is a layer of horizontally disposed neurons of two different types which associate and interrelate the activities of receptor neurons and groups of neurons. The third group of neurons, described as ganglion cells, receive the findings of the receptors, further interrelate them and transmit the results back over their own sending fibers which are gathered in the bundle which is called the optic nerve.

A few of these neurons send their terminals to autonomic neuron centers which evaluate intensity of light, sharpness of image, etc. and send back return fibers to eye muscles to adjust the pupil size, the lens focus, etc. The remaining fibers of the optic nerve are divided, and part of them are crossed to the opposite side to permit the comparative evaluation for judgment of distance, speed and perspective. The optic nerve fibers terminate at what are called the lateral geniculate bodies where another group of neurons receive their messages, perform some mediating or evaluating function, possibly the spatial relations, just noted, and then relay the signals over their own sending fibers for final projection or reproduction at the visual area of the cerebral cortex located near the rear of the brain. Here at last we have reached the large mass of brain cells assigned to the storage of the meanings of things seen. Here we put away the form and color of things recognized, the shape and meaning of language learned, the appearance of things, to which we may wish to refer. It must be appreciated of course that so brief a description of the visual nervous system involves oversimplification and ommission of supporting evidence.

Next, the sound analyzing, reporting, storing and recognizing mechanisms of the sense of hearing are remarkable in their perfection and compactness compared with the effective but awkward audio devices which human engineers have designed.

Air is made up of atomic particles of nitrogen, oxygen, carbon, hydrogen and other elements alone or in simple combinations. These are floating freely and well spaced apart in the manner of gases. A sound wave such as that imparted by the vibration of a drum head, sets these particles into vibrating motion which spreads like the visible ripples imparted to particles of still water by the blow of a stone dropped into a pool.

Such a sound wave is picked up by the ear, Figure 3 and funneled in to set up an equivalent vibrating movement on a receiving diaphragm or membrane, TM. The other side of this diaphragm is cushioned against still air, T, from the throat which is controlled as it passes through a connecting tube, E.

A delicate system of bones and msucles, IN, attached to this receiving diaphragm transmits a controlled portion of its movement across the dead air space to another diaphragm, FR. This imparts the adjusted vibrations to liquid which fills the analyzing chambers containing the specialized receiving tips of the neurons which are assigned here.

The analytical devices include two discs set at angles to each other, the semicircular canals and an interesting spiral chamber which tapers smaller toward the far end. The chamber is really divided into two paralleling spirals separated by a layer of hairs growing out of the tapering central column. The column contains the hair-cells which are receiving tips for the frequency analyzing neurons which are within the column. The liquid of the lower spiral is cushioned at a window or diaphragm, F, on the dead air space. The liquid of the upper spiral is set in motion by the vibrations of the diaphragm FR. The wave length or frequency of this motion will therefore disturb the hairs to a proportionate distance up the spiral. High pitch sounds are registered near the large end of the horn and deep low pitch sounds toward the small end.

This selective movement of the hairs is registered upon the receiving tips of the hair cell neurons. An electrical pressure reported to be about 80 millivolts is maintained by these neurons and the hair

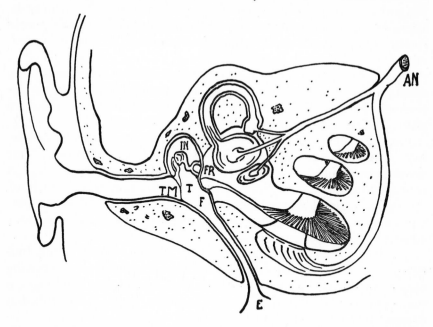

Figure 3. Mechanisms of the ear which detect the variations of direction, distance, frequency, etc., of incoming sound waves and send their findings, as electrical waves, through appropriate brain areas for evaluation, interpretation, and possible storage. (After Czermak; from P. H. Mitchell, Physiological Psychology, by Clifford T. Morgan, by permission McGraw-Hill Book Co., Inc. New York, copyright 1943.)

movement alters the resistance in the haircells which initiates the signals transmitted over the fibers gathered at AN enroute to the brain area.

The (first) groups of neurons in the analyzing chambers of the ear selectively identify relative frequency, direction, distance and duration of sound waves. They dispatch their electrical reports through two relay stations or groups of neurons before they reach the brain areas which are assigned to storage and the trained identification of combinations of sound such as musical numbers and language.

It is probably that the first group of intermediate neurons are charged with autonomic evaluation of the reports for direction, clarity and intensity in order to make the necessary operating adjustments at muscles of the neck (for direction), at the tiny transmitting and damping linkage between diaphragms and at the equalizing tube to the throat.

It seems likely that the second set of intermediate neurons perform an evaluating service of an autonomic nature such as appraising whether the sounds ring true or false, whether they are pleasant or alarming and if they comprise an item worthy of storage for future use.

The sense of touch differs from sight, hearing, taste and smell in that its receptors are not concentrated in local areas but are widely distributed, requiring a major network of nerve fibers and a large number of neurons. The brief description must obviously be generalized but it is adequate for our present purpose. Under the heading of touch we appear actually to be dealing with three distinct sensory systems; the thermal, pain and pressure systems, each of which have distinctive receptors and are separately grouped as their fibers traverse the spinal column.

The receiving bulbs or nerve tips of the thermal system are scattered selectively over the body near the surface of the skin and report variations of temperature both above and below normal body temperatures. They selectively report local contacts with hot or cold objects and drafts as well as general temperature changes and are subject to some adaptability of range. The neurons which receive the local reports put their findings into the form of an electrical evaluation for transmission to the secondary series of neurons in the spinal column near the points of entry. These relay the reports directly to the cerebral cortex (the outer brain areas). At successive steps appropriate actions are taken with respect to local opening or closing of sweat glands, autonomic increase or decrease of the bodily heat from stored fuel supplies and final conscious consideration of clothing requirements, open windows and furnaces or fans.

The pain receptor neurons deliver their electrical reports at convenient levels of the spinal column in the same way but make intermediate connections with quite a series of neurons before reporting to the thalamus and thence to their conscious area of the cerebral cortex. The system observes local cuts, bruises, irritation, infection, fatigue, etc. Its successive neurons presumably order local action to isolate the damage, general autonomic action to correct it including increased blood supply, increased white corpuscles or iodine contained in thyroxin, etc. Quickly enough, but last in the series comes conscious consideration of splinter removal, first aid applications and possible retaliation.

The presure system utilizes free nerve endings in the skin, groups of nerve ends arranged around the root of each hair to detect movement of the hair and specialized corpuscles in the hairless regions such as the finger tips. Here again successive neurons in series pick up, coordinate, evaluate and report to the autonomic and then to the conscious system, on their findings. They must determine degrees of pressure from a passing breeze and a firm grip to a blow, areas of contact by group operation, movement by progressive contact, and must give a check on muscular performance as a part of the smooth coordination of movement. Subconscious routine movements are presumably supervised by second or third order neurons of this system.

Sub-conscious reflex reactions detecting the presence of a fly and locally ordering the muscular movements of skin or hand to get rid of it are attributed to the second order neurons in the spinal column, before the report ever reaches the brain area. At this lower intermediate level all three of the touch senses, possibly with the help of others, may cooperate in the ordering of reactions which are instinctive or practised. This is a more rapid response than is possible when the messages must travel on through various time consuming connections for conscious consideration.

So much for the conscious *receiving* system. The specialized receptors of initial neurons, or nerve cells, in the several receiving senses detect and pass on their findings through intermediate levels of neuron responsibility until they finally reach the cerebral cortex. This is the wrinkled outer layer or rind of the brain, composed of several layers of neurons specialized for memory storage of consciously usable information.

The *storage* or memory function (b) is largely but not entirely

distributed over this area. It must be remembered that large groups
of neurons or nerve cells belonging to the other, the autonomic system are in protected areas well below or within the area of the
cerebral cortex and that still others of the subordinate reflex group
are distributed down the spinal column.

The consciously used storage areas of the cerebral cortex are
mapped about as well as we are able to do at this time in figure 4.
The locations of particular responsibilities have been charted by the
testing of people having accidental or other damage in various areas
of the brain, and further checked by experimental work during
operations and by laboratory work on animals.

This voluntarily utilized area of the human brain has been greatly
developed by comparison with animals, especially in those localized
areas associated with sight, hearing and manipulative skills.

It has been observed that the invention and development of language has contributed tremendously to human advantage. The learning of word sounds, spoken meanings, wisdom of all sorts brought

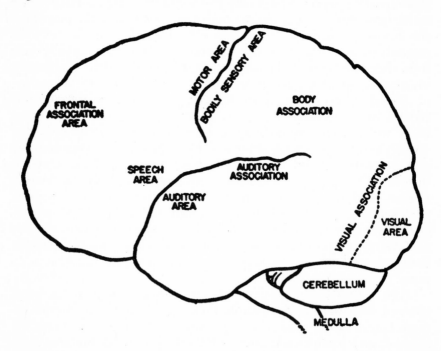

Figure 4. The human cerebral cortex, the outer portion of the brain where things
which are learned find storage in assigned areas. See also Figure 9, a section through
the brain. (page 16, Physiological Psychology by Clifford T. Morgan; by permission
McGraw-Hill Book Company, Inc. N. Y. copyright 1943.)

in through hearing, is founded upon language. College lectures, business conversations and such are catalogued and stored away in the side areas of the brain which happen to be near to the ears and are assigned to their service.

The auditory area is that in which the analyzed sounds are scrutinized for primary meaning and identification and then rerouted to appropriate portions of the auditory associations where greater complexity of things heard are put away and drawn upon as required. It is natural also that the speech area should be close to the auditory area for there we put away the means of forming the words and sounds we wish to send forth. These are sounds which the ear should check for satisfactory formation. The great development of the human-speech and hearing-storage requirement is probably responsible for the deep convolution which increases the brain's surface area in this section and there-by increases its usable neuron space.

The visual area is at the rear of the brain, opposite to the position of the eyes. It is reported that meticulous nerve checking has shown that reporting nerve endings take positions in this area corresponding to the positions of receiving nerve tips in the back of the eye. Thus the image seen is projected or reproduced at "the mind's eye". We can only surmise at present that intermediate connections should make it possible to project at this same point the things which we mentally visualize or which we see in dreams.

Visual associations in adjacent areas are the stored and available records of things seen and things known by reason of having seen them and learning to understand them. The human invention of writing and printing made it possible to set down and to transmit the stored experience and organized knowledge accumulated, through the eyes. This area therefore shares with hearing, the basic distinction of man, the learned background for his inventions and development.

The body sensory area where movements and "touch" are reported, the body associations area where manipulative skills, the arts and crafts, the sports and daily dozens find storage and the adjacent bodily motor areas are also large areas, for man has learned how to do many things physically.

The frontal area of the cerebral cortex, back of the temples, seems charged with the greater complexities, the combinations of the responsibilities of the other areas and particularly the abstractions, the methods and routines and habits of thinking. This is the area most greatly differentiated between man and the lower animals. Its conscious thinking importance is borne out in tests and particularly in those following operations known as lobotomies and lobectomies in which frontal lobe neurons are destroyed completely or are severed from their connections down to the thalamus. Reports following such operations state that the patients show deficits in the synthesis of acts into a complete pattern and often that they lack ability for planned administration of their daily business activities.

The *operational system*, (c) of the conscious circuit utilizes an entire nerve network of its own. It branches and spreads from the cortex through successive contacts until its terminal neurons extend their sending fibers to contact and actuate all of the muscles which make the skeleton and the skin mobile, and which operate the voice and tongue and move the eyes. Each individual neuron is a one way creature. It receives through one nerve fiber and sends out through other fibers so that a sending system requires an entirely separate set and series of neurons from a receiving system. Thus the pressure and movement sensing neurons which bring in their reports from the extremities through progressive intermediate levels to the cerebral cortex are paralleled by another series of neurons taking instructions back from the brain to the muscles of the extremities.

The motor cells or neurons, those wherein we store the ways of doing things are described as larger and more pyramid shaped than those which store interpretations and understandings. The motor cells are distributed among the appropriate areas of the cerebral cortex and in general are several layers down from the surface.

For the golfer who takes his position before the ball and gauges the distance for his drive, there are instructions to be sent out by practiced motor neurons to direct muscular movements from the eyes clear down to the feet. These instructions emanating from pyramidal cells here and there in the brain pass through, or are radio interlocked by the cerebellum at the base of the brain for it is charged with the coordination of bodily movements into a smooth flow. Thence the signals pass down through nerve fibers of the spinal column and out of it at proper levels to branch to each of the muscles involved in the "swing". Depending upon practice, judgment, calmness and execution, the ball may go straight and far or dribble off to one side into the rough or the woods.

This is a complex train of action which many of us wish we could master. The neurologists have done extremely well in fathoming the nervous pathways and connections involved but there are still many details which are not fully understood. The general scheme of this operating system of neurons is enough however for our present purposes. We may still marvel to ourselves as we issue a conscious order to the left little finger to wiggle slowly and think of the number of connections to be made between neurons as we watch the order carried out.

The *organizational system*, (d) of the conscious circuit has been left to the last even though it is obviously the intermediary between (a) the receiving system, (b) the comprehensions and action-storage neurons of the cerebral cortex and (c) the operational system of neurons which carry out the orders by directing the suitable muscles. There is a specific assignment and wisdom to be stored and utilized at each tiny neuron along the way in each of these three systems. But the major role is yet to be done.

I, as author of my conscious considerations and decisions may not reside or have my office in the cerebral cortex at all, but in the corpus striatum behind it. And in evaluating my considerations I may use autonomic facilities even farther back in the inner brain area. But those are matters for later discussion.

But how do I bring together for consideration the items of knowledge, understanding, experience and alternative procedures stored in the outer brain. The organizing means is found in the network of nerve cells and fibers which constitute the inner layer of the cerebral cortex. This layer of neurons reach their receiving nerve fibers up into the stores of wisdom above and branch their sending fibers in a wide spread and massive maze of interconnections. Known as the association fibers, they form the floor of the cortex and shroud the autonomic systems inner brain areas.

Injury to no one part wholly incapacitates the cerebral cortex and there seems to be a remarkable capacity to relearn, reconnect, and restore the wisdom of a damaged area. It has been observed that the complexity of association increases from the rear toward the front of the brain so that the height of conscious consideration trends toward the frontal area. Experimental work indicates that the motor neurons of the frontal area are utilized for the storage of habits, routines, and skills of thinking. Thus it is found in studies of the maladjusted that those habits of thinking which are long-practised fears and worries, self-pampering irritability and feelings of frustration are stored in motor neurons of this area and may be destroyed by operations which also destroy useful habits of thinking. The undesirable habits of thinking noted above are among those described as emotional by reason of their stimulation of the autonomic hormone controls which give an emotional vehemence to the outward expression of feelings. (This an another controversial point in that inadequate understanding has given an unwarranted flavor of maladjustment to many psychological appraisals of the emotional function.) By operative sever-

ence of the nerve fibre connections between the neurotic motor
neurons and the autonomic areas back of them, these delinquent
neurons are deprived of their capacity to mis-stimulate or over-
stimulate the hormone flow and upset autonomic control balance
and the emotional aspects which go with it. That however is something to be considered later.

*   *   *

Our third question was, How does the conscious system function? We have answered the question in part as we described and
located the various members which go to make up the circuit. But
now it becomes an electrical problem. The system itself, the sum of
its components, is electro-chemical in nature as was brought out in
describing the neuron, the nerve cell, of which some ten billion comprise the system.

To picture a "thought" as an electrical wave motion in space or
in transit over some part of the nervous system is difficult except
as we think of the same sort of transmission of a message over a radio
or telephone system. To picture a thought or an explanation snugly
stored away an as electro-magnetic shadow or a photoelectric picture on one or a group of the neurons of the cerebral cortex is equally
difficult except as we think of a wire recorder. Or perhaps we may
think of a motion picture film having a sound track so that it pre-
serves simultaneously the form, color, voice and music of a scene in
a tiny space.

A thought stored away, presumably by ionizing rearrangement
of atomic pattern of the complex neuron molecule is still micro-
scopically small. It might be compared roughly in size with a vitamin,
a hormone, a microbe or a virus, but so far it has defied examination
by any method other than the obvious one, conscious observation.
Its minute size must not be underestimated for its power for good or
evil may be as great as that which Napoleon crystalized into bloody
empire. Most thoughts are not that exciting fortunately, but psychiatry and religion are on common ground in finding that a motor
neuron practised in hate or greed or fear can be as damaging to the
electrical mechanism as a microbe or virus can be to the physical
system. On the other hand, a mind cleansed of such trouble makers
can indeed be a pleasant abode.

The fourth chapter of this report was not merely to imply that
the mind's nerve system resembles a group of electrical devices, but
actually that it *is* such a system. The man-engineered devices which
we know, relatively cumbersome devices though they are, help us to

understand God's engineering of our own communications and operating system for both comply with the same laws. The human system, to be sure, makes far better use of its materials and has built into its devices features of living, adapting, rebuilding and double checking which we engineers have not been able to approach. Furthermore, even with the free will feature of conscious decision, its average of performance is so much better than the laws of chance would suggest that there is indicated the wise provision of God's forgiving guidance which most of us come to appreciate is present. That conviction would seem to be an aspect of the spiritual maturity, the autonomic utilization which we seek to evaluate.

My good friend Freeman Crampton balked at about this point in the manuscript. In his prepublication reading, his legal mind objected to so "text bookish" a discussion of the "science of thinking" and we will probably be judged guilty as charged. Yet in defense of the report it seemed unwise to remove any appreciable portions of it as it endeavors to lay the ground work for our inquisitive exploration of the less familiar inner mind.

The instinctive direction of many non-conscious activities is interesting enough. The higher evaluating functions which aid conscious decision are even more intriguing, and any glimpse we may get of distinctively spiritual contributions will require humbly careful attention.

Before approaching that major objective it seemed imperative to be sure of what we mean by conscious and subconscious activities even at the risk of boring ourselves with some perfectly obvious notes.

On the other hand we are finding it necessary to undermine some of the STOP signs posted in the literature of current opinion. The remarkable outer brain area does distinguish much of the human advance. To consider relegating it to a possibly subordinate position cannot be undertaken lightly. One helpful critic in New Orleans warns us that "it is an axiom of psychiatry that you cannot know your own subconscious except perhaps remotely . . ." To try to do so identifies one as a "potential schizophrenic", which sounds terrible but will turn out to be both true and quite normal.

In such sections as the following effort to describe electrical and physical details of the nervous system I believe we have used as few technical terms as possible. If those used are unfamiliar a few paragraphs may be skipped as they are inserted particularly for supporting value to those who are following the technical aspects of the undertaking.

In 1856 Köliker and Müller used a nerve from a frog to conduct an electric current in demonstrating the variations of potential (electrical pressure or voltage) at the muscles of a beating heart. That demonstration was about a century ago.

Now in our more complicated language we find that a neurophysiologist describes a nerve fiber as a tubular membrane with a protoplasmic core and lying in tissue fluid. Electrolytic dissociation or ionization in the core produces positive and negative charges in the core. These disperse to opposite ends of the fibers so that the neuron of which they are a part, achieves opposite polarity at its receiving and sending termini in accordance with its direction of transmission. The charges pass through the permeable membrane in the transmission of a message. Thus the proper cathode of one neuron is thought to make contact with the anode of the next neuron as it delivers a stream of electrons, a current, a message.

The generation of power occurs within each successive neuron from the chemical supplies which it draws from the surrounding liquid, which is supplied in turn from the bloodstream. This gives the particular neuron an influence over the message which it is delivering. It also influences which one of its sending fibers it will select for the build-up of potential which stimulates the next neuron to its cooperative effort. The ionization of molecular structure of each neuron is presumably the inherited, developed or educated basis for its influence upon the electrical message which it relays. The research professor who described each neuron as also having certain characteristics of a radio tube, presumably had in mind the problem of how my control can order the choice of the correct series of contacts to permit me to wiggle the left little finger instead of the right thumb.

Each of the numerous contacts between successive nerve tips in the transmission of a message constitutes a chemical or electrolytic reaction in the mind of the chemist, or a switching make-and-break in the terms of the electrical man. Whatever it is called it constitutes a point of resistance calling for a voltage or pressure to overcome it and to move the tiny current along its way.

In the human body the voltage required to gather and to move a message from its origin to the muscle which it is to "kick-in" is extremely small and this indicates the remarkably low resistances of the nerve circuits. Thus measurements indicate 5 to 100 microvolts (millionths of a volt) as being a normal requirement. Pressures as high as 300 to 500 microvolts are considered pathological or abnormal, indicative of excessive nervous tension.

In nature's system each individual neuron incorporates a battery function whereby it generates the power required for its own reaction and transmission. A relatively simple thought and movement might energize a few thousand neurons so that the individual effort is small compared with the overall measurements above.

A major mental effort might require the cooperation of millions of neurons, and one prolonged over an extended period further increases the fatiguing power demand. In that the energy is generated as required this withdraws oxygen, the battery chemical (cholesterol) and other elements from the cerebrospinal fluid which cools and supplies the neurons. At the same time waste by-product materials (acetycholene, etc.) are returned to the fluid and must be disposed of. This puts a demand upon the bloodstream at its autonomic centers which cleanse and replenish the vital fluid.

An electric current in motion has momentum as shown by the spark which jumps the air gap as a switch is opened. A line of thought in motion has a similar electrical momentum as any business man knows who works right up until bedtime and then tries to sleep without a diversionary slowdown or damping period. The line of thought just keeps bobbing up. Similarly, when a line of thought is interrupted by a telephone call it must be damped out and another line of thought gotten into motion. If the concentration is deep, requiring large numbers of neurons, and interruptions are frequent, the stopping and starting shocks and their accompanying energy demands are distinctly fatiguing and disturbing.

Nervous fatigue involves the same need for a rest period and chemical rebuilding or refueling as is involved in physical fatigue after muscular effort. I find as I work on this report that it is necessary to stop occasionally to have a drink of water and lie down a few minutes. To be sure at fifty-three, one fatigues more easily than at twenty.

Prolonged nervous fatigue, continued operation under high nervous tension, exhausts or runs down the neurons involved to the point where they require an extended rebuilding period. Evidences of such fatigue are found in certain headaches, dizziness and jitteryness from inadequate replenishment of chemical supplies. Later they appear in improper functioning of nervous services or controls and emotionally accentuated expressions of fatigue. If rest and refreshment are not provided, neurons may be seriously rundown so that they do not function in their duties, or may literally die so that a long period and new training are required to build new nervous pathways.

*　　*　　*

Our fourth question, what are the activities of the conscious or voluntary nervous system, has been answered in part during the discussion of its elements. I beg leave to submit the following as four major activities, of which modification and subdivision may occur to you, and for which different terms and descriptions are used at times:

1. Reception and interpretation of reports received,

2. Association and consideration, bringing together of pertinent information and belief.

3. Decision, selective discrimination and the ordering of appropriate action.

4. Imagination, my private wanderings which may be purposeful or not, constructive or not, beneficial or not, a fine field for controversy and the place for mental hygiene.

1. Reception and interpretation considered together as a single conscious activity seem to me to be an essential simplification. To be sure, there is a considerable train of operations and there are many neurons involved in focusing conscious attention however briefly, on an object, a sound or a sensation, but it is not until that train has been completed and the identification added that the item becomes usable for conscious purposes.

We may recognize also that a whole conscious collaborative effort involving activities 1, 2 and 3 was involved in the original learning of the meaning of the particular sight, sound or sensation and in the repeated consideration or observation essential to store that meaning or interpretation in the appropriate area. The meaning so stored may have been precise or biased or colored or wholly incorrect with consequent influence upon further thinking but that again is beside the point. For any particular item of reception, *the meaning* brought to the point of conscious appreciation, the command post through the interlocking association layer of neurons, *that* is the vital unit of reception so far as "I" am concerned.

2. Association and/or consideration. "My" number two conscious activity is the consideration of the item upon which I have permitted my attention to concentrate, the item which the psychologists like to call the stimulus, the externally applied starter of a line of thought or action. Actually, "I" will quickly run through stages 1, 2 and 3 identifying, considering and rejecting a number of items, a number of the papers or memos in my office before selecting one of sufficient interest or importance to proceed with.

Then having read and interpreted the meaning of the item, (a letter perhaps) one may pursue the next step, consideration of it, gathering together all pertinent information which may assist in decision. This association of ideas calls into play many more of the layers of neurons which send their transverse fibers connecting and cross connecting with different areas and sections of the cerebral cortex. "I" search the visual area for things I may have seen which are pertinent and the auditory area for things I may have been told about the customer or the job. "I" go forward into the frontal area among my habits of thinking to see how such things have been handled in the past. In this search I go up and down between layers or neurons reconsidering alternative meanings and data which I have learned, and which we suspect is stored in the outer layers and in the more basic neurons around incoming areas. I consider also the action alternatives stored on the pyramid-shaped motor neurons which are stored at a lower level. Then:

3. Decision, selective discrimination and the ordering of appropriate action. Perhaps I decide that information in mind is not adequate and external search is needed. This then involves orders to muscles to go to a file and look up prior correspondence or to pick up the phone or walk outside and ask someone else about the status of the inquiry or job. Alternatively I may decide to undertake a practised series of calculations, using other motor neurons or groups of them, or I may table the whole thing and go on to something easier.

Decision and action, even if the action is evasive, the two go together as the conclusion, the completion of each conscious undertaking. Of course one might break this series, 1, 2, 3, down further and into more detailed history but for present purposes the three are enough. (Alternatively of course one might follow the procedure of the behaviorists and lump the whole thing as one external reaction to an external stimulus for they seem inclined to bypass the internal part as purely automatic. Forgive this little aside on one of the very controversial points-of-view. The behaviorists have made worthy contributions despite some confusion of the issues.)

4. Imagination. Should this be numbered as a separate activity of the conscious mind? Perhaps not. Certainly it may and often does include all three of the normal, purposeful activities. Is it just idle ramblings without purpose? Yes and no. It may be used to high purpose. Is it a court of review for our conflicts and troubles, a place for self-sympathy and self-justification? Is it a private and unpoliced area for thoughts which would not bear public scrutiny? It may be such as these but to our sorrow as we shall observe. Such swamps breed the diseases of mind, the undesirable habits of think-

ing which have many repercussions, both internally and externally. Then purposeful or not, constructive or not, beneficial or not, it is certainly an activity and one which will bear study, but later. We will be in a better position to examine it after checking the subconscious level and then studying the autonomic level so far as we are able.

X

THE SUBCONSCIOUS LEVEL

The term "subconscious" is old and full of meaning. While it was originally a catchall for everything not clearly conscious, the recognition of the province of the distinctive autonomic circuit has opened the way to clarifying that former confusion.

Recognizing the subconscious as a distinguishable mental "level," observes its subordinance to the conscious level and also the fact that it evidences an autonomous capacity to direct and govern action, both physical and mental. It is subordinate, for any subconscious act may also be consciously controlled. It is independent, for several examples were cited in the last chapter of subconscious and conscious operations proceeding simultaneously. It may also operate with conscious attention retained but at a faster rate than conscious consideration would permit.

The province of the subconscious is to receive a conscious stimulation, suggestion or instruction and thereafter to carry out a physical and / or mental operation or sequence of operations or movements. The operation will continue to completion or until interrupted or until receipt of a conscious order to desist. It should also be part of the definition that the operation was previously established or stored away upon its motor neurons as a skill or routine or habit. The process of learning it normally includes conscious intention and subsequent practise or repetition. This practise develops a preferred sequence of mental or physical moves which improve the efficiency of performance and establishes it more firmly as a habitual routine.

Thus by long practise the skilled baseball player develops a fast and effective coordination of his visual observation of the speed and path of the ball and his muscular reaction in timing and directing the swing of his bat. His conscious attention is probably present throughout the operation, but there is not time for a conscious analysis of the pitcher's delivery and a consideration of stance, the contact point on the bat and the weight of blow to reach the hole in left field. Such things must wait for "post-mortem" analysis and coaching correction. Rather in the brief instant after the ball leaves the pitcher's hand there must be a flash recognition of a set of conditions and the application of a practised set of learned reactions, bypassing or short circuiting conscious consideration. There remains the conscious decision whether to strike at it or not. But rapid decision would not help the batting of an unpractised greenhorn who did not have the skilled reactions all set up and ready to carry through.

Can we recognize and check a sequence as follows:

1. Stimulation; something which calls for mental or physical action. This stimulus may be external, an observation, instruction or reminder, or it may be internal recollection of a routine duty or obligation.

2. Conscious decision and instruction. In that we are dealing with an established sequence or routine, a fully evaluated and organized practice, no particular consideration is likely to be needed. It is only necessary to bring the stimulus and the reaction together and give the order to proceed.

3. Subconscious procedure may then take over and carry on to completion or interruption.

Knitting was mentioned as an example in which various series of finger movements have been learned, which will produce various types of stitches. Conscious attention was devoted to the initial repetitive practise which stored them for future use on motor neurons, together with visual and touch checking procedures.

In starting a new knitting project, conscious decision is made of what needles to use and the order is given. Thereafter conscious attention may proceed to count stitches as required or it may depart to reminiscence or to conversation. But at the end of a row, or if touch or sight reports that a stitch has been dropped due to some faltering of the routine, then the conversation must be stopped and conscious attention devoted to the change of procedure which is involved.

I was interested to observe one day, how such interruptions to subconsciously directed routine movements may occur. The memo of it was made at Minnewaska and dated 1948. One of the mornings during that vacation I was doing my usual daily dozen, a group of the old army calisthenics, prior to shaving and dressing. At the moment my arms were pursuing a familiar sequence moving to the front, side, front, in; front, side, front, up; etc. It was one which I repeated day after day without a hitch and I left it on repetitive control whilst my conscious thoughts ambled back over the previous day's doings. Eleanor and I had been sitting on an age old slab of broken granite extending out into the lake. We were watching the swimmers and particularly a couple of them who were approaching us. They did not climb out onto the ledge which would have required quite an effort, but as I idly reconstructed the scene in my mind, I visualized how they might have done so. My arm muscles started to illustrate what would have been required and in so doing, they interrupted the subconscious routine of the calisthenics. I was chagrined for a moment until I realized how well the incident illustrated both the simultaneous operation of a conscious and a subconscious procedure, and the way in which interruption of subconscious operation may cause an accident. It has become a recognized fact that the mere thought of a movement sends a partial stimulus to the muscles involved.

Women quickly develop into fast and skilled operators of punch presses in manufacturing plants. With one hand they remove a formed metal part from the tools or dies in the press. With the other hand they dexterously select another piece from a box and place it in the correct position to be formed. At almost the same instant they coordinate the pressing of a foot treadle to trip a clutch and release the tremendous stored energy of the press for the forming operation. The pressing action is fast and with practice and earning incentive the skilled operator develops a high production rate. But familiarity breeds contempt and despite warnings their conscious attention wanders to conversation or thoughts of the evening before. The natural tendency to assist the expression of one's thoughts with one's hands makes it easy to alter the subconsciously directed routine. A scream follows for the press responded to the tripped clutch even though the fingers were not out of the way. Safety devices are helping in a variety of ways but damaged hands all through the manufacturing states bear mute testimony to absent minded interferences with a practiced routine.

I watch in horrified wonder as automobile drivers speed merrily along, carrying on an animated conversation and punctuating it with hand motions and turning of their heads to regard the one to whom they are speaking. To be sure, they have practised driving for years and are confident that they can get conscious attention back on the job quickly if need be. But at times they don't and no one knows just what happened. Subconscious routines can only be entrusted with practiced reactions. They can't exercise consideration, for that requires the conscious hook-up, and they *can* be unintentionally interrupted.

Dr. A. C. Wyckoff of Spring Valley and the Biblical Seminary in New York, wrote me on February ninth of 1954, in part as follows:

"I wonder whether you have read Lindbergh's, "The Spirit of St. Louis"? * It has in it his frank statement of the way his unconscious mind took over and guided his plane, when he no longer

* Published by Charles Scribner's Sons, New York.

could keep awake. When the story appeared in "The Post," I copied down this entire part of his account because I was afraid that when he came to publishing his story, the publishers would delete this part as fanciful. But it is all in the book. And is worthy of careful study by you in your work. Something similar is to be found in Admiral Byrd's, "Alone". The psychology of this problem belongs most clearly in the field of psychology of Religion, where prophets and mystics have been presenting material for study for centuries. I was interested to note that when The Reader's Digest published its review of "The Spirit of St. Louis" it left out all of this part of his account of his experience, as if it were of no consequence. And yet Lindbergh himself believed that it was the most essential part of his being able to make his flight. It deserves study, and you should be able to add some valuable physical, or soma, contribution to the explanation of what took place. You have something in this field that seems to be overlooked by both the soma and the psyche scientists."

As Lindbergh arrived in New York the French team, Nungesser and Coli, were lost over the Atlantic. He was handed a clipping expressing the opinion of a Canadian flier, that a man could not physically maintain flight control alone to cross the Atlantic, even assuming adequate rest before hand. Reporters, well wishers, promoters and his own concern over planning details, resulted in his having only two hours of rest, but not sleep, before leaving. Between that last day, the thirty-three hours of flight and the celebration on arrival, he faced 63 "sleepless" hours.

His detailed account reports with care the sort of marginal experience that psychological theorists find it difficult to visualize, in calm surroundings.

Eighteen hours out, about halfway across, Lindbergh was still keeping up his hourly log records, but was experiencing great fatigue.

On page 358 he notes how extremely tired he is and wonders whether it would be possible to sleep and yet to live. Then he recounts how his attention wandered and his mind drifted off in dreamy reminiscences of past experiences.

On page 361 he realizes that sleep is becoming inevitable but also makes a reassuring discovery. Without being able to name the three mental bodies which are collaborating in the situation, he *recognizes* them *and* their functions!

For the moment he lumps the subconscious motor routines of muscular operation with his tired body. Later it became apparent how much the long practiced flying skills stored in cerebral cortex were doing their part in mechanical flying of the ship.

Second he recognizes his conscious mind which was weakening in its ability to maintain attention for purposes of decision. As this center drifted off in sleep, its capacity to consider and decide upon corrections of the subconscious routine was lacking for the time being.

Third, he recognized a directive and guiding force and observed that its paternal authority increased as his fatigued conscious control weakened. An experienced authority might have confirmed his new discovery, for truly this body of the autonomic inner mind does take over when conscious control lapses, due to panic, exhaustion, extreme confusion or conflict in the voluntary mental circuit. The best current evidence would indicate that it is the thalamus, immediately back of the conscious center, which stores in its motor and informational neurons the drives and evaluating standards which supplied the help he needed. Their unlearned wisdom is described as "instinctive" by the materialist or "God-given" by the theologian. In normal living we take this endowment for granted and rarely observe its vital services as Lindbergh was forced to do.

On page 365 he recognized the instinctive factor in his non-conscious flying. The study of autonomic functions are of major interest to us and it will become apparent that subconscious learned routines and autonomic evaluations and drives must often collaborate, even though the conscious command center is relaxed or attentive elsewhere.

On page 374 he reports one of numerous times that he was providentially awakened as the plane started to turn or dive. There was ample evidence of his conscious center having been asleep. He was equally sure however that his eyes had stayed open. Again the physiological psychologist might have told him that visual signals from the eyes and balance signals from the ear go direct to the thalamus for evaluation of urgency and thence to cerebral cortex areas for subconscious interpretation in the light of learned wisdom. This combined capacity to evaluate and sense urgency, and to stimulate the conscious center to reawakened attention, saved him repeatedly.

On page 375 he expresses the hope that he can carry this secret revelation of the mental capacity which lies beyond the conscious range, back into ordinary life. Certainly it is a facility which we can and should use much better than we do. It will identify itself with the sensed evaluations of judgment and the collaborative efforts in the organization of thought.

On page 377 he recognizes the limitations of will, of the conscious mind's scope, and the precise evaluation of danger limits by his new found power (thalamus). He doesn't quite appreciate that his receiving senses, subconscious learned skill and autonomic evaluating capacity are all collaborating under the instinctive urge to self-preservation, to hold the line or to reawaken the conscious center for corrections when external wind forces upset the routine.

On page 378 he discovers that he can give up conscious command with increasing confidence. It is a humble respect for the mental bodies beyond the conscious range which we do well to develop.

"The Spirit of St. Louis," (Scribner's, 1953) is a valuable account of the workings of the mind under a revealing condition of stress which cannot properly be reproduced in the laboratory. Such marginal experiences have been one of our most valuable means of checking the validity of current theories.

Whether or not Lindbergh's new found faith in his God-given assets was reinforced by urgent prayer was not disclosed. He did mention however, (page 321) that, despite conflicts in scientific thinking, it was difficult to remain agnostic under such circumstances.

Even as I write I find that my writing cannot be fully entrusted to subconscious control. Consciously, my attention may be wandering several words or phrases ahead, weighing meanings or looking for better means of expression. It has left the actual writing down of familiar words, with the long practiced finger movements which form them, to subconscious routine. My eyes seem to have been assigned to check the results as part of the routine. Frequently they call back conscious attention with the discovery that I have skipped a word or two or indulged in phonetic spelling or tried to combine two words in one. For such absent-mindedness I keep a large eraser handy. The specialists have a long word for it, but it is just trying to do two things at once.

Electrically or nervously how can we picture a particular subconscious activity? Suppose we compare it with the operation of the switchboard of a small office telephone system. A stenographer is also switchboard operator. A buzzing sound attracts her attention to an incoming call. She answers it to find out what is required and then "plugs in" the necessary connection which makes possible the desired conversation or conference call. Thereafter she may go about other business until the disconnect signal comes through.

In a similar manner the knitter must plug in a circuit among the connecting fibers of her association neurons. The connecting group must make contact at their receiving and sending tips with surface neurons in the visual area toward the rear of the brain, which have learned what the chosen knitting stitch should look like, and with motor neurons in the more central body function area which have learned, what finger muscles must be moved in sequence to produce the stitch. Further connections are made from those motor neurons down through the coordinating cerebellum, a short portion of the spinal column and the arms to the finger muscles. Return connections are set up from finger-tip touch receptors, to check the position of needles and wool, to aid in coordinating the procedure.

All the little intricacies of the procedure and the many little muscles involved may require the interconnection of dozens or hundreds of neurons to complete the required circuit. Yet this is a very small percentage of the whole. It sets apart a group which have learned by practice to perform a repetitive operation which can carry on by itself.

At the same time it might be desired to hook-up another circuit linking other body function motor neurons down through other nerve connections of the spinal column to muscles of the feet and legs. The instruction this time is to maintain the rythmic pressures essential to keep the chair rocking.

The knitting group of neurons and the rocking group had to be associated or interconnected by independent conscious decisions and instructions. Once the connections were made and the results checked, conscious attention might go on to some other areas. Most likely it would utilize connections with the hearing area, the throat muscle motor neurons and the frontal area neurons of habits of thought, to carry on a conversation with the lady in the next rocker.

An inconsiderate fly landing on the knitter's hand will stimulate the touch receptors at the base of a hair which will in turn short circuit through some reflex connecting neuron in the spinal column. This will result in a muscular arm movement, which will disturb the fly and will also be likely to disturb the knitting sequence. Conversation will have to stop briefly to permit conscious attention to restore the sequence. And so on and on until lunch time.

*   *   *

A wide variety of terms describe subconscious jurisdictions and operations. Physical routines, practiced skills, and habits such as muscular twitches and distinctive gait involves motor neurons of the body control area and the coodinating facilities of the cerebellum.

Absentmindedness, inattention, mistakes and getting into a rut usually denote that the subject has left the subconscious in control whilst his conscious activity is preoccupied with woolgathering, aircastle building or more serious but distant activity.

Mental attitude, point of view, specializations, mental reactions (worthy or unworthy), inhibitions, frustrations, complexes and neuroses denote a variety of practised routines, skills and habits of thinking. They are mental practises, the motor neurons of which are found in the frontal areas of the cerebral cortex, back of the temples. This area, in its relation to outside environmental evaluations and relationships, internal autonomic system relationships and reactions, and psychosomatic equilibrium or malfunctioning, is the seat of the trouble in the problems of self-determination and mental hygiene or maintenance of "self."

The subconscious operational possibilities in which some of these motor neurons are hooked up in imaginative or directive associations for better or worse, is a major part of our problem. The examination of autonomic operational functions and controls will be needed before the picture can be completed, but some examples may be in order before that is undertaken.

Prayer itself, can illustrate to most of us how a practised mental routine can carry on subconsciously and without interference with conscious thought. How often have you caught yourself mechanically reciting the Lord's prayer and at the same time consciously planning the day's activities or picking apart the hat of the lady two rows ahead. The prayer had been well impressed upon the mental motor neuron which directed the throat muscles, but it was failing in its purpose of assisting in mental or spiritual hygiene, for you were not paying attention to it, not giving thought to its meaning.

Getting into a rut is a descriptive term applied to business men, preachers, teachers and what-not, people who have been on the same job too long and have become ineffectual or careless. In the course of the years, during which these people have practiced certain procedures, they have established skilled routines of thinking which seem to adequately take care of their responsibilities. The point at which they (or we) let the routine take over the run by itself without paying strict conscious attention to it would hardly be perceptible. It is the easy way, but such subconscious functioning without conscious checking is subject to diversion by stray influences. Suddenly we make the embarrassing discovery that we have made a serious mistake. It may have been a mathematical error due to diversionary upset of a familiar calculation. Or it may have been an error in judgment, really lack of judgment, as a routine solution was applied without conscious consideration. Perhaps in the course of repeating the same old lectures or procedures year after year we overhear some remark which leads us to discover that the old routine is no longer up to date. Our rutted subconscious practices need renovating.

If we are not too deep in the rut we will undertake the renovation. But here another mental routine may interfere. The teaching profession, the engineering and the medical profession, the theologians, in their dispensing of wisdom are likely to fall into the rut of regarding themselves as the infallible source of wisdom in their line, and looking down upon the receivers of their benefactions as a lower order whose thinking is subject to no serious consideration.

The term "laymen" is applied almost contemptuously to other people by some who reach moderate eminence in their specialties. The mental disease, egomania, describes these self-centered habits of thinking which are so long practiced and so well ingrained that they amount to a neurotic inability to consider or evaluate differing points of view.

I worked many years for an ex-Prussian army officer, a capable engineer who had made real contributions to the industry. He was quite impressed with those contributions however and as he grew older he fell into the habit of characterizing those who differed with him as "Gott-dam fools". It reached a point where there were few who had not so qualified. "All out of step but my Jim." Most of us could name several (other) people who we think have such habits of thinking.

Planning for activities which are ahead of us, appears to be one of the responsibilities utilizing the frontal lobes of the brain. Often we take advantage of periods of subconscious operation to do our planning. Time and again I find myself mapping the day's procedures while I am washing and shaving or eating or even driving to work when I should be paying attention to traffic.

We also plan to utilize subconscious hook-ups or neuron connections without thinking of it in that light. While I am undressing at night I give the order to set the alarm clock for next morning and then go on to think of something else. A while later I wonder whether I did set it for I can't remember doing it. I was not paying attention to the act when performed but I find that subconsciously the act was properly carried out.

In my youth I do not recall observing such things. Perhaps it was merely a lack of interest in them or possibly I had not yet developed such confident utilization of the subconscious procedures. Absent-mindedness is usually associated with old age (and I hasten to add that I do not feel old). Still I have looked for my hat when it was on my head. The order to find and put on the hat had been given and executed by appropriate motor neurons with so little interruption to some conscious activity that I did not even notice that it had been carried out.

Subconscious operations are mental and physical or just mental practiced habits which may be valuable *or* undesirable. They utilize motor storage neurons, association pathway neurons and observational checking neurons of the cerebral cortex, the subconscious domain. There functioning as a group, subordinate to conscious control may proceed with or without conscious attention. This we have observed thus far.

The interaction of subconscious routines with autonomic circuit reactions, which may result in psychosomatic disturbances or in peaceful well being, are yet to be explored. In a better understanding of the autonomic system and its interrelationships with conscious and subconscious activities we hope to appreciate the meanings of neuroses, complexes, sins and mental conflicts. In their elimination we seek the achievement of mental balance and peace of mind.

XI

THE AUTONOMIC, GOVERNING OF SELF

The very existence of the autonomic system came as a surprise to me when I first found reference to it in browsing among the medical texts. That was back in October of 1945 in the beautiful new Brooklyn library. It was after the rebuff at Columbia which was probably stimulating in itself. Why had I never heard of this primitive or primary system which is apart from the conscious?

The first thing was to look up the meaning of the name. Autonomic meant "self-governing". We have already noted that the system includes the governing within itself of many functions which are apart from the conscious circuit and which we will want to examine more closely. We have also noted the implication of the name that the system serves as a governor or stabilizing influence over self, *my*-self, as represented in the conscious function of decision. That has become a fascinating feature as the evidence and the controversial aspects of the problem have accumulated.

The elements of the system bear a certain similarity to those of the conscious system in that they include brain areas and a complex system of receiving and sending nerve pathways. The system also includes the endocrine glands, the group of glands, which accumulate and dispense hormones through the bloodstream making it into another communications system for psychosomatic control purposes.

Endocrinology is the title of the study of these glands and their hormones, considered by themselves, and it is fascinating enough as a subject. In a book under that title, a Harvard professor questioned whether the mind affects the glands or the glands affect the mind. The influences both ways are now quite clear.

Portions of the autonomic nerve pathways are separately named as the sympathetic and the parasympathetic nerve systems, Figure 5. These pathways connect between the centrally located autonomic brain areas and the endocrine glands, the digestive tract, sex organs, lungs, heart, salivary glands, tear ducts, etc.

In a general way the sympathetic train of neurons have to do with *mobilizing* and *dispensing* of our reserves of strength, courage and vitality. These are chemically available in a variety of forms including fat, water, blood components, muscle and brain restoratives, digestive juices, genes, adrenalin, thyroxin and other hormones.

The parasympathetic system or sequence of neurons generally carries the responsibility of *producing* and *conserving* these resources of body and mind. Consciously recognizable signals of fatigue may indicate extreme depletion of these vital reserves but, without conscious note, the normal dispensing and replenishing carries on under the marvelous system of checks and balances, checking the needs and balancing the budget.

It becomes obvious that considerable powers of evaluation and

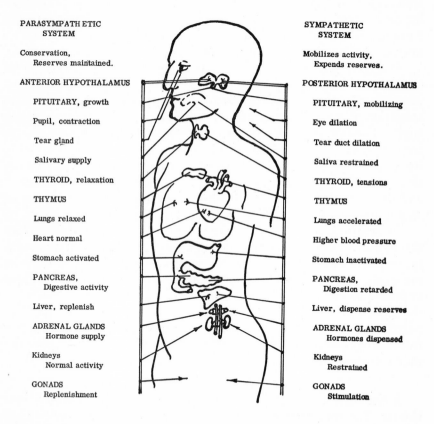

PARASYMPATHETIC SYSTEM	SYMPATHETIC SYSTEM
Conservation, Reserves maintained.	Mobilizes activity, Expends reserves.
ANTERIOR HYPOTHALAMUS	POSTERIOR HYPOTHALAMUS
PITUITARY, growth	PITUITARY, mobilizing
Pupil, contraction	Eye dilation
Tear gland	Tear duct dilation
Salivary supply	Saliva restrained
THYROID, relaxation	THYROID, tensions
THYMUS	THYMUS
Lungs relaxed	Lungs accelerated
Heart normal	Higher blood pressure
Stomach activated	Stomach inactivated
PANCREAS, Digestive activity	PANCREAS, Digestion retarded
Liver, replenish	Liver, dispense reserves
ADRENAL GLANDS Hormone supply	ADRENAL GLANDS Hormones dispensed
Kidneys Normal activity	Kidneys Restrained
GONADS Replenishment	GONADS Stimulation

Figure 5. The autonomic nervous system sends two major networks from its inner brain area to major glands and organs indicated, as well as to the many involuntarily controlled muscles of the face, throat, heart, stomach, rectum, skin, and gland cells. Bloodstream connections to all the organs involved, furnish pathways for coordinated hormone distribution and for supplies. This is all separate from the voluntary nervous system which directs consciously ordered muscular activities.

discretion are essential in the operation of this system. Keep in mind that it is quite an autonomous system. It must have information from the conscious system upon which to act, whether to quail in fear or rise in anger or to rest and rebuild with a feeling of security, just to note the psychologists' three favorite emotional reactions. The activities of the autonomic system in such fear and anger, and their psychosomatic implications will be developed later.

The external expression of emotional or autonomic or involuntary reactions has been observed. Autonomic muscular controls may order expressions of frightened warning, of nervously depleted fatigue, of well replenished exuberance, or of concern, distress, panic, dislike or happy contentment. The chuckle or sigh, tears or scream may rise naturally or be suppressed by conscious effort and hidden under an unemotional and expressionless mask.

We have noted that the emotional reactions may be fooled or elicited unnecessarily or improperly by reason of improper reporting. A prank may elicit a scream when there is no real danger. A private recitation of gripes or imagined unfairness may build an unwarranted anger. The conscious domain, receives reports from the outside, interprets them, works them over in considering them, and then gives its picturization of the situation, whether accurate, colored or seriously distorted. From this the autonomic must make its further evaluation and then order whatever preparation or reaction it deems advisable among the muscles, glands and nerve centers of its domain.

In return, conscious reception *from* the autonomic takes place through a "sixth sense", a receiving service using the interconnecting nerve pathways between the two circuits. We have noted that we recognize among these communications:—a wide variety of sensed impressions, emotions, intuition, inspiration, the flash of an idea and the reports of internal environment of the autonomic circuit (as compared with the external environment which is reported by the other five receiving senses). We will learn more of the origin of these communications in the autonomic circuit as we proceed.

*   *   *

It has been a tedious process for my poor comprehension to get this far. The organizing of bits of data from many sources and the evaluation of conflicting points of view and experiences have progressed slowly month by month and year by year. I have recited some of the stumbling blocks and landmarks to you in the belief that we have a common interest in the problem. Looking back upon them, many of the conclusions seem so obvious that I wonder why they were not apparent to me long ago. One of these dawned upon me one early morning in 1952.

Both from the negative aspects of psychosomatic maladjustments and mental unbalance, and from the positive problems of normal balanced thinking and spiritual values, many have stated or intimated that the autonomic circuit exercised a restraining or advisory or governor influence over conscious decision. I sensed that they were correct in spite of contrary opinions and objections. Evidence and experience both gave strong support but it troubled me that I could not see how it functioned. What is the seat of an emotional reaction? Obviously it must be a neuron or a group of them for those are the building blocks of both nervous systems. But how does this important group act so decisively and so consistently generation after generation? Where do the laws of nature and the laws of human behavior, morals, enter into the activity?

Even before my confusion had been resolved into questions as definite as these, I sought an answer which brought me a good clue in Dr. H. G. Wolff's words, "inherited tendencies", although I didn't properly evaluate it at the time. My effort to frame the question was as follows:

September 18, 1948

The National Research Council
2101 Constitution Avenue
Washington, D. C.

Gentlemen:

In the course of work in what might be termed mental engineering the writer is interested in developing the concept that the current position concerning the relative levels of the autonomic and somatic systems is based upon an insupportable assumption and is highly misleading to research. The counter-position is that the conscious facility has evolved out of and with the autonomic circuit from primitive prototypes and remains, in spite of its responsibility for ordinary decisions, in an inferior and subordinate position. The thesis into which this fits has proved highly revealing with respect to the problems of mental hygiene, etc.

Dr. Shields Warren of the Atomic Energy Commission has advised me that your organization is undertaking comprehensive study in this field. Can you advise me how this is set up, including details of scope, plan, limitations and progress to date. Under whose general direction has it been organized?

Thanking you for your courtesy in this matter,

Yours very truly,

Dr. Lewis Weed of the Council forwarded the letter to Dr. Wolff who responded on the letterhead of the The Society of the New York Hospital. One of his former students, now practicing in Canton described him to me as eminent in his practice and meticulously thorough in his teaching.

He was properly cautious in not taking sides as to whether the voluntary system was in the superior or inferior position.

Rather the evidence implied to him a coordination which is not haphazard, but has plan and direction. This, even though the direction may be at variance with the conscious purposes of the individual.

In meeting such a simple problem as change of weather and temperature, he noted the voluntary actions of closing the window, walking rapidly or putting on long underwear. He noted as automatic the evidences of action taken by the other system in sweating, shivering or increased muscle tension. Both systems aimed to maintain a balance between heat production and heat loss.

Some serious threat to a man's security . . . . offered a second and deeper example. Autonomic adjustments thereto might result in muscular tremors, asthma, or ulcers. The voluntary decision might be to fight or run away, or to sidestep the issue by making a joke of it.

Factors affecting the resultant pattern of reaction include experience, habits, cultural background and *inherited tendencies*. Dr. Wolff correlated voluntary choice, health (autonomic reactions) and resultant survival as focal points of the problem. He concluded with the acknowledgement that there was as yet no centralized research underway despite broad interest.

It is unimportant from his biological and medical point of view whether the voluntary or the autonomic circuit were the higher as long as they function in harmony for the security of the individual. He used the word automatic rather than autonomic but attributed to this system the *direction* of feeling states, attitudes and emotions, linked with physical functions of glands and certain muscles. He associated with this directive capacity such involuntary maladjustments as are rendered observable in the tremors, ulcers, etc.

His well chosen examples included both conscious and autonomic participations. This again raises the question in my mind of the common but baffling back-ground of the autonomic wisdom directing these so called "reactions".

According to my notes the morning of September 6, 1952 represented a step of progress worth noting down. We had stopped for the night at the little Queen Hotel in Barrie, Ontario, to have some work done on the car.

I awakened at about six that morning with the project and the problem of emotional reactions and conscience very much in mind. The first order of business each morning is the prayer period and in the course of it I tried to formulate the question.

Arising I sensed the answer:

Those autonomic neurons, the source of emotional "reactions" which are so universally similar, are instinctively equipped, an inheritance through the ages. *They serve as a series of standards*, measuring sticks, *representing* the laws. With these standards the autonomic circuit compares and weighs each consciously gathered and interpreted report of a current or potential situation or occurrence or intent.

As each such *elavuation* is made in the autonomic circuit, "we" in the conscious circuit receive back and sense the "reaction". This may be a feeling of approval or satisfaction, or perhaps it is one of extreme distress or of moderate discontent, if the proposal or situation reported meets the standard or fails to meet it.

We may list many more types and shades of meaning which we sense in these reactions or reports. We will have to resolve separately the reinforcing or opposing influences of subconscious habits of thinking and their effect upon the next step of autonomic activity, the dispensing of hormones. We will have to clarify our ideas of instinct and of heredity. We will have to distinguish autonomic activities other than this *evaluation by the standards, standards* which men have tried to interpret in our "laws" of nature and of behavior. We will consider the rising pressure of autonomic guidance upon conscious equanimity if we endeavor to ignore the standards.

There are and will continue to be things which are yet to be resolved. But now in the light of hindsight this concept of our inheritance of standards and their place in the organization of the mentality, seem to be obvious and so logical that one wonders why I did not see it before. Yet that morning after prayer I could not help but rate it as one of those visualizations or dawnings or bursting of the light of understanding which biblical writers described as visions. There accompanied it a feeling of accomplished calm, of peace of mind, which properly should follow the long period of discontent for want of an adequate answer. Glenn Clark had described such a feeling of peace with answered prayer but I had not observed it before. This recording of my private feelings is just in keeping with the idea that the important things of life have not changed much through the ages, so far as the individual mentality and soul are concerned.

Fig. 6 charts the contributing influences in an emotional reaction.

The cooperation of mental bodies of the two neural systems, which it illustrates, will have to be demonstrated as our search proceeds.

*   *   *

Before undertaking a plan for the study of elements of the autonomic circuit perhaps we should tabulate tentatively the activity of this system, as distinguished from that of the conscious circuit. This tabulation may then serve as a checking list as we consider the elements and accomplishments, and the potential power of the system.

1. Autonomic Receiving Services:
    Communication between the conscious and the autonomic circuit

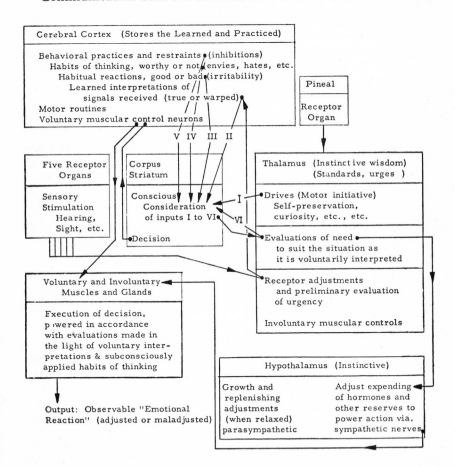

Figure 6. An Emotional Reaction. The contributions of the several mental bodies to an adjusted or maladjusted emotional reaction, which are to be demonstrated in succeeding chapters. The three mental bodies charted at the right are members of the autonomic system.

is a two way affair with groups of neurons, nerve pathways conduct-
ing messages both ways. Thus, just as the conscious can sense the
reactions or opinions of the autonomic, so also the latter can sense or
receive a picture of what is going on over the association network of
neurons during any conscious activity. We have noted that the picture
which it gets in this manner may be an accurate and reliable one, or
it may be a highly misleading one by reason of imaginative distortion
or prejudiced discoloring or by entry of the myriad envies, hates,
fears, worries, greeds, glooms, inferiority complexes, etc. etc., which
we may nourish in ill kept subconscious swamps.

The autonomic circuit also has its own connections to the receiving neuron groups of sight, hearing, taste, touch and smell. In the
brief description of the way in which these functions are organized,
it was noted that autonomic neurons appear to be involved in such
operations as the evaluation of intensity of light and sound, and the
compensating adjustments of pupil size and ear linkage muscles. But
the autonomic brain areas do not receive a direct interpretation of
sounds heard or an identification of objects seen for that requires
taking the signals received through the cerebral cortex of the conscious system. They do appear however to sense urgency and to report it directly, ahead of the conscious reports. I recall an experience
in which an apparent danger of collision caused that frightened
sinking feeling at the pit of the stomach which is an autonomic
reaction, whereas a fraction of a second later the conscious circuit
analyzed the illusion and reported that all was well.

There remain the radio and radar wave receiving functions which
were discussed at length in Chapter VIII. Whether their receptor
neurons are located in nasal or pineal areas or elsewhere is not yet
known. Radar receptions might be assumed to be projected on the
visual receiving area of the cerebral cortex, which might be explained
by the passage of the optic nerve pathways through autonomic neuron
centers. Radar or television receptions may occur while the conscious
activities are de-energized in sleep, as I will try to illustrate in a moment, which seems to bear out the assumption that the receiving
neurons are a part of the autonomic circuit. Radio receptions appear
to be consciously sensed through the sixth sense receiving connections
of the conscious from the autonomic, and therefore their receivers
also seem to be autonomic.

The television illustration of which I was reminded was related to
me on September 29, 1952. The young man gave me permission to
relate the experience though I said I would not mention his name. He
is a college graduate who majored in mathematics and physics. Dur-

ing World War II, he was radar operator in a large bomber. On one of his missions over Japan, the bomber was shot down and he was one of those who reached ground alive. This happened about six months before the end of the Japanese War and he was confined as a prisoner of war. There were nineteen among the airforce PW's at the time of whom three survived the food, disease and other conditions of imprisonment.

His father and mother were notified that he was missing in action but could not check whether he was alive. Then one night both of them experienced an identical "dream". As they compared their recollections of it, both had seen him on his knees, looking up at them and smiling reassurance.

As a matter of fact, at that time he was forced to spend sixteen hours a day in a semi-kneeling position in a tiny cell. His great concern was for his parents for he knew that his mother would worry and that his father had a heart ailment. The visualization or vision of him which they received was quite accurate and it may be noted that night time in their little town in West Virginia would be daytime in Japan. As in other instances related, the urgency to raise the sending voltage, the waiting attention to aid reception and the attunement or community of interest of parents and son were all present, and the message got through!

2. Autonomic Consideration:

As in the case of conscious consideration, the message material which is received must be subject to analytical association and evaluation before ordering action.

We have noted before that logical thinking, the organizing of consciously accumulated information into creative or conceptive thought, is one of the functions assigned to the autonomic system.

Evaluation of the material received and organized is the next step. Evaluation must precede reaction. Potential injury must be sensed before ordering a danger reaction. Accomplishment must be sensed before responding with satisfaction.

Evaluation by comparison with a set of predetermined standards is an old trick of industry. Measuring a part for an automobile with a "go or no-go" gauge will tell whether the dimension being inspected is too large, too small or within an acceptable range. Chemical and physical test standards are set up to check whether a metal is acceptably pure or properly mixed and has requisite strength. Specifications for machine tools or for airplanes are written so that inspectors may determine whether the thing which is received is acceptable or should be rejected.

In the same way those autonomic neurons which are charged with evaluation of the data or situation or conditions reported to them by the conscious, are surely equipped as standards with specifications, codes, means of judging adequacy or acceptability. This wisdom is presumably stored by ionization pattern on their complex molecular structure.

In court we must sense whether the testimony is honest or not and whether the decision is just or unjust. In our daily life we may react vehemently or cautiously to a sense of wrong or of injustice. The instinctive urge to freedom of thought and freedom of action has been strong enough to supply the vital drive to heroes and martyrs throughout history.

Those endowed with musical genius must superimpose on their practiced skills at their chosen instruments, an autonomic evaluation of their creation. Is it adequate by comparison with their sense of rhythm, their sense of harmony and their sense of the overall beauty of the composition?

3. Autonomic action.

After reception and evaluation comes action and this may be mental or physical or both. The physical aspects are apparent in the regulation of digestive juices, hormones, energy reserves, waste products, etc. and the muscular movements evidenced in the frown or grin, the chuckle or scream. The mental aspects are noted in the sensed feelings of happiness or frustration or ire. . . .

The mechanistic idea of emotional "re-"action suggests a prescribed response to a prescribed stimulus. Up to a certain point this is so. A depletion of the reserves calls for a feeling of hunger. The chewing of food calls for a dispensing of digestive juices. A reported injustice calls for a feeling of displeasure or more, even to violent rage with the whole system's reserves mobilized for action. The degree is coupled with the vehemence of the voluntary report.

The solitary wasp hollows out a suitable hole, lays its egg, deposits a supply of food, seals the hole and departs to die. The next year the larva hatches from the egg, eats the food supply, emerges to dry its wings and flys away to repeat the cycle. It has never seen its mother to receive a proper education, but its procedure and behavior are adequate and normal. Its endowment of instinctive wisdom, stored upon autonomic neurons has provided requisite direction.

In man the process has become more and more complex. The means of acquiring and dispensing temporal understanding and wisdom has greatly developed. The instinctive urges to reproduction and to self-preservation, etc., persist and form an interesting part of our study of the autonomic circuit. Curiosity's urge to evaluate, an urge to service and a frequent urge to creative effort often link their drives to goad the consciously directed activity to exceptional accomplishment. Inspiration, intuition and the sensed ideas which flash from the autonomic realm of conceptive thought, climb far beyond the mechanistic confines of the predetermined and into the refreshing reaches of originality.

Obviously this is rich ground for controversy for some take quite contrary points of view.

It is bound to be a very difficult field to search and to clearly set forth. Our hardest work is still ahead of us.

One more point to be watched and appraised is the vehemence with which the autonomic system may make its recommendations known. Men refer to the still small voice of conscience, and I have often wondered, as perhaps you have, why it has seemed so hard at times to distinguish the right and true amidst the confusing din of personal prejudice and self-biased habits of thinking. Yet we shall see that if one persists in ignoring the standards, the voice becomes more insistent. Nervous discomfort rises to emotional conflict and on to hysteria or panicky escapist addictions.

Thus far we have had a preliminary look at the autonomic system, what it comprises, how it operates and how it is related to the other nervous system and the physical structure. As we go on to examine the more specific details of its operation, which can be searched out, two questions arise.

Should we try to organize our material by mental functions such as the instinctive drives or related character responsibilities, or should we start from the physical centers, the endocrine glands, and their responsibilities? There is a two way communication and influence between the mental and physical centers, though the mental influence is presumably the primary one. The glands are probably more easily isolated but they collaborate on so many activities that it is not easy to examine them individually. Associated neuron activities are also complex. The approach selected is something of a compromise, but endeavors to recognize that the glands are in the secondary position.

In what order should we examine the several centers and their related responsibilities and activities? An ascending order suggests itself. The sex glands have probably received more study than any of the others and are blamed for more mental disturbances by the specialists in such problems. Above them are in turn, the adrenal glands over the kidneys, the pancreas which is near the stomach, the thymus above the heart, the thyroid at the throat and the pituitary and pineal glands in the head. Each of these has sending and receiving nerve pathways communicating with the neuron groups which are known as the hypothalamus and thalamus in the central (autonomic) brain area. These centers appear to shelter the instinctive drives and to furnish discriminative direction to the glands. The bloodstream, we must recall, provides a further connection between each of the glands and other members of the body for the dispensing and restoring of their precious hormones. In following the ascending order of discussion, the instinctive urge to reproduction and the sex glands, will be the first to consider.

XII

HEREDITY, URGE, PERPETUATION

There is a certain natural or instinctive feeling of restraint concerning public discussion of sex. This would appear to be an autonomic provision to keep the old and experienced from disrupting the natural educational sequence for the young and curious. It seems to be part of the laws of common decency.

To be sure, it does not take much conscious effort to ignore the sixth sense in this matter up to a certain point. In smartly decadent circles of society an aura of worldly wisdom surrounds sexy inuendo. The stage thrives upon it, but even the public law feels called upon to restrain it. Just where the line should be drawn will probably continue to be a matter of debate between the rigidly proper and the libertine.

When Eleanor read my first effort to discuss the urge to reproduction, her Quaker inheritance stirred a strong feeling of resentment. While she approves the major objectives of the project, I cannot help but sense her feeling that the whole thing should be abandoned rather than include this part of the discussion. On the other hand, research has progressed farther in this field than elsewhere. It provides the clearest picture of the strength of an instinctive drive, the contaminating effect of acquired mal-education and the powerful psychosomatic retribution for violation of the moral law.

Dr. Sigmund Freud gave psychology great impetus with his observations of his patients' mental difficulties ranging from conflict with morality to insanity, which he traced to sexual misadventure. The evidence would seem to permit us to take issue now with his self-excusing effort to rationalize that the moral law is at fault. Heredity and the proper perpetuation of it calls for a sequence of worthy sensed objectives, logical control and peaceful satisfaction. The evaluation of conflict and calm in the matter involves the relative contributions of the three levels of mentality and the resultant physical behavior.

The instinctive urge to reproduction and perpetuation of the species, the nature of it, its messengers or means, the autonomic drives sensed by the conscious, the conscious stimulation of those drives, the subconscious habits of thinking which wisely restrain or honestly reinforce or dishonestly mislead the autonomic functions and finally the conscious decision and action which is ordered after consideration of (1) the external situation, (2) the sensed drives and (3) the subconscious habits of thinking; these are the components of the sex problem for better or for worse.

That the urge to reproduction exists and is a vital bit of our wisdom need not be discussed. Without it life would cease to exist. That it is instinctive goes back to the definition of instinctive; a natural impulse, an involuntary urge. Now we may trace it back to the autonomic, the involuntary circuit and to the neurons of the storage areas of that circuit. The tiny neuron (or group of neurons) which stores this bit of wisdom is basic to every creature down to the microscopic amoeba. It is an inheritance which has been passed along since the beginning of time.

The hormone-like messengers which convey this, as one of many items of our physical, mental and spiritual heritage are the sperm of the male and the ovary of the female. The storage and dispensing of them is entrusted to the sex glands of the autonomic circuit. Nature is bountiful as always in its supply of seeds but the individual seed is so small that no ordinary microscope can properly show it. A. Cressy Morrison, a former president of the New York Academy of Sciences, described his reasons for having faith in God. In the course of doing so, he marvelled that a thimble would contain all of these tiny seeds responsible for all the living people in the world.

A three inch photograph of a human spermatozoa was reproduced in Electronics Industries for January of 1946. It was reported to have been obtained by an electron microscope capable of magnification up to 180,000 times. It showed a curious shadowy fishlike creature with head structure and tail propelling mechanism.

The specialists in their studies subdivide the individual sperm or ovary into twenty four subdivisions called chromosomes and these in turn into still smaller genes. Each of them develops some portion of the physical or mental structure and equipment of the child. Individual chromosomes and genes differ and carry thereby the heredity differences which genetic studies trace in blue eyes, red hair and other distinguishing characteristics of children of the same parents. At the same time they convey the common characteristics which guide the development and growth of the embryo into the child. Certain of them transmit such instinctive wisdom as guides the life cycle of the solitary wasp or which provides the basic drives and guiding standards underlying emotional reactions.

In a fascinating little book, "What is Life", Professor Schroedinger of Dublin University begins with the studies of chromosomes and genes of the fruit fly as they control similarities and differences in succeeding generations. To be properly technical, he shows that the mutations which alter heredity are isomeric changes occurring in the individual genetic molecule, that is to say, stable rearrangements of the atomic pattern with a corresponding gain or loss of energy (ionization).

Patiently assembled theory indicates that the minute governors of heredity are gigantic as molecules go. Each is a distinctive and orderly system of perhaps a thousand or more atoms. The changes or mutations may involve an electron more or less in an individual atomic sphere. He felt that despite the large element of chance at certain levels an overall guidance prevailed. He concluded that a gene "is the finest masterpiece ever achieved along the lines of the Lord's quantum mechanics."

Before leaving the genes and the mental endowment which certain of them transmit, some controversial definitions should be set up to be subject to scrutiny as the discussion proceeds. The controversy traces to the schools of thinking in psychology which seek to reason that instinct and heredity do not exist. They argue that all such wisdoms must be acquired through education and environment even though this may occur at a very early age.

The discrepancy here is probably only a matter of degree and not as serious as it seems. It is an important finding that conscious learning begins at a very early age. Fearful, malicious and other distorted habits of thinking may be sensed and established even before language is learned. Injury to important neuron or gland centers may occur before or at birth.

But now we are able to distinguish the autonomic responsibilities which are apart from learned habits of thinking of the conscious. It seems clear and should be made clearer as we proceed, that the basic wisdom represented in their standards and drives is a substantially identical and universal heritage differing primarily in the strength or robustness of its influence. The confusion which must be clarified, traces to differences in conscious training and experience which modify the consciously expressed reactions to sensed autonomic influences. Thus my elderly reactions with respect to an attractive young lady will differ from those of an eligible young man or a mentally ill sex pervert, due partly to subordinate habits of thinking stored on motor neurons of the conscious area, the cerebral cortex.

Instinctive drives are one of the items for which we seek an improved definition. Physiologists and psychologists now generally recognize them. Most define them as unlearned or inborn patterns of response, tendencies or propensities. Some further identify them as universal or at least common to a species. Many prefer to limit their research observation of these instinctive patterns of response to animals. In that the end result, the observable response is consciously ordered, human subjects introduce so many variations that a basic autonomic influence is difficult to observe externally.

The term "drive," "influence," "pattern of response," recognize the tendency to action of one sort or another. The storage element is therefore a motor neuron, a nerve cell which tends to initiate action when properly associated in an operational circuit. The urge to reproduction, the urge to self-preservation, the subsidiary autonomic drives to actuate the heart muscles, to digest food or to evacuate waste are among those to be recognized. Then let us define tentatively:-

An instinctive drive is an active influence stored upon a motor neuron of the autonomic circuit, an influence which is common to the species if not universal and which is essential to survival, including therein the physical, mental and spiritual aspects of survival of the fit.

The latter part of this definition is difficult and debatable. The field of action is one which we should try to define, however. Perhaps it will clarify as we proceed.

Instinctive standards. These may be part of the drives themselves, but it seems to me that we will clarify our understanding if we recognize them as separate and distinct. In the conscious area there are association neurons, motor neurons, and an outer layer of neurons which store acquired wisdom for purposes of knowing, understanding and interpreting. It would seem logical that the autonomic circuit would departmentalize its files in a similar manner. Therefore we would set up another tentative definition as follows:

Instinctive standards are a heritage of wisdom stored upon information neurons of the autonomic area, which are common to the species if not universal and which represent data which is essential to the exercise of judgment. We will undertake to see whether these standards represent the fundamentals of the laws of decency, of behavior and of maintenance for the physical, mental and spiritual activities.

Instincts and heredity are two words which may require some distinction. I find that my own understanding of the meanings of words changes somewhat as I get older and endeavor to absorb or eliminate different points of view. In this instance may I offer the following:

Instincts, the instinctive drives to action and the instinctive standards for guidance are long range heritage tracking back into antiquity and dealing in general with the similarities, the common characteristics of the things which the genes pass on from generation to generation.

Heredity as it is ordinarily discussed, seems to deal more with the differences in the heritage, the special characteristics distinguished one from another, the field in which the laws of chance may play their part.

On the negative or deficient side this includes family tendency to baldness, to frailness, to weak-mindedness, to astigmatism, to certain diseases, etc. Actual deformities, Siamese twins, extra toes or fingers or shortages of them, and similar distortions in the mental or nervous equipment may trace to mix-ups or deficiencies in the mating of the parental genes or to parental misadventure.

Positive advantage accrues in heredity in a fine physique, a strong mentality or special talent or trend to technical or artistic or literary proficiency. Whether the old observation of "three generations from shirt sleeves to shirt sleeves" traces to heredity or environment or a mixture of both, is still a good question.

*   *   *

Mating behavior is observed to precede reproduction. This procedure is guided by; (a) An instinctive pattern furnished to all alike, in the form of successive drives and the standards for guidance; (b) Heredity forces supporting the instinctive motor neurons, utilize the adequacy, inadequacy or over-adequacy of the several hormone supplies which are husbanded and dispensed; (c) Education, proper or improper, adequate or inadequate, stored on neurons of the conscious circuit and utilized consciously or subconsciously; (d) Environment, the current external situation which is reported and interpreted or misinterpreted through the conscious facilities to furnish the immediate stimulus to the successive steps and decisions of the pattern of mating behavior.

The success or lack of it, or catastrophe which may result has obvious effect upon human lives. Furthermore it seems to be subject to review at the period in the forties which has come to be known as change of life, with positive or negative influence upon peace of mind.

Note in the outline, for it is important, that two of the groups involve autonomic forces which are *not* subject to voluntary control, and the other two involve forces which *are* under conscious control. Our primary interest is in normal operation of the system but the abnormal and maladjusted operation is often revealing. Particularly in the case of sexual misbehavior, we are inclined to selfishly blame the involuntary forces of our instinctive endowment. The strentgh of these forces of the autonomic does seem to spiral to a position of dominance over the conscious forces at crucial times. But I believe that intellectual honesty will permit us to see that errors in conscious interpretation, in *habits of thinking* and in *voluntary decision* have sufficient lead time to bear the responsibility.

Mating behavior has been described by biologists, physiologists, poets, cartoonists and song writers. The insight and medium of the last group is perhaps the most popular if we may judge by record sales. More somber theologians, in their effort to interpret the fundamental laws, describe responsible mating as "an honorable estate." Involuntary or emotional (autonomic) approval is expressed in the smiles which follow the oblivious couple, holding hands, for truly all the world loves a lover. The observation of romance, submitted for autonomic evaluation against the standards, brings back to the sixth sense a pleasant feeling of approval.

Misbehavior brings forth a sense of revulsion or of pity which may be drowned in a worldly smirk. If so, this consciously controlled reaction is biased by a self-centered effort to condone one's own behavior or habits of thinking. The abnormal aspects of sexual misbehavior terminates in criminal conviction, disease or insanity. The much more common intermediate stage is characterized by a consciousness of conflict, a sense of dissatisfaction, mental disease the source of which we seek to clarify.

Returning to the autonomic circuit and its participation, we recall that the sympathetic and parasympathetic groupings of its functions have to do respectively with the utilizing and the replenishing of its precious working store of hormones. Heredity differences apparently can have at least a marginal effect upon these resources. Sheldon, Stevens and Tucker in their books on The Varieties of Human Physique, and the Varieties of Temperament have studied at length, physical differences in largeness of structure, hairiness, tendency to fatness and cranial variations with respect to mentality trends. All of these differences trace back to parental genes, and the autonomic pituitary function of growth control. It seems safe to accept similar parental or ancestral influence upon normal or abnormal potency of other endocrine glands with consequent reinforcement or retarding influence upon corresponding instinctive drives. That is, the resource reports of the glands to the autonomic motor neurons will influence their reaction to the conscious report of the external situation.

A variety of these instinctive drives in turn influence the progressive pattern of mating behavior. Perhaps the first is curiosity, the instinctive urge to learn and to evaluate. This drive obviously begins at an early age and devotes its initial interest to relatively simple problems. In the teens, the moonlight maneuvers of young couples savor strongly of the inquisitive.

Shortly the urge to romantic adventure, the aspect of daring will advance the pattern. The adrenal glands are called upon at this point to mobilize the action, to supply the courage. The thrill of an embrace is presumably the sensed coursing of some adrenal hormone through the bloodstream.

Offsetting and balancing the daring is fear and the urge to self-preservation. The evidence seems to associate this with the pancreas gland and the neurons of its directive hook-up. This restraining influence has been a saving grace often enough.

At the higher level of logic and the urge to orderly thought, the lovers' questions of compatibility and common interest, of livelihood and responsibility may be raised or dismissed. A little more weighty perhaps are the urge to service and the creative urge. The pituitary gland and its neurons are associated with certain of these aspects. Medical research has found considerable reason to associate the pituitary with the gonads (the sex glands) in the problems of reproduction. The creative urge is paritcularly strong in man, and accounts for much of his progress. His participation in the creation of another man is certainly the highest attainment of that urge, and is a remarkable privilege in itself. The drive attains its utmost satisfaction in the proud happiness of the young mother as she fondles her new creation, her babe.

All of this is vital, fine and beautiful as it should be. The responsibilities of worthy parenthood have carried their own reward down through the ages (and vice versa). Each successive step in the pattern of mating behavior may be checked against the instinctive standards and sensed to be acceptable, right. Yet people do get into trouble, into situations which they sense are wrong, disturbing even to the extreme of suffering insanity.

Psychologists have realized that things which we learn with regard to behavior participate with the sensed drives in influencing decision and action. Others have emphasized the need for mental hygiene or discrimination with respect to things learned. Our observation of subconscious activities indicates that things learned, practiced routines, even unintentionally acquired habits of thinking may exert a directive influence without conscious attention. Bear that in mind as we consider habits of thinking fostered by "liberal" teachings, obscene stories and suggestive plays as they influence decision in this problem.

A small child pampers its ego by showing off, acting smart. The youth endeavors to appear less youthful by talking big, evidencing worldly experience. Obvious among the devices of worldliness are lewd and obscene stories and creating the impression of "having been around." The college humor magazines feature moderately screened "stories." Year books emphasize the "wine, women and song" features of college life. Inuendo in public entertainment contributes further. This unscrupulous "worldly" repetition of the point of view that sexual misbehavior is commonplace and smart constitutes a major educational effort with the apparent approval of organized education. It cannot help but establish habits of thinking, mental routines which will participate in decision at critical times. It is the basic training of the libertine and the pervert.

It begins at a time when the natural mating drives have been delayed by the unnatural lengthiness of the formal educational program. The social scheme of things is out of time with the natural timetable.

In matters of juvenile delinquency we must go farther back to childhood environment. Suggestiveness, improper behavior, obscene conversation in the home and homes broken by infidelity, all contribute to the mistraining of impressionable young minds. But the difficulty obviously goes back to the training and resultant habits of thinking of the parents. The sins of parents *are* visited on their children.

"Free thinking" is the excuse of the educator for the teachings of the libertines upon his staff. I quoted in Chapter V from one of my son's university text books which was written by a college professor and endorsed by a college president. The author presented to my son as a basic concept of psychology, the libertines' self-justifying excuse that morality is wrong. That concept was among the things which Ed was required to learn, and store away to guide his future thinking.

The Freudian concept of psychology recognizes the wretched conflict in the minds of those who grasp the brief illicit thrills of sexual violation of the moral code. It seeks to dispel the conflict by endeavoring to root moral teachings out of the patient's mind and to substitute a habit of thinking which justifies the misbehavior. *If* morality were no deeper than habits of thinking instilled in the process of conscious education, it might work. But honest thinking psychiatrists report a "Poverty of results", "the orthodox (Freudian) method is powerless," this from the Psychiatric Quarterly.

What permitted such misconception to achieve such popularity? The desire for self-justification in the conscious thinking of the reprobate who conceived it, and of some or many who have promoted it, may be contributory. But the basic error was the assumption that morals are *only learned*, acquired as part of the conscious education of cells of the cerebral cortex.

To be sure, at that time little was known of the autonomic circuit and that little was assumed to be in a subordinate category. The theological recognition of spiritual *and* temporal interests had a basis of centuries of observation and inspiration, but it was easily waived aside by the bright young men whose shiny new wisdom was so impressive to themselves. Perhaps that is being too caustic with them for we all enthuse about man's progress in conceptive and creative thinking.

After all, it is the capacity for observation and organization of thought which permits us now to clear up what appeared to be a hopeless conflict between psychology and theology. As we progress we may match the activities of theology's temporal and spiritual realms with physiology's voluntary and involuntary circuits. We may observe that conscious decision and education characterize the former and that instinctive wisdom and guidance to the conscious realm, characterize the latter.

Note therefore that conscious training in the moral code as we understand it, may supplement the sensed influence of the instinctive standards in matters of decision.

Unmoral efforts to instill conscious education at variance with the autonomic standards have been made by the communists, fascists, and Freudians. Such training does influence conscious decision, but it does not alter the spiritual standards of the autonomic. It can only result in conflict with those standards, Schizophrenia, loss of peace of mind, mental misery.

Let us return to the problem of those conscious decisions which may lead to sexual misbehavior. The instinctive drives are *stimulated* to exert their influence *upon* conscious *decision, by* conscious observation *and* interpretation of the things observed. That interpretation in turn is based upon consciously acquired education as are the habits of thinking which restrain or encourage decision. The conscious therefore bears a major responsibility.

The teachings of the anti-moral Freudian psychologists have had a favored place for a generation or two in formal education. They did not do permanent damage in all cases for psychiatrists like Menninger in Kansas, Blanton in New York and Watters in New Orleans thought their own way through to the unity of wisdom and effectively discounted the misconceptions. But on the other hand, the unintended malicious influence of those teachers who perpetuated the anti-moral approval, has left its mark upon the first half of the century in the form of an increasing ratio of broken homes and disturbed or broken minds.

A professor of Zoology made a major contribution in his books on sexual behavior. His report of youthful misbehavior and lesser mature misbehavior lends support to the childish excuse to mitigate inevitable punishment; "well *everyone* else was doing it." The extent to which the behavior pattern he reported was influenced by conscious miseducation and a pattern of conscious thinking based upon obscene stories, unmoral plays and anti-moral educational influences should have an equal position in an intellectually honest report which purports to be scientific.

The author showed his position in endeavoring to represent science as opposed to, or doubtful of the position on morals represented by Christ, ancient analysts of what constitutes desirable behavior, and modern theologians, and jurists. The report strongly raises the question of rightness or wrongness of sexual loyalty or disloyalty to a mate in human society. Therefore it cannot honestly ignore the modern evidence of the divorce courts, the insane asylums, the social and religious councilors, if not of personal experience. The wealth of current data on peace of mind and happy homes where fidelity is practised, grading to the opposite extreme with infidelity, quite naturally supports the observations of the ages.

Yet an educator contributes this work which is bound to have serious influence upon habits of thinking at the formative stage. What may be a reasonable report of the trial and error method of self-education in sexual matters, goes on the record with a slap at the (experienced) moral teachings which endeavor to set up habits of thinking to help one avoid the error and its consequences.

Christian psychiatrist Karl Menninger defends his profession against the charges leveled at its Freudian branch. In the Register of the Chicago Theological Seminary he explains that "Psychoanalysts do not favor promiscuity, do not encourage it, do not attempt to relieve any patients' guilt about it, and in short, are no more to be considered immoral inciters to crime than anyone else who is doing his best to diminish the errors of mankind. Quite the contrary, most of them spend hours and hours attempting to relieve patients from the compulsive feeling of need for these very immoralities." (Perhaps we can recognize the compulsive feeling of need as a neurotic habit of thinking growing out of misunderstanding of the periodic relief of the glands and fostered by obscene stories and old wives' tales.)

Menninger also argues that psychiatry is not down on all sense of guilt but only false guilt, a patient's sense of guilt about something he did not do (or about some natural enough act which he imagined was wrong). Here again we are dealing with erroneous habits of thinking consciously instilled into the trainable and mistrainable conscious storage areas. Autonomic reactions are internal and can consider only the precise or distorted data submitted by the conscious mind. The mistraining must be undone by mental hygiene or housecleaning at which Dr. Menninger has shown worthy talent.

No such subject as this is quite complete without a tale of an otherwise dignified male dashing out of the back door in inadequate attire. I must pause to relate that story for the benefit of those of my neighbors who may have missed it when it happened yesterday afternoon. I know that some of them were away at the Canton-Massillon football game which ended in a dismal 41-8 defeat for Canton. I heard the end of the game over the portable radio while I was bathing and shaving for the evening. A radio in the bathroom sounds a little odd perhaps, but undershirt and shorts were a sufficiently dignified costume for shaving.

Eleanor had been out doing some weekend marketing and I heard the car return as she stopped in the drive by the side door, I glanced out of the window and saw the car beginning to roll down the slight slope of the drive. The hand brake on that thing is about as impotent as I am. She ran back to the car and was trying futilely to hold it back with her slender weight.

I made it down the stairs and out to the open door on the far side of the car in substantially nothing flat. As we caught our breath my sweetheart told me that scared as she was, she wouldn't call out because of my alleged heart condition. I was all right but observed to her, she would have to find me a bathrobe to get back into the house.

It wasn't until then she noticed my undignified, scant attire; and in mid-November at that. She had to laugh.

That instinctive sense of humor is a valuable asset. It must not be condemned even though man's selfish desire to be smart may trot out sexy wise-cracks at ill-advised times when they "contribute to the delinquency of a minor" or even of a morally shaky adult.

This chapter has endeavored to explore the relationships of

learned point-of-view and instinctive forces in sex matters. Out of the combination of sensed instincts, acquired thinking habits and external observations we pick and choose to reach vital decisions.

The discussion would hardly be complete without emphasizing the part played by an instinctive sense of responsibility. Surely the heavenly happiness of young love is compounded, not alone from the basic urge, but also from a new found sense of mutual responsibility. That responsible feeling, considerately nurtured to avoid mutual hurts, is essential to continuing happiness, to peace of mind. It will require our further consideration.

XIII

COURAGEOUS ACCOMPLISHMENT
AND THE ADRENALS

In these chapters we undertake the interesting task of correlating successive functions of *character* in man with *instinctive drives* underlying them in his endowment, and the *physical means* of implementing them.

In this instance the qualities of character are Courage and Determination, major supporting factors to a man's *confidence* in himself. Deviations to be considered are excessive combativeness and bad temper on the one hand and various forms of "spinelessness" and inadequacy on the other.

The instinctive heritage which we believe can be recognized involves the urge to accomplishment and the urge to freedom of thought and freedom of action, both personal and general, underlying the human yearning for liberty. It includes the urge to daring and adventure in youth and the driving spark for self-assertion.

That does not mean for one moment that these drives in each of us are backed with equal vigor in the glands which supply their motive power. Heredity, varying from generation to generation, deals out differing proportions according to the laws of chance and to parental nourishment, both physical and mental. Furthermore both we and our parents may so molly-coddle us as to set up fearful habits of thinking which completely nullify these assets.

The physical means which implement and power our courage and determination are the adrenal glands as we shall see. The hormones dispensed by these glands do many things, and at times other glands participate with them and even direct them or restrain them. Yet the adrenals' accomplishment warrants their title, "the glands of combat," and their more common recognition in the vernacular term, "guts." It is the quality which we admire in the good athlete, whether winning or losing, and in the builders of great buildings, great nations and great religions. Perhaps we might also call them the glands of success.

Bear in mind that these assets are part of the autonomic system. (1) The instinctive drives stored on neurons among the protected inner brain cells, (2) the glands themselves down near the base of the spine and over the kidneys, and (3) the connecting network of (sympathetic) nerve pathways and hormone pathways of the blood-stream which have access to the many areas and activities to be in-fluenced, are elements of that system.

Bear in mind also that the other circuit, the conscious responsi-bility brings in and influences the true or biased reports to which the autonomic expresses its "emotional" or instinctive reaction. There-upon we may accept or reject such recommendation:-

Thus, when the boss comes into my office and gives me an in-struction with which I have reason to disagree, there are three gen-eral courses of action open to me. (1) The straight and narrow path is to express my position with courage and in as clear and unbiased a way as I know how. (2) The "safe" yes-man alternative is to express complete agreement with a face-saving mental reservation to the effect that he ought to know better but it's up to him. (3) The third alternative is to color his instruction with a hatred of his authority, as being overbearing and malicious, calculated to get me into trouble. Having chewed on that point of view imaginatively I would burn up a lot of adrenalin by getting hot under the collar and flying into a rage. I was fired once for doing just that for the works manager was in the same mood that day.

Such an utterly obvious illustration of possible human deviations to the right or the left of proper decision is disarming in its simplicity. It is a useful device however, by which we may test the physical, mental and spiritual forces entering into this study of reactions in human relations. Perhaps it will demonstrate to us before we are through, that autonomic instinctive standards act as a spiritual com-pass to keep bringing us back from the deviations introduced by environment, misconception, vicious propaganda, mistrained selfish habits and what-not. It is remarkable that so many of us get along as well as we do.

Functions of the adrenal glands have been described as the mobil-izing of body and mind to meet stress, emergency or danger in many forms, and less dramatically, the ordinary demands of growth, work and sport. There would also appear to be a de-mobilizing effect at times.

These glands of combat are called upon in physical defence or attack, but also in fighting disease, injury, nervous shock or infection, in meeting the hazards of exposure to the elements and in mental combat, tense working or living conditions, external argument or internal conflict. In their more quiet moments, their dispensing of our reserves contributes to activating growth under pituitary direction.

Observe as we proceed that the adrenals may be misled, erroneously activated by misconceptions, and pure flights of the imagination. Overworking, mal-functioning and mistreating of them result in a variety of retribution, diseases and discomforts.

We sense the functioning of the glands as their hormones course through our blood in thrill and excitement, enthusiasm and pugnacity. At the other extreme are the petrifying chills and shock effects. Some of these nerve system sensations are reports of secondary results in circulation, breathing or what-not, initiated by the hormones.

Two small more or less oval adrenal glands nestle down near the lower part of the spinal column and over the kidneys. They produce and dispense over two dozen hormones according to the present count. They have liberal vein and artery connections which permit them to take essential nourishment from the blood, to receive STH and ACTH hormones from the pituitary gland in the brain area and to send forth their own messengers to heart, lungs, liver, muscles, digestive system and brain area.

There has been some question whether adrenal activities were started entirely by pituitary hormones but now it is agreed that autonomic nerve messages also initiate their action. Whether it is a safety provision that either the nervous system or the hormone system may stimulate them, or whether it is a matter of convenience depending upon urgency or duration or specific character of the demand is not yet clear. The fact remains however that there is a two-way intercommunication system, between the glands and the autonomic brain area over its nervous systems as well as through the blood stream.

The adrenal medulla, the inner portion of the glands, produces and administers adrenalin which is also known as epinephrine. (The medical profession uses ephedrine to achieve some of its results.) This hormone is credited with bringing about results similar to many of those obtained by stimulating the sympathetic nerve system. The heart rate is accelerated and its efficiency is increased. The carbohydrate stores of the liver are mobilized and the elevated sugar supply of the blood make more fuel available to the muscles for physical effort. Blood vessels to the heart and muscles are dilated increasing resistance to fatigue. The spleen is contracted, forcing its reserves into the blood to increase its oxygen carrying capacity. Increased intake of oxygen is made possible by dilation of the breathing passages and increasing the rate and depth of breathing.

As a protection in case of injury the coagulability of the blood is increased and constriction of skin capillary passages discourages loss of blood from superficial wounds.

Evidences of emotional excitement are induced. The hormone causes contraction of tiny muscles in "goose flesh," makes hairs to stand up and withdraws skin pigmentation causing the pallor of white rage. Pupils of the eyes are dilated.

At the same time, services not essential to combat are restricted or eliminated. The supply of blood is reduced to a gastro-intestinal (digestive) system and its activity is reduced. Thus nervous indigestion results when eating under stress. The bloodstream is by-passed at the kidneys so that poisonous wastes are not eliminated, especially at times of severe injury.

The outer portion of the gland, known as the adrenal cortex developes and dispenses two groups of hormones. In some respects these two can have opposite effects upon the system to regulate it or to keep it in balance.

One, the mineral group, regulates the body's utilization of mineral salts. Its best known hormone is DOCA (short for desoxycorticosterone). It increases the blood pressure as needed so that repeated overstimulation of its activity becomes hypertension (chronic high blood pressure). This group also produces or controls production of germ destroying cells in the blood, and the subsequent production of immunizing globulin, the blood fraction which carries immunity bodies to fight future infections by those germs.

The other group regulates the use of glucose (sugars) and the conversion of sugars into body-building proteins. Cortisone, the best known hormone of the group, reduces blood pressure. Its administration medically reverses the crippling effect of rheumatoid arthritis, rheumatic fever and other crippling ills. It is claimed that inflammatory manifestations and certain allergic reactions are held in check by this group and aggravated by the first group.

The identity and functions of many adrenal hormones are not yet clear. It is clear however that the glands are governed by nerves and/or hormones from the hypothalamic, involuntary area of the brain. Operations performed on both animals and men have shown that these autonomic decisions are, in turn, influenced by the frontal lobes (conscious) which have already received any external or environmental influences from the rear, side or upper areas of the conscious brain, (areas which have to do with sight, hearing and other receiving and interpreting services of the conscious system.)

It is also clear that, as the glands spend these reserves in re-enforcement of the system to meet the reported emergency, they reach successive stages of depletion and exhaustion. The depleted stage seems to be evidenced in jittery, spasmodic or hysterical functioning of pertinent physical and nerve-system elements of the individual. The completely expended stage is evidenced in exhaustion and shock. Repeated heavy demands are more easily met in youth when recuperative capacity is at its peak. With increasing age the recuperation or restoration of reserve is slower. Eventually chronic over-demand results in shortages which are recognized as diseases. Some of these have been listed.

Hardening of the arteries and the clogging of circulation in various forms seem to trace to repeated excessive stimulation of the adrenals. The various blood enriching reserves which they cause to be pumped into the bloodstream to meet emergencies eventually precipitate out or fall by the wayside to some extent. These collect as a scum along the inner walls of the arterial pipe lines, stiffening them and occasionally breaking loose and clogging capillaries or larger tubes.

*   *   *

Battle fatigue, which was the subject of much wartime observation, gives an excellent illustration of both the use and the misuse of the adrenal function. Courageous men going into battle proceed with caution until the shooting starts. Then the stamina of the man, the adequacy or inadequacy of his adrenal hormones and the body's reserves which they mobilize, must meet the test.

The sequence of autonomic events begins with the report from the conscious circuit that danger is present. The mobilization which follows, is essentially the same for the soldier, the prize fighter, the gladiator or the lion. The message evaluated and relayed by the hypothalamus and pituitary stimulates the adrenals to select and send out appropriate hormones in suitable quantity. One part in a billion has been reported to be enough for most purposes.

These electro-chemical messengers traverse the bloodstream (which takes time). They increase the speed and pressure of the heart's pumping action to get supplies around faster. They increase the rate and depth of lung action to make more oxygen available for distribution by the bloodstream. They withdraw fats and sugars from the fuel reserves and deliver them to be burned with oxygen under enzyme control to furnish the energy which is to be used up by muscles and the nervous system and brain. They withdraw additional supplies of blood from the liver to take care of wounds, and furnish coagulating control to seal the damage. Their direction of tiny muscles and glands in the skin makes the hair to stand up at the back of the neck, goose pimples arise, the palms perspire, the face flushes or turns white.

The resultant fatigue of such a mobilization of resources is apparent. Prizefighters may be "worn out" before the fifteenth round. A man with a nagging wife becomes less efficient at the office. Soldiers, after a severe series of engagements, must be rotated back through less dangerous activities to the rest areas. Care must be taken however for too sudden a let-down from severe strain in rotation, retirement and relaxation can apparently constitute something of an emotional and nervous shock.

General Eisenhower reports, "I saw a major general, one of the finest athletes of his time, definitely break down because he could no longer sustain the agonies of combat. He could not talk to me without shaking, and he had to go home." The symptoms include the physical fatigue expressed in pain or discomfort in the adrenal region and the nervous fatigue expressed in shaking or crying. It's a very real malady found in the ordinary routines of business and living as well as in battle.

The rage reaction to persistant annoyance has been subject to considerable study. Rage is a primary emotional reaction to the behaviorists in psychology. The outward expressions of it are those resulting from adrenal stimulation and preparation for combat. Enlarged adrenal glands have been found in men who have had lives of tension and strife. Whether the large glands were the result or the cause of such a life is not yet clear.

Chronic irritability and bad temper are frequently observed in conjunction with rheumatism, arthritis and hardening of the arteries. Medical men have pointed out the connection between such habitual repetition of adrenal stimulation and the maladies resulting from inadequacy or exhaustion of the adrenal hormones which would otherwise rectify such troubles. Self-pampering (neurotic) habits are frequently the psycho-somatic root of such mentally induced physical ills. Obviously it is not the valuable adrenal capacity for meeting emergencies which is at fault. Rather it is a lack of conscious discipline, a lack of restraint, in deciding what is an emergency, or mental fatigue in which trivial irritations cannot seem to be forgiven and ignored.

Wartime hysteria brings a lot of pertinent problems to the foreground. The army labels over two million men as psychoneurotics. Men endeavoring to avoid military service "threw away their false teeth, hid in coal bins, jumped off harbor boats, paid up to $1,000 to civilian physicians to show them how to fake illness." "Their officers tried discipline, doses of salts, a little psychiatry, but failed in most cases to salvage them; those who returned to duty after treatment usually landed back in the hospital."

General George S. "Blood and Guts" Patton of World War II fame defended the famous incident in which he slapped the face of a (scared) soldier, in his book, "War As I knew It." Said he; of 34 instances, "my personal intervention had some value," and of the incident in Sicily, ". . . had other officers had the courage to do likewise, the shameful use of 'battle fatigue' as an excuse for cowardice would have been infinitely reduced."

Psychoneurotics? "Nuts," said the colonel to General Elliot D. Cooke at a forward command post in North Africa, "Somebody has just thought up a new two-bit word for being yellow." Psychiatrist Edward A. Strecker, in a book, "Their Mothers' Sons," argues that maternally pampering "smother love" was the root of the psychoneurotics' trouble. The newspaper sob-sisters, however, played up the sentimental side of Patton's slap, on the ground that the boys were really mentally sick.

Now that the facts are more clear we can see that all the points of view were more or less right. The soldiers who suffered battle fatigue without ever seeing battle were definitly sick. Their symptoms were the same as those of men who suffered it from excessive front line service, and for the same reason.

They had exhausted their reserves by overstimulation of their adrenals. They had done so by imaginatively living and re-living the battle conditions in anticipation of the real thing, imagining alarming conditions and thereby stimulating the glands. Possibly the grueling training had something to do with helping their imagination. And maternal pampering and soft civilized living built up the imaginative differences as to what constituted emergency. Certainly materials provided to conscious education by youthful environment and contrasting indocrination provided the grist for the imaginative flights which kept prodding the adrenals until the man was literally worn out nervously and became physically ill.

Soon we will consider the truly neurotic nature of conscious habits of thinking developed by repetitious practice of fears and worries. The character-robbing accomplishments of warped thinking and ill policed imaginations must be considered in the same class with communicable physical infections so far as the human mind is concerned.

Rabble rousing techniques of mob psychology are highly perti-

nent. Oratorical appeal to the fears, hates, greeds, and generally selfish and self-centered habits of thinking, which imagination tends
to nourish, are grist for the mill of the demogogue and the Red. On
the other hand in the worthy causes of liberty and justice, the appeal is made to the habits of thinking developed in moral training
and in support of the instinctive urge to freedom and justice. In
either case it is the object to cause stimulation of the adrenal glands,
to picture a state of emergency which actually initiates the physical
mobilization of reserves and raises the heart and lung action and
nervous tension to a fighting pitch. That such opposite objectives may
originate the stimulation merely illustrates the dependence of the
autonomic circuit upon the internal reporting of the conscious
circuit.

Inciting to violence and murder may be an entirely private matter, but based upon the same principles. Jealousies, fears, fancied
injustices or inequities may be played up imaginatively to infuriating
violence. In the extreme stimulation of the innocently hoodwinked
adrenals the temperature rises and the urge to attack in fancied self-
defense is no longer subject to voluntary restraint.

Fortunately the normal activities associated with the adrenals are
not so exciting. They function normally in providing means to
growth, means of adjusting to changes of temperature and means of
meeting the rather tense daily demands of twentieth century stress
and strife.

Adrenal control over heart action gives some check on such
activities. A close friend of mine reports a check made upon him
thirty-odd years ago when he was training for research work at
Harvard. His normal pulse rate was observed to be about 68 to 72.
Then he was asked to perform a one hundred yard dash at which he
was proficient. After it, his pulse had risen to 97. A short time later
he was playing a chess game, at which he was also proficient. His
pulse was checked again after the game and had risen to 110. Collegiate chess teams have been much kidded by the athletes, but here
we see that mental effort can place a heavier demand on the system
than physical effort. Other research attests the same fact.

A check of the hormone directed draft upon bodily reserves in
athletics is provided in a blood count of the eosinophils which are
specialized cells in the blood stream. "Time" for June 11, 1951
reports a test made at a Yale-Harvard boat race which I hestitate to
set down, for Yale lost. However, "random samples when there was
no stress, got an average eosinophil index of 123 for the (Harvard)
varsity crew. After a practice pull, the oarsman's eosinophil count

dropped to 19. When the day of the Yale race came, the counts were down to an average of 64 before anybody had lifted an oar. The coxswains' was down to 33."

"It was a gruelling race over four miles; Harvard won in the last seconds by a quarter length. The eosinophil average at race's end: 3 for both oarsmen and cox. Harvard coach Tom Bolles' own drop: from 101 before the race to 6 after."

The results were related to proportionate physical and mental exhaustion and depletion of the control hormones of the adrenal cortex. Compare the nervous mental exhaustion of the coach and the cox with the indicated physical exhaustion of the crew.

Note also the drain caused by imaginative anticipation before the race started. Like imaginative battle fatigue, thinking about it ahead of time actually wastes reserves.

For that reason football coaches try to teach their teams to relax before the game, to stand in a relaxed position. The object would seem to be a proper one, to assume a mentally relaxed attitude which would conserve resources, rather than a tense anticipation which stimulates and wastes reserves.

Relax; a proper warning to all of us in this tense modern life. Relax the thinking which otherwise unnecessarily stimulates the mobilizing activity of the adrenals.

The troubles of advancing age have their utility in giving point to a study of this sort. As my 57th year draws to a close, the more insistent pressure of angina in constricted arteries above my heart illustrates again the sequence of mental and physical controls.

Usually the warning pressure is for good cause. I have been hurrying or otherwise stressing the system physically beyond what it could take. On two recent occasions, however, I was entirely relaxed and the pressure built up wholly through mental misguidance.

Eleanor and I vacationed this year at lovely Newagen Inn on the Maine coast. After dinner the Inn provides entertainment which, on the evening in question, was a motion picture of the Crusades of Richard the Lion-hearted. We had been sitting completely relaxed for half an hour before the film started. When the action began there was plenty of emotional stimulation, plotting, fighting and exciting horsemanship. We naturally let ourselves go along with it to enjoy it fully. In about the third reel the psychosomatic sequence had my heart working hard enough to meet the strain of combat. I had to argue with myself over the unreality of it to keep the discomfort of angina within endurance.

A few weeks later, back home in Canton, I turned in very early to get some rest before catching the midnight train to Detroit. The radio by the bed was turned on as it is quite often to block recitation of the day's problems. I had lain quietly relaxed for about twenty minutes when my old friend, the Lone Ranger came on. Of course I have complete confidence in his author's capacity to bring him triumphantly through the most impossible situations. But as the plot thickened he illustrated for me again the nature of the thrill we get out of such blood-and-thunder portrayals. My hearing reported the wholly fictional situation to my consciousness. My autonomic evaluations sensed the danger as reported and flashed the urgency to my instinctive adjustments. Pituitary and adrenals responded with a stimulating flow of suitable hormones. The old pumping muscle responded in turn with increased output until the angina congestion set up a serious complaint. I laughed at myself but the lesson was potent. The picture painted in the conscious area, whether true, mistaken or fanciful, might actually go on to kill a man.

The heavy demand upon the body's resources of mental stress and strain is no news to engineers and business men. My own experience and the troubles of my friends and associates are a major impetus in this effort to present data for their understanding and guidance. We are among the group of professional people and people over 40 to whom the psychiatrists frankly hold out little hope for help from their current art, in times of trouble.

Two weeks ago I stopped in church to talk with a man who was leaving for a rest which he feared would not restore his flagging energies. He has been for years a top-flight executive of a large manufacturing organization here in town and had just been struggling with the problems of budget making for his department.

As we talked tears came to his eyes and an emotional catch to his voice. His grip on my hand was almost frantic. He insisted that he was a failure and had let down his family, his friends and associates. That of course, was not so, but he was worn out, his reserves were depleted which he sensed. Treatments offered hadn't helped, he had lost confidence as I had once years before. The (adrenal) fight had gone out of him. The recitation of his troubles during the long hours of the night coupled with ill-advised self-sympathy-building solicitousness on the part of his friends and relations, had nourished frightened habits of thinking which were neurotic, detrimental. They contributed to the tearing down process, accelerating the drain on his resources by imaginative stimulation of the adrenals.

Rest alone was not enough. To be sure, it could restore the reserves if the drain upon them were not continued by neurotic stimulation.

Confidence is a quality which must clearly be associated with adequacy of our adrenal supply and of the reserves of physical and mental energy which they direct. Confidence rests upon our capacity thus to meet stress, strain and emergency. When these reserves are at a low level so also is confidence, and nervous and physical reactions become jittery to hysterical.

When the reserves are in good supply we thrill to exuberant enthusiasm. Confidence is at its height. Courage and determination are backed by the power to go on to the heights of success.

Yet even when the power plant is in good order and well stocked we have observed that bad mental management fostered by mistraining may squander the reserves or even block their proper usage.

Healthy young soldiers wasted their resources ahead of time as they imagined and exaggerated the potential emergencies which others met with courageous confidence, when the time came. Others waste the reserves, building pent-up fury over fancied wrongs and slighting remarks or in chewing over some frustrated selfishness.

Healthly mental hygiene, good housekeeping, is essential to police the conscious area and throw out the habits of thinking which are contrary to the things Christ taught, the laws of human behavior.

When this has not been done and mischievous to vicious habits of thinking have run us down, when rest, medication and the best efforts of our advisors fail to restore confidence, the conviction develops that no power on earth can save us. Then if we think of it, we wonder if even God has not forgotten us.

It is at that point that some angel must come along and start the restoration of our confidence, our lost faith in God's presence with us. "He restoreth my soul." Alcoholics Anonymous earn recognition as being such messengers of God. These salvaged derelicts of discouraged alcoholism have found the meaning of unselfish love of their fellowmen. They expend themselves and their time to bring the vision, the understanding of faith which restores courage and confidence.

It is in things of this sort that we see the substantial identity of Christ-like courage and confidence and faith. It is anti-climax to point out from this, the essential place of the conscious habit of thinking which is represented by faith, in the adequate functioning of the adrenal-autonomic support for our instinctive urge to just accomplishment, to worthy success.

XIV

DISCRETION, THE PANCREAS, AND
THE URGE TO SELF-PRESERVATION

The grouping of mental, physical and instinctive aspects in this title is dictated because the pancreas at the center of the digestive system is the autonomic agency which physically controls the accumulating and conserving of the resources which are essential to self-preservation and are basic to an internal sense of security. Its physical control in turn is influenced by coordinated conscious and autonomic evaluations of the need for such resources. Prudent discretion becomes necessary in the gratification of attendent appetites, and cravings.

Conversely its fatigue or depletion influences the conscious and autonomic brain functions to feelings of insecurity and even to hysterical reactions which are among the disease results of its unwise exhaustion. In the vicious cycle of maladjustment, such depletion or exhaustion can, and often does result from unintentionally practiced conscious or subconscious habits of thinking which are indiscretions, such as worries, fears, inferiority complexes, miserly hoarding and greedy overindulgences.

The psychosomatic (mentally induced physical) disorders which trace to such self-pampering indulgences or craven self-gratifications are now believed to include diabetes, stomach ulcers, diarrhea, possibly tuberculosis, fear-sterility, apoplexy, many ordinary headaches and indigestions, sleeplessness and sleep walking. Alcoholism, drug addiction and suicide are related problems.

All of these of course are negative aspects, maladjustments, evidences of misuse overtaxing and exhaustion of the control hormones and their auxiliaries. There is a growing tendency in experimental work and diagnostic observation to correlate such resultant ills with the mental attitudes and habits which contribute to them or cause them. After examining the activities of the pancreas we should consider some of these correlations. In them we can observe the aspects of self-sympathy, self-pampering, self-indulgence, selfish greed and general selfishness. This self-centered point of view seems to underlie the neurotic habits of thinking at the root of the nervous overtaxing of the function and the ultimate physical disorder.

We may go back to Christ's teaching of unselfishness and Gautama Buddha's teaching of selflessness if we will, for a glimpse of the underlying laws of human behavior. From these and the observations of normal and abnormal functioning we may formulate for ourselves a concept of the discretionary instinctive standards among the autonomic brain cells, which advise us concerning our gratification of our appetites.

Self-esteem and the character problem of proper evaluation of self for purposes of mental balance are closely related to the operation of the checks and balances in this service of supplying the physical and neural system. How can we give proper weight to self-esteem and pride? At my present age, recently turned fifty-seven, I have become convinced that a pride in the marvelous piece of equipment with which I am endowed and a faith in the infinite wisdom of God, to whom I am responsible, is as far as I can go. I may derive a sense of satisfaction from such accomplishment as has rewarded my use of it, under such portion of inspiration and guidance as I have been able to discern. Back when I gave little thought to any higher responsibility and felt smugly self-satisfied, I came up hard on the end of my rope. My physical, mental and spiritual equilibrium went sadly out of balance and I suffered in all phases of my being.

Some of the specialists are content to consider only the physical, or the mental or the spiritual alone, but on the not-so-novel theory that there is a unity in all things, let us consider what is available at present on the subject as a whole.

*   *   *

In re-reading this chapter it seemed to me that the basic relationships of self, fear and the digestive control center were not stated clearly enough to permit one to correlate the assorted items of supporting evidence which follow. Permit me to restate:

1. Preservation of self, physically and mentally, is instinctive, present in all forms of life. The *external* aspect of preservation, organizing and dispensing reserves for combat is largely an adrenal function as was discussed in the last chapter. The *internal* aspect of self-preservation, the hunger and thirst, mastication, digestion, absorption and storage of the chemical reserves to supply physical *and mental* energy and growth is the problem here.

2. Nature's instinctively wise guidance of the function is provided in the anterior hypothalamus of the inner brain area. Parasympathetic nerve fibers from this group of neurons extend to the various organs involved and to the pancreas, the hormone producing and dispensing

agency which aids and adjusts other organs of the system in the production and maintenance of a supply of energy chemicals.

3. The operation of the critical pancreas may be maintained in good health, or overstimulated even to the extent of exhaustion, or frozen into non-functioning uselessness by conscious interpretations of the external situation upon which autonomic evaluations and instructions to the system are based.

4. Flights of imagination in the conscious domain cannot be distinguished by the inner brain from real emergency demands. Consequently fear and worry routines and the like can disrupt healthy operation which in turn can be sensed as discomfort in the affected area. To the extent that unwarranted worry flights represent lack of courageous faith, the relation of the individual self to the infinite, to God, becomes part of the problem.

*   *   *

Generalities may be quite misleading, but worried thinness and overindulged fatness are likely to be maladjusted extremes of the current problem. Unintentional and possibly unobserved habits of thinking which may have been acquired in childhood, or possibly even inherited as trends from parents contribute to the pattern of control which is evidenced in acquisition of nourishment.

Before the New York Academy of Medicine in 1947, Dr. Hilde Bruch of the Columbia University Department of Psychiatry reported that fewer than 1 in 200 fat people had an actual glandular ailment, and traced the trouble to greedy, irritable, fearful personalities, seeking to offset a conviction of inability or insecurity, (a lack of faith). Says Dr. Bruch: "Quite often it is the youngest or an only child who becomes obese . . . Mothers are the dominant influence." Coddled, overfed and overprotected by a doting mother, the chubby child grows up with a "fundamentally low self-esteem and with the conviction of his helplessness in a world which has been represented to him as a dangerous place. . . ."

The pancreas, which is the principal gland involved, is a light pinkish organ stretching about ten inches across the abdominal cavity at the level of the stomach. It is a potent member of the autonomic system consisting of large numbers of blood vessels, gland cells and nerve termini. It has ample vein and artery connections with the blood stream for sending and receiving purposes. It has parasympathetic nerve connections with the midbrain area and sympathetic nerve connections with the stomach, intestines, adrenals, bladder etc.

The pancreas delivers pancreatic hormones, enzymes, digestive juices, which it produces, through two ducts, the larger entering the duodenum between the stomach and the intestine and the other entering the bile duct near the duodenum. These chemicals participate in transforming food carbohydrates (sugars, starches, gums, dextrines, cellulose, milk sugars, etc.) into glucose which can be absorbed from the intestine and into the bloodstream.

The pancreas also produces insulin and other hormones which it delivers as required to the bloodstream. These adjust the percentage of blood-sugar (glucose) available for normal energy demands of the muscles and brain. They direct the excess available, after eating, to the places where it is converted and stored for future use, or disposed of as surplus. Thus they are instrumental in converting glucose to glycogen at the liver for storage there and into fats for energy storage at the muscles. A really excessive supply of sugar in the blood is disposed of through the bladder. In diabetes, an inadequate insulin supply results in excessive loss of necessary sugars through the bladder.

Phosphorous, sulphur and to lesser extent magnesium, manganese and cobalt, all metallic elements, are utilized in the production of the hormones of the pancreas. For the chemist it is reported that some of these act as catalysts in the reversible conversions of sugars to fats to sugars for energy and storage purposes. Intermediate products at various stages of the reaction include amino acids, pyruvic acid, lactic acid, acetic acid and phosphoric acid. Some of these serving beneficial purposes in limited quantities are poisonous or even fatal in excessive quantities when the checks and balances of the system fail. Control of acid production and balance seems to be an important responsibility of the pancreas and its autonomic brain connections.

Combined voluntary and involuntary mental activity must obviously participate in the unity of action. Neuron responsibilities involve evaluating the need for food, the digestive juice requirements, the relative proportion of sugars for energy in the blood and the disposition of reserves of energy in storage. Close collaboration with the energy dispensing responsibility which utilizes the adrenal hormones is also essential in the maintenance of the balances which constitute good health. Bear in mind the coordinated conscious and autonomic evaluation which recognizes an emergency, puts the adrenal system into operation and at the same time shuts down the activity of the pancreas and restricts the blood supply to that organ.

Nervous indigestion quite naturally results if we insist upon eating a substantial meal while our thoughts are directed to disturbing controversy. I had demonstrated to my sorrow before I read it in texts and reports, that I can't eat and argue. The emergency mobilization takes precedence and the pancreas' digestive efforts are suspended or retarded for the duration. One observes the wisdom of the dog who eats and then curls up to sleep, sensing without knowing that his digesting and recuperating services will do better thereby. Old rules about not undertaking energetic exercise especially swimming immediately after eating, are justified by the facts. Autonomic attention and energy must be devoted primarily to one major activity, either the accumulating and replacement of reserves or the emergency dispensing of reserves. More or less violent complaint will be sensed in the form of cramps or stomach ache if we endeavor to ignore the natural laws which pertain.

Therefore relax before starting to eat. Vehement business discussions during meals or emotionally disturbing situations at such times, prohibit digestive application to the job at hand as we have seen. And relax a while after a heavy meal for you have given the (autonomic) system a serious undertaking which won't be properly completed if you divert its activities elsewhere too soon.

Chronic nervous indigestion, repeated mistreatment, fatigue and depletion or exhaustion of the nervous controls and the productive capacity for hormones result eventually in a hysterical to panicky reaction. A nervous stomach or intestinal tract behave in a jumpy spasmodic manner. Cramps and diarrhea are among the results.

The ample nerve system of the pancreas and associated abdominal organs serve the normal useful purposes of maintenance reporting and directive control. At times however they express other complaining reports beside immobilizing cramps and less serious objections to overeating or inadequate opportunity for digestion.

The pangs of hunger, "butterflies in the stomach" and that "sinking feeling at the pit of the stomach" in sudden fear or in nervously tense situations are also sensed reports from the jurisdiction of the pancreas. Cold chills diffusing from this area and the "petrifying" immobilization of muscular activity, the frightened "freeze" help to associate fear reactions with the sensed functioning of this autonomic responsibility.

It is interesting to note the relation of the brain and the gland centers in these sensed reports relative to autonomic "emotional" activities. Why do we sense the fear reactions *at* the pancreas when the conscious observation and interpretation of the cause for fear and the autonomic evaluation and plan for hormone adjustment to meet the situation both take place in the inner brain area? The reports of stomach and intestinal conditions and hormone disposition are also returned to the brain area but we sense them at the point of origin of the report. This fortunate and useful provision of nature has been demonstrated in connection with the amputation of limbs. A man whose arm has been removed at the elbow will sense discomfort in fingers which are not there. Actually the discomfort may be at the ends of the severed nerves in the stump but the brain senses it where the terminals should have been. Thus when a real or an imagined or even dreamed danger threatens our security as examined and considered in the mind, we "feel" it at the pit of the stomach where the pancreas is.

In the course of fifty odd years I have been "privileged" to sample many of the fear and worry reactions, the endocrine sensations and fatigue complaints. Of late years I have made notes of some of them and have been interested to find where they fitted into the system.

One morning as I rode to the laboratory by subway, I stood looking out of the front window of the leading car. As we rounded a curve in down-town Manhattan, there appeared the lights of a rapidly approaching train and head-on collision appeared instantaneously imminent. My pancreas reacted at once with that "sinking feeling at the pit of the stomach." Yet I figured out consciously that it was the optical illusion created by the curve, even before the other train slithered past on the next track. The autonomic emotional reaction to the pancreas and back, was faster than the conscious explanation.

And silly as it seems now, I experienced that same fear reaction a number of times just entering a dark room in my own home. To be sure that was during my 1944-45 bout with extreme nervous fatigue. I have experienced a milder sense of nervous tension at the pancreas on some occasions since then in driving my car and even in anticipating a business trip by air, not that I am conscious of any real fear of planes.

A quite different fear sensation is the immobilizing cold chill, the freeze which holds a frightened animal rigid in its tracks when surprised. I know just how it feels for that chill has swept over me and held my muscles in a grip which conscious effort could not break for the moment.

Once it happened in our old four story "brown stone" house in Brooklyn. House-breaking and burglary were not uncommon. Something awakened me during the night and I was convinced that I should go down through the blackness to investigate. Then the chill came and literally I couldn't move a muscle for a few minutes. Actually there was no cause for alarm but had there been, I was temporarily helpless.

Early this year I experienced the "petrifying" experience again, and this time made a note of it. We were vacationing at a hotel on the Georgia coast but I awakened one night with a realistic dream of meeting a wild cat in northern woods. There was nothing I could recall which might have initiated or stimulated it, but that is beside the point. It was vivid and convincing. As I awakened the chill started and I observed its progress. It began distinctly in the area of the pancreas and spread as if in widening circles until it covered all of me and tingled at my finger tips. Positively I couldn't move a muscle, even though by that time I was sufficiently awakened to know that I was safe in bed.

The best I can do to explain it at present is to link it with release of acetylcholine. This is a waste by-product of normal nourishment of the neurons of the brain and nerve system. In sufficient concentration and out of its normal habitat it is reported to be a deadly poison. It is stated that it can be released at the terminals of the tubular sheaths which enclose the nerves and their nourishing supply of the cerebrospinal fluid. Dr. C. D. Turner observes that acetylcholine has an opposite effect to adrenal hormones which release or activate energy stored in the muscle areas, therefore the effect of demobilizing, rather than mobilizing the body's combative resources. The rate at which the paralyzing muscle freeze spreads from the area of the pancreas to my finger tips resembles that of hormones liberated through the blood stream. Turner also notes that "acetylcholine is inactivated quickly by an esterase present in the (muscle) tissues," which corroborates the fading of the sensation.

Among these several reports of sensing fear reactions of the autonomic circuit, there was really nothing to worry about. This and my experience of the early forties confirm professional observations with regard to neurotic worries and such. When I took time for conscious consideration I knew there was no cause for alarm or for the resultant impact upon my digestive system. But as in the practiced subconsciously directed activities of mechanical skills and athletics, the train of reaction took place before conscious consideration could be completed.

The conscious circuit is not to be excused however. The reports of a threat to our security to which the autonomic circuit reacts had to be initiated by some observation of conscious receiving organs and interpreted over some subconscious hook-up of information and motor neurons of the cerebral cortex. Those elements constituted a habit of thinking, practiced unintentionally perhaps in worrying or developed out of nightly reading of the scare stories which newspapers love to feature;—airplane accidents, with all lost, automobile crashes with gory details, well intended warnings of safety agencies oft reiterated, all coupled with an occasional close call in personal experience. Such things readily establish patterns of thought over the years, and these combined with the resultant reactions at the pancreas and perhaps at the adrenals, establish a chronic drain upon the system which the medical profession terms neurotic.

The urge to self-preservation, as an autonomic, instinctively equipped motor neuron, is an acceptable root of the reaction. A high self-esteem, a self-centered basis for worry, accounts for the implanting of the worry pattern in the conscious domain. The combination of the two, oft repeated, brings the detrimental depletion and exhaustion of the endocrine hormones.

A public recognition of responsiblility for neurosis-promoting news and propaganda is an obvious need, within limitations. But that alone is not enough.

The attitude of mind with regard to self, as a matter of conscious training is vital. Molly-coddling and pampering is obviously wrong. A devil-may-care fatalism suggests undue carelessness at the other extreme. A courageous sense of responsibility coupled with the religious concept of faith in God's will appears to be the sound middle ground.

Conscious responsibility for fear reactions to dreams may seem a bit far-fetched and I have no desire to become entangled in dream interpretations. Yet as a matter of reporting I recall recently listening to a diet of three or four blood curdling radio mystery stories of an evening and then awakening to some disturbing dream during the night. To be sure, I rarely have such dreams, but also I rarely listen to such programs. Music is definitely more soothing after a difficult day, but some evenings it is hard to get music.

Sleep-walking behavior in its association with dreams and with attitudes of mind seems to be pertinent. An investigation of 22 somnambulists at Camp Lee, Virginia, was reported in "Mental Hygiene" in June 1945 by Lt. Col. S. A. Sandler. Men who were gentle by day became dangerous to themselves and to others at night, when their fears and imaginations were unfettered. One sleepwalker jumped out of a window, rolled off an awning, broke a wrist and walked five blocks before he was caught and wakened. A boy shot his mother in his sleep and an English somnambulist killed and carved up his wife while asleep. These are extremes, but what neurotic habits of thinking motivated the plans and actions?

Colonel Sandler states that "The personality structure of the somnambulist is that of the overprotected, babied adult. . .Somnambulism, in its essence, represents to the sleep-walker an attempt to escape from (imagined) threatening dangers." Some dreamed of snakes, of being chased by men with knives, or by rabid dogs. Some dreamed that their fathers saved them. Most of their fathers had some disease, "the fathers of the entire group were feared, respected and idolized." Half of the boys were the youngest child in a very large family.

The New York Mental Hygiene Clinic of the Veterans Administration gives psychiatric treatment and encouragement to offset the worries and troubles of a hundred or more veterans a day. It has classified 370 different types of headaches and found that one way of treating them is a sedative novocaine injection to relax tense muscles and pave the way for persuading the patient that his headaches will disappear if he stops worrying. . . Psychiatrist Charles Brown who heads the clinic, believes the men's problems are no different from those of civilians. He believes that many a mentally ill veteran might easily have got over the (fatiguing) shocks of his war experience without treatment if he had not run into home and job worries, and the housing shortage which forces jittery veterans to live with jittery relatives.

At the other side of the world, Sir Charles Blackburn, Chancellor of Sydney University and "grand old man of Australian medicine" observed that modern man worries so much about his ability to measure up to the challenges of his environment that he often, literally worries himself sick. Most alarming he feels is the . . . widely held idea that "The conditions of life today are such that it is difficult for any but the most exceptional nervous system to stand up to them."

An unwise scholastic and business attitude of hurry and pressure is certainly present. At the same time a softening of religion and an undermining of its training by materialistic educators has robbed many men of a courageous confidence in their spiritual equipment and in the availability to the worthy of the strength and wisdom of the Infinite.

Mounting alcoholism has been traced repeatedly to self-pampering evasions of responsibilities, fearful neuroses of insecurity, inferiority and guilt. The curative processes of mental housecleaning and restoration of confidence have been best carried on by Alcoholics Anonymous. The appetite for the means of numbing the conscious area's worries is appreciated by those who have experienced it. The gratitude for the help of other similarly bedraggled but triumphant "messengers of God" has strengthened the urge to loving service in the AA's to a point where it really works.

Narcotic addiction may be started maliciously as it has been among would-be-smart teen-agers. More often however, it also "is a cover-up for feelings of inferiority, insecurity or depression." This is blamed by Psychiatrist Walter Adams for the fact that while Negroes comprise only 10% of the population, they number 45% of the narcotic addicts.

An orphaned lad who knew insecurity from youth got his first "lift" out of a medicinal shot of morphine for an earache. He became an addict and was sent repeatedly for the medical "cure" at the Lexington, Kentucky, hospital, but it didn't really reach the seat of the trouble. Later he became interested in the ideas of the A.A. "It seemed religious," he reports, "and like most addicts I didn't care anything about God. It might work for those drunks, but not for us. But after a while I began to feel that this group had the answer." Danny studied the A.A. code, saw how it could be applied to discharged dope victims, and founded Narcotics Anonymous for the restoration of faith and confidence which must follow the withdrawal treatment if the cure is to be effective.

Vagatomy, cutting of the vagus nerve of the autonomic system, serving the pancreas, stomach and digestive system, is an interesting and controversial treatment for sufferers from stomach ulcers. Dr. L. R. Dragstedt, professor of surgery at the University of Chicago Medical School originated the treatment after studying the secretion of the gastric juices in the digestive system. Ulcers result from the secretion of abnormally large amounts of gastric acids (hormones or enzymes from the pancreas). While normal secretion or distribution of such juices accompanies eating, Dr. Dragstedt found that ulcer patients secreted large amounts between meals and at night (when imaginative malpractices are likely to be permitted). Medical men have long observed that ulcers are what might be called an occupational disorder of business executives, taxidrivers, newsmen, doctors and others who work under excessive stress. Therefore to protect the stomach from the effects of mental stress he tried cutting the (autonomic) nerve connection from the brain at the diaphragm just above the stomach area. He found that it did reduce the flow of gastric juices to the stomach and permitted the ulcers to clear up. He still urged the normal treatment first, bland diet and a change to a less exacting job and concludes that, for nervous stomachs and the "tensions and strains of modern life," preventative psycho-analysis may be better than nerve cutting.

The storm raised over the cutting of nerves to block the psysical ill-effects of unwise thinking habits was reported * in *Time* of June

* Courtesy of TIME; copyright TIME, Inc. 1947.

30, 1947 in part as follows:—"All over the United States surgeons were cutting nerves in various parts of the body in the hope of relieving ulcers, hand sweating, high blood pressure, hiccoughs, drug addiction, schizophrenia. One hospital last week was booked solid for the next nine months with appointments for lobotomies (severing the conscious influence from the subconscious neurosis). . . Doctors were asking, "will people who are now getting their nerves cut, someday wish they hadn't?"

"Psychopathic surgeons are being swamped by demands for lobotomy by alcoholics, frustrated business men, unhappy housewives and people who are just nervous." But "Psychiatrists recommend the operation only for otherwise incurable psychotics." Dr. Leo M. Davidoff of New York does very few lobotomies and warns sternly: "Although surgery is sometimes necessary, it is a barbaric form of therapy." Dr. Winifred Overholser of Washington adds: "I look upon it as a mutilating operation. It puts out of commission the part of the brain that separates man from the higher anthropoids."

If we interpret it properly this operation damages at least for a time the group of motor neurons storing consciously and subconsciously used mental routines, habits of thinking. To get at the detrimental ones, it must necessarily eliminate useful ones. Presumably however the patient will be more careful in relearning, providing other neurons will pinch hit for those destroyed.

If such operations sever nerve pathways which eliminate the influence of malicious conscious thinking upon autonomic physical controls, do they not in turn eliminate autonomic instinctive and other influences upon conscious thinking? The complexity of nerve pathways is such that this is not necessarily so, but at least I have not yet found an answer to it.

The vital part of all this study of maladjusted and malfunctioning systems is the light it throws upon proper normal operation, good mental housekeeping. In these problems of mistreatment of the pancreas a progressive series of tensions, anxieties, worries and fears which are evidences of conscious lack of faith, confidence and discrete restraint in self management, cause physical malfunctioning which in turn adds to the load of anxiety.

An extreme illustration of anxiety was reported in October 1952 by Doctors Harvey and Levine of Boston. The old reference to people being "frightened to death" poses the problem of how seriously conscious activity may influence the autonomic psysical controls. A 29 year old woman entered the hospital for psychiatric treatment, complaining of palpitations of her heart and a "smothering sensation." She volunteered to test the effect of a drug, amyl nitrite, on heart sounds. Preliminary readings of the electrocardiograph and phono-cardiograph showed her heart to be normal. But as soon as the patient saw the drug her heart began a machine-gun beat. Scared nearly to death themselves, the doctors put the drug away and her heart went back to normal. In their report in the AMA Journal, the two doctors pointed out that it might have taken nothing more than a severe fright to cause a prolonged heart speed up. And this sort of speed up can lead to a futile non-rythmic (hysterical) quivering of the lower part of the heart which means death.

In this case the instrument set-up recorded the effect of fright at the heart rather than the stomach. It was still an autonomically ordered activity based upon the womans' conscious observation of the drug. The missing link is the interpretation which she placed upon the appearance of the drug. She had volunteered to take it, but her hysterical reaction to anything in the nature of fancied danger to her-self must have been built-up by long hours of imaginative worry about fanciful threats to her well-being. The autonomic urge to self-preser-vation is proper. The indiscretion lies in improper conscious policing of the imagination. The root of that probably is to be found in molly-coddling, sympathizing and inadequate training in the point of view of faith and courage. Where the worries trace to misbehavior and the disturbing complaints of conscience, reacting to the instinctive drives and standards, then the therapy calls for recognizing the error and the rules honestly. I am inclined to state positively that honest prayer for God's forgiveness of misbehavior and selfish thinking, and for help in changing the malicious habits of thinking is an essential part of the cure. The cleansing of mind may take considerable time and care, for long practiced worries, greeds, envies, inferiority self-pam-perings etc., etc., may be well rooted. Some outstanding men have recognized the need for close cooperation of the psychiatrist as diag-nostician and of the ministerial servant of God to guide the confes-sional cleansing and the rebuilding of thinking and of faith.

I have tried to help a few intimates and passers-by just through sharing my own experiences, although I am not professionally quali-fied in either field and am not even a really good man. But perhaps it should be observed that qualification in both fields goes beyond academic acceptance and the practicing apprenticeship. It requires achievement of spiritual maturity which is not an easy or common attainment. Glenn Clark, whose attainment I know, has expressed his findings in a number of non-professional books of great value. In one, his novel "What Would Jesus Do?", he includes a portrayal of the difficult ministerial problem of carrying out their part of cooperation with the medical profession.

Returning from the problems of helping the maladjusted and unwell, to the aspects of self-preservation in which the pancreas plays so vital a part, what are the considerations of normal maintenance? God provided as one item of our instinctive heritage, that urge to self-preservation, the motor drive back of our eating and acquiring and saving habits. It isn't wrong. We *need* it and God gave it. But it is *not* the end objective. Rather it is a maintenance function that the whole mechanism, the individual, may be preserved for useful purposes.

XV

THE URGE TO SERVE,
THE SENSE OF RESPONSIBILITY
AND THE THYMUS

As we gather the psychosomatic interrelations of physical, mental and spiritual activities, this next group bears an interesting relation to the last two. The three are the legs of a tripod which, taken together, support our balanced behavior.

First, the autonomic and conscious neuron groups, in association with the pancreas which we have just discussed, and the organic activities which it promotes, all combine to evaluate the needs and to gather and store our nutritional supplies and reserves. The urge to self-preservation with educational aspects of discretion and faith, as opposed to those of self-centered worries and greeds, characterize the autonomic and the conscious participations of this last group.

The prior group dealt with adrenal dispensing of these supplies and reserves in the interests of healthy growth and of courageous accomplishment. Maladjusted extremes of impotent sloth and pugnatious imperiousness characterized the mental aspects.

The third group, completing the triumvirate, balances the accumulating and the dispensing of our reserves with *purposeful responsibility*.

In the autonomic instinctive heritage we may recognize the urge to service, the feeling of responsibility. It is back of the high "calling" of the pastor, the priest and the physician. The absorbing interest which attracts me to engineering and analytical problems is something I can understand although Eleanor deplores it. The drive which carries the musician, the artist and the poet through probable privation is part of it. From the tense, high-powered executive to the less dramatic but also satisfying myriad of jobs which keep things going, a desire to do one's part, to pull one's weight in the boat reaps a rewarding sense of satisfaction, a sense of accomplishment.

The materialist would school himself to ignore these sensed impressions which his sixth sense neurons admit to his consciousness. Unscrupulously, he closes his heart to brotherly love and condemns religion as the "opiate of the people" because it espouses unselfish service in preference to self-aggrandizement.

Instinctively men have associated the sensed spirit of loving kindness and brotherly service with the region of the heart. Literature is filled with references to worthy men who speak from the heart, actions governed by the heart, behavior which stimulates a warm glow over the heart.

I listened recently to an emotionally stirring radio presentation of "The Littlest Angel," the Christmas story of the somewhat bedraggled little soul who offered up as his gift to the Christ-child, his soiled box of boyish treasures, white stones, a butterfly and some bits of wood. It left me with tears in my eyes, a catch in my breathing and a taut feeling over my heart. And it is the same area where I feel the discomforts of angina when I overexert myself.

Trained observation has related the tired feeling of the adrenal glands to the exhaustion of reserves in battle fatigue and other demands upon courage. Next the sensations associated with hunger, fright to the area and responsibilities of the pancreas. And now we are examining the aspects of loving service and of stress, exhaustion, heart failure, etc. which the interrelation of sensation and circumstances tend to localize with and above the heart. I note at fifty seven, that the pain of angina over the heart responds to emotional and business stress.

Across the chest in this area we find another of the endocrine glands, which knit together the external situation, our attitudes of mind and our physical functioning through the evaluation and control functions of the autonomic neuron system. This gland, the thymus, is generously equipped like the others with incoming and outgoing transmission connections in both the nerve system and the blood system. Its two lobes lie along the midline of the thorax and chest above the heart.

The human thymus weighs about 15 grams at birth and increases to about 35 grams at youthful physical maturity in the late teens. Then gradually it becomes smaller until at sixty years of age it is again 15 grams or less. It is interesting and pertinent to note the concurrent rise and fall of human nervous energy which is literally the electrical energizing capacity of the nervous system, the capacity for service.

One might suspect maximum energy at the age of three or four, and some psychologist wore out a college athlete by having him imitate all the activities of a four year old. But the energy demand does increase with growth and with the brain activities of learning. The army recognizes the beginning of decline of such energies at about 18 or 20. The prize fighter must defer to younger competitors at about 30 and the ball player at 35. Despite a few apparent exceptions like Churchhill, Root and Baruch, the brain worker begins to know the meaning of fatigue and the need for husbanding his nervous energies as he reaches the forties.

A recent report of research with radioactive tracer elements introduced into the bloodstream indicates that the heart action follows a similar pattern. From the Yale Scientific Monthly, "Results showed a progressive reduction of blood flow with increased age. In 18 year olds the maximum flow of blood occurs;—25 cc through 1 liter of tissue per minute. At 25 years of age the flow is reduced to 15 cc and at 35 it is 10 cc."

This change of flow rate is significant for the bloodstream carries the energy producing supplies, fat and sugars to the muscles and fatty alcohol to the brain and thence to the rest of the nervous system. Electrical energy as such participates in the activity and health of both the nerve system and the bloodstream.

A person's blood is normally charged during good health with either negative or positive ions of electricity, Rh, positive or Rh negative. A positive or negative ion rides each red corpuscle. As any science high school student knows, like-charges repel each other, and it works out that way. In the tiny capillary tubes which nourish body members and which connect the system of outgoing arteries with the system of veins to return blood to the heart and lungs, there is only room for the 35 trillion corpuscles or red cells to slip through one at a time. In good health, the electrical ions keep them nicely separated in neat single file.

In many types of ill health however the electrical charges are more or less absent. The red corpuscles tend to bunch together in a sticky sludge. They interfere with proper circulation and clog or stop it entirely. In that case the tissues in that area fail to get needed supplies and die. Dr. Melvin H. Knisely and research associates at the University of Chicago announced in November 1947 that they had found red cell clumping associated with over fifty conditions from common cold and malaria to hysteria and mental illness. Dr. Knisely found the central nervous system of one psychotic patient "showered with permanent plugs" that had destroyed many of the nerve cells. He suggested that even aging and senility may be accounted for by such accumulated damage from injuries and illnesses.

Presumably it is the passage of electrically charged red cells close to the surface of the skin which makes possible the recording of the actions and irregularities of the heart by the electro-cardiograph. Its electrodes detect their pulsing passage, for amplification and recording by the instrument.

The sequence effects of conscious reporting and thinking upon the heart's action, as registered by this instrument, were observed by doctors of the New York Hospital under Dr. Ian P. Stevenson in 1948. They were finding that emotionally stirred people who claimed;— "my heart skipped a beat," or "my heart stood still", are probably stating a literal fact. When patients were under test with the electro-cardiograph, the doctors deliberately stirred their (love) emotions. One patient developed a noticeable arrythmia (irregular beating) when the doctor mentioned his in-laws (whom he didn't love). A woman patient's heart began skipping when the doctors referred to her illegitimate child. Premature contractions of the heart (extrasystole) were recorded when they asked a 61 year old spinster why she had never married.

We know that hormones from the adrenal glands may increase the heart action as a part of emergency mobilization and that they may draw from emergency supplies at the liver to enrich the blood for refreshment of the muscles.

We know that insulin hormones from the pancreas also have their effect upon the preparation and maintenance of sugar reserves, a shortage of which may demand excessive heart action.

We are not yet clear about the part played by the thymus but we have several clues to add to the instinctive and sensed attributions. The rise and decline of heart action and of nervous energy with the growth and shrinkage of the thymus relate it to heart beat activity and to the electro-chemical reserves of the nervous system, which will have to be discussed in some detail.

Cholesterol, the fatty alcohol which the heart delivers through the bloodstream to the brain and nerve system, supplies the chemicals for their production of the electrical energy they use in thinking and in muscle stimulation. Some agency, possibly the thymus, must catalyze the natural fermentation of sugars to alcohols for this purpose and store a reserve supply.

Beverage alcohols do not have to await such a process and go direct to the brain. Such rich diet taken in excess overstimulates the brain, as rich food in excess upsets the digestive system. Turner reports that "it has been determined that a variety of infections and *intoxications* cause the thymus to involute (shrink in size) more rapidly than it does normally." If it does not have to participate in the production of the required alcohol, would not the reduced need for it permit its reduction in size?

A de-energizing malady known as myasthenia gravis may also lend a clue. *Time,* November 10, 1952, reports the story of young Billy Lucas, an apparently hopeless invalid in his early years, with expressionless eyes and so feeble he could hardly swallow or raise his arms. A British neurologist prescribed neostigmine, a stimulant which began a gradual revival until Billy became a normal boy, requiring the stimulant, however, every three hours. The report continues that the disease seems to be connected with (some malfunctioning of) the thymus gland. About half the victims of the disease get better after removal of the (defective) thymus.

Cholesterol is described as the battery chemical of the nervous system, the significant contributor to nervous energy. At the same time it is the villain of the piece in the heart attacks which kill older men, driving themselves under excessive nervous tension.

Having had a number of my friends bow out with heart troubles I am naturally interested. My own angina which is not at all serious, thanks be, appeared last winter at the climax of three very tough years. I had lived in three cities, built up three engineering departments, dealt with some rather difficult personalities and tackled some engineering problems beyond anything I had ever known. I began to get pretty tired and, after a couple of warnings, went to our very fair president and told him I was going to have to cut down the hours. The peak average was about sixty hours a week which was a lot under stress for a man past fifty, but now it is down to about thirty five. And I have cut out "homework," except this project.

The nerve nutrient, cholesterol is described as a chemically complex molecule which indeed it must be. Egg yolks, butter, milk, cream and animal fats are said to contribute to its formation. Described as a fatty alcohol, there must also be a conversion of starches to sugars to alcohols. Oily constituents produce the insulating needs of the electrical system in the form of an oily or fatty film over the nerve fibres.

In the form of cholesterol it is delivered to the bloodstream from its source (intestines?) and delivered through the arteries to midbrain areas where it enters the cerebrospinal fluid. As we get older some of it tends to separate out as a fatty or paraffin-like substance to gather along the walls and contribute to hardening of the arteries, and to gather near the entrance to the heart to interfere with the flow of blood sufficiently to be reported in the complaint pains of angina pectoris. The surplus formations may break loose at times under the circulatory rush of some sudden excitement or hard exertion. Then they may carry through the main blood stream to clog some critical point and stop its supplies as a thrombosis. This is a present understanding of the mechanisms of heart trouble and failure under mental pressure, responsibility and physical effort beyond the age and state of the individual.

My good friend and neighbor in Brooklyn, Dr. Lohman had a little poem in his office which I wish I could set down for you. It was advice to men over forty and under considerable nervous tension, to slow down and take it a bit easier. It ended up, "Do as I say, and not as I do." That was all too true for it was the wartime period of shortage of doctors and the demands upon Lohman at the hospital and in the office were terrific. He seemed to be in fine health but he was tired, and he wouldn't let his patients down. One day at the height of his career he dropped, dead. Heart attack was the verdict. He was truly a dedicated servant of his fellowmen, and one who felt a great responsibility for them. So also in religion was the late great Dr. Peter Marshal, who would not spare himself. At a less dramatic but equally conscientious level, my friend Pete Lorenz was production manager through a very harrowing period and gave of himself without stint. Then one morning at the height of the pressure, he died on his way into the office. The diagnosis again was heart attack.

One heart specialist described the angina reaction as a hysterical cramp of the heart muscle. This would explain how anticipatory worry routines seem to stimulate it at times.

Doctors now tell me that heart patients "need not retire to a cloistered life," but do need to adjust their responsibilities to their energy level and to reduce the cholesterol producing diet.

On the other hand it has been observed that the thymus reacts to malnutrition, checking its reservoir service. Its abnormalities are reportedly found in people who are irresponsible, quite the opposite to those "big-hearted" men who took their responsibilities more seriously than their lives.

Kneeling at prayer one October morning and considering the problems of this undertaking, it became apparent that the Golden

Rule and the command to "love thy neighbor as thyself" were the positive expression of the natural laws against the debilitating neuroses of self interest. They are the clue to the responsibilities of the thymus-heart-mind group. The time honored association of the "heart" is with love, the sort of love George Washington Carver lavished on his plants and his people. It is also the sort Lohman, Marshal and Lorenz lavished upon their responsibilities. Even the negative aspects of the maladjusted reactions registered on the experimental cardiographs are pertinent.

Darwin's finding is more properly expressed; the law of survival of the fit. In it for modern man there is the implication of worthy accomplishment as well as physical adaption. The survival aspect is not to be confused just because some worthy men did not readjust their responsibilities to their declining energy level.

Christ expressed the same natural law in many ways and at many times. "*Do* unto others as you would that they should do unto you," with the emphasis upon the word "do," the accomplishment of service. Negatively, in the parable of the salt, he urged the discarding of the unworthy, and again in the parable of the non-productive fruit tree. Positively again, "Let your light so shine before man . . ." The obligation of loving service was urged repeatedly.

At the change of life period, when men and women must readjust to the reduced capacities of their physical and nervous system we observe also a review and readjustment of their mental and spiritual position. It is then that their shortcomings overwhelm them in psychosomatic disaster, or that they courageously ask God's forgiveness for the errors of the past.

Then they may be figuratively reborn to the revered responsibilities of the patriarch. The elder statesmen, the experienced and matured advisors in all walks of life, the retired folk who lead in civic and spiritual responsibilities, and the worthy grandparents through all generations, these are the folk who have successfully negotiated the change. Thereafter they may achieve their greatest heights of worthy service.

Faith, hope and charity, or perhaps in the terms we have been using, Faith, Courage and Loving Service, these three respectively we may interrelate with the pancreas, adrenals and thymus as executive agents. Related neurons of the autonomic brain area provide their standards and driving agencies. But to utilize them, the consciously trained and (often subconsciously) used habits of thinking must be in proper order. Purposeful responsibility with the aspect of brotherly love would appear to be the healthy point of view, as opposed to selfish ambition on the one hand, (the viewpoint of responsibility only to self) and indolent irresponsibility at the other extreme.

XVI

THE THYROID, CURIOSITY AND
THE URGE TO EVALUATE

The thyroid is an interesting gland spread like a bow tie across the throat. Early observation linked it to nervous tension. People in the extreme tension of panic, tore open their clothing at the throat due to the swelling feeling of discomfort there. Under other conditions goiter swelled the glands due to insufficient dietary iodine supplies to meet normal living stresses, or due to excessive stress (hypertension), be it real or fancied, in the life of the individual.

Now we find that the healthy thyroid with its associated areas and activities in the two brain groups has to do with the attentive, stimulated and alert mentality. The group responsibility deals with adjustment of nervous tension and relaxation; adjustment of sensitivity of the perceptive senses; adjustment of rates of conversion (metabolism) of foods to reserves, to energies, to activities; adjustment of natural rhythms, rates of activity of organs and muscle groups; adjustment of rate of development and growth in both the physical and mental system.

In this adjustment of rates and tensions there is a necessary close collaboration with other elements of the autonomic system. In the maintenance of checks and balances, thyroid hormones affect the hormone activities of the pancreas, adrenals and pituitary and are influenced in turn by some of them. And nerve impulses intersperse and influence the activities and report status and requirements in a variety of ways.

To make all of the adjustments of nervous, physical, mental, recuperative and constructive activities in which the thyroid participates, it requires considerable mental support. Specifically it requires first the conscious observation and interpretation of the external situation. Interpretation must be emphasized, for in misinterpretation are found again important sources of maladies and unnecessary exhaustion of the organism.

Finally it requires the exercise of its autonomic perceptive capacities to evaluate such observations against the standards of value, sincerity, importance, danger, utility or opportunity. The resultant evaluation must determine whether or not its hormones are to be dispensed and to what extent. This instinctive urge to evaluate, to perceive value, necessity, and utility is inherent in the curiosity of the youngster as he seeks to learn, to grow mentally as well as physically.

*　　*　　*

Illuminating maladies of the thyroid function may trace to infection, dietary (iodine) deficiencies, developmental defects (inherited or otherwise), excessively tense living and neurotic habits of thinking which have the same effect. Sometimes the patient may swing wildly from ecstacy to depression with hysterical spasms of the heart, stomach or throat. This is particularly so if the cause of the trouble is subconsciously stored thinking routines which intermittently exhaust the glands.

Excessive supplies or capacity for secretion may result in irritability, nervous tremors, shortness of breath, high body temperatures, sweatiness, or the extremes of epileptic fits, characterized by excessively high nervous tension (high mental voltage and frequency).

Inadequacy of organic capacity or of chemical supplies are evidenced in dull, languid apathy, fatness, weakness, low body temperatures (feeling cold), emotional immaturity and the extremes of shock, dwarfism and idiocy (physical and mental under-development). It is reported that nervous exhaustion of the gland and dietary iodine deficiency exhibit rather similar mal-effects. The gland gives observable warning of fatigue I find, with a feeling of discomfort and swelling or contraction. The medical profession warns us that exhaustion may be carried to a point where the glands may never recover. I have also found that the thyroid may get into a neurotic habit of expressing discomfort and may continue to do so long after extended relaxation and recuperation have eliminated the actual fatigue.

One is hesitant about such recitation of symptoms although it seems an essential part of the record. The danger is that some sensitive readers who lack adequately courageous faith may indulge in imaginative excesses and really make themselves sick.

A variety of goiters, overdevelopment or swelling of the glands, have been identified. They may be due to a poisoned condition, possibly due to arsenic salts or cyanide, a lack of iodine or a surplus of calcium or proteins. Or they may trace to excessive nervous tension demands in the face of limited dietary supplies. One of my friends, in charge of a large engineering group with accompanying evaluation problems, has recently required the goiter operation.

*   *   *

Hindu philosophers are reported to have been notably successful in sensing the higher circuit functions associated with the endocrine glands. Perhaps they are not as handicapped as we are with the great mass of ill-digested research and educational material which confronts us. Be that as it may, they have associated with the throat (area of the thyroid) perceptual ideas and the capacity to observe.

We frown upon such unscientific methods as sensed perception of a function in our current research enthusiasm. But perhaps we are now in a position to add up the evidence and agree that their conclusion is pretty well demonstrated.

The thyroid draws its name from Greek words meaning, "shield-shaped." Its right and left lobes spread across the lower throat in a position which I have found can make a close fitting collar quite uncomfortable upon fortunately rare occasions. This morning, struggling with the perceptual problem which is involved here I am more comfortable in a soft open-necked shirt.

The normal human thyroid weighs about 25 to 40 grams and fluctuates very considerably in size as the demands upon it vary and its nutritive supplies are liberal or scarce. More blood flows into and out of it, in proportion to its size, than any other organ except possibly the adrenal glands. From that blood stream it takes the iodine and other supplies necessary to produce its own hormones, and also receives pituitary hormones which tend to limit its productivity. Nerve connections report back concerning its reserves or exhaustion, and control the muscular squeezing out or dispensing of its hormones to the bloodstream for delivery to all or most of the other six glands.

Four tiny parathyroid glands at the back of the thyroid are vital to the system. Their removal from experimental animals gives information upon their functions and results quite soon in convulsions and death. They secrete a protein-like hormone containing considerable nitrogen and traces of iron and sulphur. It resembles vitamin D in its accomplishments and regulates the rate of absorption and dispersion of calcium, magnesium and phosphorous ions by the blood stream. Thereby it regulates healthy maintenance and development of bone and tooth structure. Its excesses and deficiencies are connected with a variety of bone troubles, brittleness, weaknesses and shrinkage.

It also regulates the excitability and irritability of the nervous system associated with pH acid balance of the hydrogen ion in blood acidity or alkalinity. Inadequate supply of the parathyroid hormone results in muscle twitching, spasms of the face, larynx or intestines (cramps), or convulsions of the whole structure. An excess of the hormone reduces sensitivity and causes general weakness, loss of appetite, pains of bones and spinal column, deformities and even death. Loss of calcium in the bones may be accompanied by excesses of calcium deposited in the heart, lungs and medium sized arteries.

The apparent beneficial effect of sunshine upon excessive nervous tension may be explained by the statement that "vitamin D is formed in the skin through the action of ultraviolet light upon such steroles as ergosterol." Vitamin D resembles the parathyroid hormone. It is credited with facilitating the absorption of calcium, magnesium and phosphorous from digesting foodstuffs. The hormone regulates the balance of these elements through the blood stream to the bones and to the cerebro-spinal fluid which nourishes the nerve system. Magnesium and calcium ions are natural nerve sedatives, exerting a quieting or restorative effect upon an overexcited or fatigued nervous system.

The thyroid hormone is given the tongue twisting name of iodothyroglobulin. It is a complex protein molecule made of hydrogen, oxygen, carbon, iodine and a dash of nitrogen. A major portion of this large molecule is an amino acid called Thyroxin. One M.D. asserts that only $3\frac{1}{2}$ grams of thyroid secretion stands between intelligence and idiocy. That tiny amount is actually large compared with other minute quantities of master chemicals imperative to vital functions. It is indicative of the critical correlation of the physical and mental departments. It has been observed that thyroid-plus people are more acute of perception, more sensitive and more energetic than others.

Metabolism is a term used to describe the life process by which plants and animals convert the chemical supplies of foods and the atmosphere for purposes of replenishing and of new construction, growth. A major function of the thyroid is found experimentally to be the supervision of this regenerative life process, the control of the *rates* of metabolic processes carried on in other organs and cells of the body. Dr. Turner credits Magnus-Levy as having established first that the rate of energy exchange and the consequent heat liberated in the oxidative process of breathing is increased by an excess of the thyroid hormone and decreased by deficiencies of it. In the latter case food consumed is converted to muscular energy relatively slowly and there is a tendency for the excess to go into fatty obesity.

Administration of thyroxin increases the rate of conversion and heat production so that temperature regulating neurons must dissipate heat in profuse sweating. Hyperthyroid people, oversupplied with thyroxin, keep warm easily, wear lighter clothing, complain that the room is too warm, and squander energy perhaps to the extent of shortness of breath, muscular exhaustion and low levels of sugar supplies and cholesterol in the blood. Conversely a (hypothyroid) deficiency of thyroxin lowers the metabolic conversion rates and leaves larger supplies of sugar and cholesterol in the blood, unconsumed. The lethargic victim lacks the energizing stimulus to use these reserves.

Growth and development of young animals and birds are materially retarded by removal of the thyroid so that there is a shortage of the thyroxin needed to keep up the metabolic rate. The infantile period is abnormally long, organs and structure develop slowly with abnormal quantities of fat. Mental inactivity and physical sluggishness are characteristic.

On the other hand, the rate of structural development is abnormally accelerated by feeding thyroid substances to certain species of tadpoles. They become (dwarfed) frogs so quickly that they omit the relaxation periods when growth should occur. A small amount awakens hibernating animals.

Thyroid restraint of rate of growth is an inverse matter for when the thyroid is stimulated some of its hormones go to the pituitary gland and restrain it from dispensing growth stimulating hormones. Relaxed periods, when the thyroid is inactive or relatively so, are therefore the periods of reconstruction and new growth. That introduces what is to me the most interesting aspect of thyroid activity.

Nervous tension which is electrical tension, the voltage of the combined nervous systems, is assigned to the thyroid for control. That is to say, periods of excitement, alert attention, tense mental activity require thyroid stimulation. Emergency conditions, nervousness, and on to hysteria, and panic are periods of extreme demand upon the thyroid.

Actually this is just another aspect of thyroid control of metabolic rates. Thus the accelerated conversion of blood sugars, etc. to muscular energy suggest adrenal cooperation, or dispensing of adrenal hormones, at rates directed by thyroid hormones. And next the rate of conversion of cholesterol in the cerebro-spinal fluid into electrical

energy to power the neurons of the brain and nerve trains becomes
a major thyroid responsibility. It is intimated that the thymus which
grows and shrinks with the life span of nervous energy may be the
intermediate link in this process. That has been difficult to demonstrate however.

We may reconstruct here my own experience with nervous tension and fatigue to typify some of the experiences which other
people meet. The sequence of happenings may be setup as;- (1)
Conscious observation and interpretation of the environmental situation, (2) Autonomic evaluation of the requirement, and reaction in
the form of calling upon the thyroid to send its hormones out to (3)
increase my nervous tension or my rate of conversion of food elements to nervous energy, and (4) ultimate fatigue and drop in energy
due to inadequate relaxation for recuperation of reserves.

My major experience with nervous fatigue extended over the
period from about my 39th to 47th birthdays, as represented in
Figure 7. I have used the general figures for thymus change discussed
in Chapter XV for the basic curve of energy level. Perhaps there
should be added a minor rise and fall to represent relaxed recuperation during the vacation periods when I began to feel the need of
them.

As charted however I have only tried to show two periods in
which nervous energy was maintained at a falsely high level under
stress, followed by that let-down feeling or depression when the
stress was relaxed, and then the proportionate recuperation to the
normal curve with mental and physical relaxation.

As I related in some detail in the first chapters, the nervous
fatigue took eight years building up to a point where it really began
to affect my health seriously. Worries about the amount of work
to be done and the conviction that I never would get caught up
maintained nervous tension constantly at a high level. I rarely went
to church for there seemed to be too much to do. Even when things
did let up the mental habit was so well ingrained that the nervous
tension did not let down. I drove much too fast in city streets jam-
ming on the brakes at each corner and then accelerating madly.
Telling myself how foolish that was and to stop it was only effective
for a few blocks for my mind would wander back to the job and
I would be at it again. The worry discomfort at the pancreas and the
tension discomfort at the thyroid had me taking sedatives more and
more steadily.

Then the let-down came with disrupted digestion, low blood

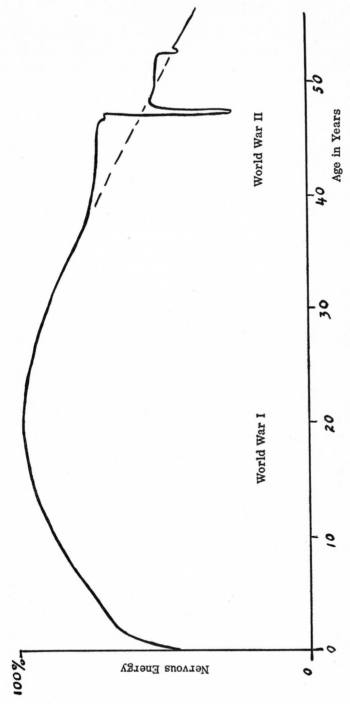

Figure 7. A schematic approximation of the normal rise and decline of human energy modified to illustrate the forced periods of high nervous tension and the subsequent let down periods of my two experiences with nervous fatigue.

pressure, loss of my job and finally glaucoma. The dip in nervous
energy came uncomfortably close to bottom. The story of rebuilding
and restoration of faith and confidence was told in the second
chapter.

The second period of unduly high nervous tension accompanied
a three year period of extended overtime hours and difficult responsibility. Then a little angina and a little glaucoma attack in the good
eye gave warning that the nervous energy reserves were running low
again. By this time however I knew what it was about and what to
do. Medical treatment of the eye lowered the pressure in it from
48 to a normal 18 or 20. A four week period of let-down and relaxation proved hardly enough to restore the reserves. But reduction of
hours at the office (from around 60 to about 35) and stringent attention to relaxation at the end of the day have made it possible to carry
on comfortably even though the technical problems remain very
difficult. It was necessary to readjust my energy demands to my
somewhat lowered capacity to regenerate.

I find myself to be enjoying a somewhat marginal state this
winter. The engineering work must not lag and I am determined that
this project should not lag either. A short rest period at noon and
good relaxation at night seem to be maintaining the balance.

Maintenance of the marginal status does favor observation of
autonomic reactions, a number of which have been noted as we have
progressed. Excitement is a state in which the thyroid participates.
An engineer can and does experience a feeling of excitement, an
exhilaration in the solution of a knotty problem or under other chal-
lenging or stimulating circumstances. Under such conditions I have
observed a taut feeling at the thyroid as it strained a bit at its reserves.
It is accompanied at times by some tightening at the pancreas in
natural concern, if not worry.

We are discussing thyroid stimulation to raise nervous tension or
voltage, to raise the *rate* of conversion of nervous energy. Any such
discussion must also be concerned with the opposite situation, the
relaxation of thyroid stimulation to reduce the rate of conversion
(of cholesterol). Just as we observe the need to think, to concentrate,
to attack a problem, so also we must consciously learn to take the
opposite path to permit regeneration, rebuilding of hormones reserves.

Relaxation is something of an art, something to be learned. I can
recall doctors telling me to relax but I cannot remember anyone teaching me how to go about it. Athletic coaches must stimulate tension
at times and at other times teach relaxation to restore and conserve

the nervous energy which will be required in keen competition.

Thinking processes, whether idle worrying or constructive problem solving activities, are consumers of nervous energy. Relaxing requires cessation of such effort. Stop thinking. Drive *all* thoughts out of the conscious mind. Relax.

Sometimes that is not easy to do. When we are working under tension, pressure to get things done, or solved, the thinking processes achieve momentum which is not easy to stop. Just the conscious instruction to stop thinking is not enough, for ideas and memory items keep popping up. Then such diversionary tricks as reading, listening to the radio, chewing gum, indulging in the light conversation of the cocktail hour, or as a last resort, the medication of sedatives may be in order. But whether we resort to such devices or not we must learn to relax, in order to permit restoration of our essential reserves.

Nervousness, jittery nerves, nervous twitches and up the scale to allergic, spasmodic and hysterical reactions and even to panic and epileptic fits, all of these are evidences of the current problem. Various aspects of fatigue, exhaustion shock, structural deficiency or neural damage may contribute.

I can recall in my own experiences with nervous fatigue, various twitches of the eyelid and fingers and facial muscles. The X-ray specialist who checked on my troubles with diarrhea explained the spasmodic activity which he could observe in my colon, a phase of nervous stomach. Since my appendix operation in 1935, I have had an allergic reaction to meat fats. I have no good reason for associating it with the appendix but the hysterical rejection of the fat is an allergic (frightened) nervous reaction.

A good friend whom I have known for almost thirty years has a disconcerting nervous twitch involving his eyes, facial muscles and throat muscles. He acquired it during the worrisome depression of the early thirties when he was out of a job two or three times. The twitch still persists when problems come up. He hardly seems to know that he does it but can control it if he is reminded to do so.

We may observe that these twitches are involuntary autonomic expressions of fatigue or tension. We may have some tendency to perpetuate them as a means to sympathy or as a matter of habit. I recall requiring considerable conscious effort to get rid of them on a couple of accasions.

Cerebral palsy, smokers' trembling fingers, writers' cramps, etc. may be associated with the cerebellum which has been found to function in the coordination of muscular activities. Consider with this the findings concerning thyroid or parathyroid rate control of electrical rhythms of the brain and nervous system. Undoubtedly thalamus or hypothalamic brain areas also enter in connection with instinctive timing standards. And to all of these must be added the conscious influence in furnishing stimulus from external sources, neurotic habits of thinking or imaginative flights.

The "wiggle test" was described in an interesting report of the nervous reactions of children to fighting, love scenes, and monkey shines as they sat watching movies. LIFE for August 23, 1948, pages 16 and 17; illustrated results obtained by a device developed by the Children's Film Library as a means of rating instinctive curiosity reactions of the youngster. Photos taken by infra red light showed the attention or restless boredom or ecstacy of the kids, with the corresponding scene appearing on the scene. The wiggle test results were plotted on the chart, Figure 8, which lacks the dramatic emotional excitement of the children's faces. Their ages appeared to range from six to twelve.

Thyroid-autonomic adjustment of rhythms, rates and tensions is found also to include the adjustment of sensitivity of the nerve receptors. It is another inverse deal in which reduction of thyroid secretion increases thresholds to light and sound stimulation. This I can check to some extent. In periods of nervous fatigue I find my sense of touch to be more sensitive to irritation of its receptors. The nerve endings in my skin report more little tickles and itches. The nasal membranes are more allergic to the irritation of tiny weed pollens. Their receptor reports result in dilation of nasal glands to wash away the pollens and at times this washing reaction is inclined to become hysterical in the excessive flood of an "attack." During the height of the hayfever season even the sight of the miscreant weeds or a reference to them seems to have been enough to set off a minor attack, an interesting psychosomatic aspect of interference by other receptors, plus conscious interpretations.

However that may be, hayfever illustrates a temporary disruption or overstrain of the system of checks and balances. Two interesting chemical molecules or messengers are involved. Both are poisons in excessive quantities and perform useful functions in small amounts. Both are products of plants as well as the human system. The nettle uses them for its protective sting and itch stimulants.

Acetylcholine is a by-product of cholesterol in the electro-chemical reactions which take place for nourishment of neurons. It is

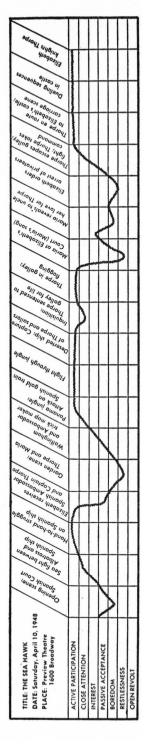

Figure 8. The "Wiggle Test" charts electrically the instinctive nervous tension adjustments or emotional reactions of children at an exciting movie. (Device of the Children's Film Library reported in *Life* magazine, Page 16-18, August 23, 1948.) Life Inc, copyright 1948.

ordinarily delivered to the bloodstream to be broken down as a waste product, but at times it is released from certain nerve terminals to dilate tiny smooth muscles of blood vessels, glands, etc. It is probably the source of the burning sensation about the nose in hay fever.

Histamine may be produced in the laboratory by combining vitamin C (ascorbic acid) and an amino acid (histidine) and the body appears to do it the same way. Its primary function also seems to be to cause dilation and increased flow. In that respect it aids digestion by causing flow of digestive juices; it improves circulation of blood through the capillaries; and increases nasal discharges which get out of hand in hayfever. It is also said to be responsible for itching sensations. The powerful antihistamines which I take occasionally during hayfever season effectively restrain it, performing a contrasting function in much the same manner as adrenal hormones. Such medical correction highlights what a wonderful job Nature ordinarily does in maintaining checks and balances.

Just how the thyroid influences the rate of dispensing the dilating agents is not yet clear but the general train of voluntary and involuntary nervous system influences forms an interesting pattern.

Clearly there is a conscious or subconscious observation and interpretation of need or of calm which is the stimulus for the various thyroid activities in adjustment of rates, tensions and rhythms.

Clearly there must also be an intermediate autonomic observation, weighing and evaluating by comparison with the instinctive standards, in order to determine the suitable amount of thyroid hormone to be dispensed.

Unnecessary panic or excitement is not the fault of a healthy thyroid but of an exaggerated report of the current situation as received over the interconnecting nerve pathways from the conscious domain to the autonomic brain area.

"Life isn't easy," as the Reverend Templeton pointed out yesterday, "and it wasn't meant to be." The emphasis has shifted somewhat from physical strife to mental effort. A remarkable provision to meet our needs has been furnished us. The rules of the game would seem to charge us not to waste our energies on useless activities, worries, etc. nor yet to conserve them to the extent of evasion of our proper responsibilities.

The motor neurons of curiosity urge us on instinctively to seek out potential wisdom and opportunity and to weigh its worth and urgency. Next the instinctive standard neurons of sincerity, value and necessity appraise the findings that we may sense their worth and deliver the "emotional reaction" which adjusts the thyroid secretion to the report received.

Christ urged "Seek and ye shall find." "Ask and it shall be opened unto you."

Habits of thinking in the conscious domain may assist or mislead the instinctive autonomic evaluations which govern the thyroid. Proper training to alert and searching scrutiny must be taught to appraise good faith and to shun flattering insincerity, threatening compulsion and otherwise prejudiced sources. Similar caution must be exercised with respect to habits acquired, however unintentionally, of coloring, or distorting facts observed or things heard. Of such are selfish bias, tendency to over emphasize or exaggarate, to understate or evade embarrassing implications, love of flattery, fear of compulsive influence or of personal disadvantage, greedy or envious misinterpretation and so on and on. Again these generalizations are a warning against the selfish and self-centered subconscious point of view. The healthy aspect is the unselfish position which Christ taught.

XVII

THE INNER MIND, THE PITUITARY
AND COMMON SENSE

This morning completing the review of texts, clippings and notes for the section, I must confess to a feeling of excitement, as the meaning of it unfolded. At the pituitary gland and the protected inner brain are centered the autonomic controls of the living man which are beyond the conscious range. Here are the controls over growth, development and health, both physical and mental. The gathering evidence shows that here also are the basis for poise, judicious evaluations, and common sense.

We would like to think of these as conscious assets. And certainly the conscious decisions which characterize both you and me to our fellow men must rest upon recognition of our endowment for comparative evaluation if we are to remain in good repute.

But as in the case of the other autonomic functions, such assets may be obscured or offset by ill chosen habits of thinking in the conscious realm. We will observe later the headstrong folly of conscious thinking which chooses to misinform the inner brain or to ignore its sensed recommendations.

Before summarizing and examining the responsibilities of the autonomic brain areas and the pituitary gland let us see about where they are located. In Figure 9 note the group in the protected central portion of the brain. The pituitary gland, nestling in a private recess in the sphenoid bone above the throat, has been described as the best protected organ in the body. Above it are the hypothalamus and the thalamus, the two major brain centers of the involuntary, the autonomic (self-governing) system. They are comparatively small, possibly a hundred million neurons or so, but their responsibilities are great. Above them and to the rear is the pineal gland, last and highest of the endocrine group, which will be discussed in the next chapter.

The autonomic group is surrounded, above and on all sides by the cerebral cortex, like the seed mass in a melon.

It must be recognized that any effort to draw a chart of the human brain is bound to be oversimplified. The estimated ten billion brain cells send out their receiving and sending nerve fibers in orderly

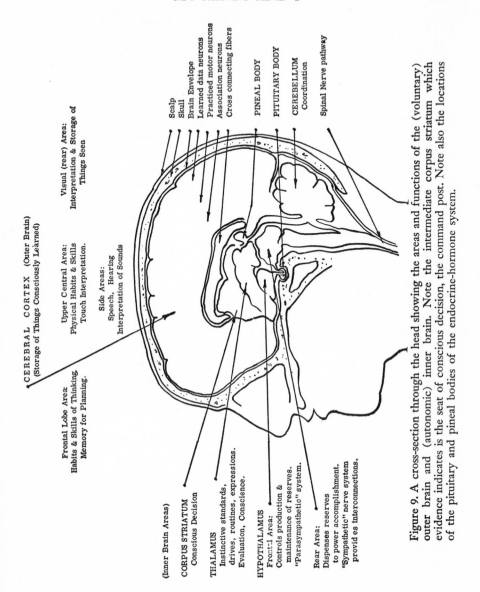

CEREBRAL CORTEX (Outer Brain)
(Storage of Things Consciously Learned)

Frontal Lobe Area:
Habits & Skills of Thinking.
Memory for Planning.

Upper Central Area:
Physical Habits & Skills
Touch Interpretation.

Side Areas:
Speech, Hearing
Interpretation of Sounds

Visual (rear) Area:
Interpretation & Storage of
Things Seen

Scalp
Skull
Brain Envelope
Learned data neurons
Practiced motor neurons
Association neurons
Cross connecting fibers

PINEAL BODY

PITUITARY BODY

CEREBELLUM
Coordination

Spinal Nerve pathway

(Inner Brain Areas)

CORPUS STRIATUM
Conscious Decision

THALAMUS
Instinctive standards,
drives, routines, expressions.
Evaluation, Conscience.

HYPOTHALAMUS
Frontal Area:
Controls production &
maintenance of reserves.
"Parasympathetic" system.

Rear Area:
Dispenses reserves
to power accomplishment.
"Sympathetic" nerve system
provides interconnections.

Figure 9. A cross-section through the head showing the areas and functions of the (voluntary) outer brain and (autonomic) inner brain. Note the intermediate corpus striatum which evidence indicates is the seat of conscious decision, the command post. Note also the locations of the pituitary and pineal bodies of the endocrine-hormone system.

but highly complex patterns. Definitive boundaries are few as the various responsibilities merge in interrelated collaboration. Nevertheless brain specialists, psychologists, and research technicians are piecing together evidence to give us an ever clearer picture.

Across through the center of the brain is a great mass of cross nerve fibers, which interconnect related areas in the right and left halves or hemispheres of the cerebral cortex. They form something of a roof over the autonomic inner mind.

We have already noted that the cerebral cortex, the great outer mass of neurons, is developed in man far beyond other life, and accomodates his distinguishing learned wisdom. Its outer layers of neurons appear to devote their services to the retention of experiences, education, material for interpretation and understanding. The next layers, perhaps not as uniformly distributed, are pyramidal motor neurons interested in ways of doing things, routines, practiced skills, athletic and mental prowess and activities, speech, writing, physical habits and habits in thinking. Together such things constitute the learned wisdom, the point of view, attitudes, utility and acquired characteristics of the individual. The inner layers of neurons extend longer sending and receiving fibers to find and correlate or associate and to transmit the material which they have previously reposed in the two higher groups.

The general assignment of top, side and rear cortex areas to the interests of the five external receiving senses was discussed in connection with Figure 4 in Chapter IX. The frontal lobes are concerned with more abstract wisdom, memory for planning, motor routines of the thinking process and the sixth sense receptions from the autonomic inner brain areas. They shelter habits of thinking and when dangerous compulsive neuroses are built-up these areas are destroyed by operation or severed at their connecting nerve fibers to and from the inner brain.

* * *

The *corpus striatum* is the neural body which we are forced to designate as the vital seat of self, the command post, the area of conscious decision and self-determination. Laboratory proof of this is still to be perfected, but the results of operating procedures, the implications of location, observations with respect to it and to functions of adjacent areas, all combine to indicate this conclusion.

Its name, meaning striped body, refers to the grouping of gray neuron cell bodies and of white nerve fibers traversing it.

Its location is in the protected inner brain area, just back of the important frontal lobes of the cerebral cortex and just ahead of the thalamus and hypothalamus, the "involuntary" autonomic bodies. It sits astride the communication pathways between these vital areas.

In operative procedures on the violently insane, effort is made to sever it from the frontal lobes where the neurotic habits of thinking are stored or from the thalamic areas which provide and adjust physical energies to power the misguided violence of the patients' reactions.

In lower forms of life the corpus striatum is smaller but is still recognized as a vital center. Decision is still a characteristic of such life. Removal of the corpus striatum leaves the body uselessly rigid with muscles tensed, ungoverned. Sleep which stills conscious direction of muscular activity is believed to be distinctive of this area and activity.

The characteristics of the command post, of self, includes wakeful consciousness of that to which we may be "paying attention," and the capacity to make voluntary decisions and initiate voluntary action. In the pattern of segregation and delegation of responsibilities which we have been observing, note that the bodies to the front and the rear have their own duties, which do not include decision, and that their activities continue while the command post sleeps. Of the three groups:—

1. Conscious or voluntary decision is not a function of the thalamus or hypothalamus to the rear, because these are members of the separate autonomic system, the operation of which is recognized to be involuntary or instinctive. The ample responsibilities attributable to these areas will be discussed shortly. Growth and other control functions of this system carry on during sleep.

2. Conscious or voluntary decision is not a function of the cerebral cortex, but outside of it because:—

(a) The functions of the cerebral cortex are largely subordinate to, but distinguishable from the conscious command. They are the functions of storing and supplying learned data, interpretations and motor routines.

(b) Subconscious activities, control of muscular skills from cerebral cortex motor neurons may function independently, while conscious attention is being devoted to another activity as was discussed in Chaper X. It was noted that conscious attention may be required to set up or restore one or more subconscious routines, but is limited of itself, to one thing at a time.

(c) Subconscious motor neuron controls may function when conscious decision is relaxed in sleep as in rolling in bed, or sleep walking.

(d) Supervision of the cerebral cortex seems to be shared by the conscious command, with the instinctive autonomic evaluations, because the pigeon-holing of learning in the uniform areas which are used, and the provision of nutriment as required would both be involuntary functions.

(e)   The difficulties which conscious self encounters in memorizing things it wishes to store away in the cerebral cortex, and in rooting out learned routines which it discovers are unhealthy, suggest its remoteness from the storage areas.

(f)   Destruction or severing of the frontal lobes of the cerebral cortex to abolish compulsive habits does not abolish conscious decision (even though background data for such decision may have to be relearned).

3. The operating center of the conscious and decisive self does appear, therefore, to be a substantially independent unit between the other two because:—

(a)   It was observed in Chapters IX and X that self can pay active and decisive attention to only one thing at a time, even though it may alternate attention rather rapidly.

(b)   Balanced decision, as will be emphasized later, must draw upon both learned data (cerebral cortex), and sensed evaluations (thalamus).

(c)   Maladjustment and mental conflict as examined in Chapter XIX places self in a cross fire between neurotic habits of thinking (cerebral cortex) and the evaluations of conscience (thalamus) which may force withdrawal, disconnection, insanity (in which both of the other neural bodies continue to function).

(d)   Blacking out or relaxation of consciously controlled activity, by means of sleep, is periodically essential to permit nonvoluntary combinations to function in physical and mental growth, recuperation and organization.

(e)   The physical location of the corpus striatum, substantially between the thalamus (discussed below) and the frontal lobes of the cerebral cortex, and its mentally intermediate position in balanced thinking appear to be confirmed in the results of operating procedures.

The *thalamus* is the name given to the highest of the autonomic brain areas. It is a mass of neurons which share the protected inner brain area with the corpus striatum and the hypothalamus. Our texts describe it as a great relay station, an elaborate switchboard mechanism, coordinating and interconnecting several ways: between the five external receiving senses, the voluntary areas of the cerebral cortex (and corpus striatum), the autonomic areas of the hypothalamus and the voluntary and involuntary nerve networks to the body. In this task it seems obvious that its neurons must exercise extensive evaluating and discretionary powers.

All signals, all information received from external or internal sources come first to the thalamic area. The optic nerve cables or bundles from the two eyes meet here, as do those from the ears. The touch, pain and temperature observing systems bring their reports here.

First, analysis must be made of the intensity and quality of the signal, and autonomic muscular or other adjustment ordered. Thus the eyes' pupil size are corrected to suit light intensity and the lens system is focused. The head may be involuntarily turned in the direction of a sound or movement. The sensitivity of touch receptors may be improved for better observation. The involuntary direction of attention to a disturbing commotion is ordered here, possibly accompanied by some "reflex" reaction, such as flicking of eyelids.

Next a preliminary evaluation of the various reports received from sight, hearing, touch, etc. is made for the benefit of the hypothalamus and endocrine gland system. This permits an advance stimulation of the hormone producing agencies pending conscious consideration and instructions. Thus I sensed alarm and the sinking feeling at the pit of the stomach as we rounded the curve and before I figured consciously that the approaching train was on an adjacent track in the dark tunnel. Similarly at this level of observation may be evaluated a state of calm, adequate to permit relaxation, recuperation and growth.

Next the report must be weighed if it is worth sending up or calling to the attention of conscious circuit which can only devote itself to one thing at a time. Many movements, sounds or tickles are ignored at this level and real urgency may have to be registered to break into conscious concentration on a line of thought. At this stage the autonomic conceivably introduces the instinctive drives, the urges to impel conscious consideration and decision to order mental and physical action.

If the item of information or experience is considered worth saving or acting upon, then the nerve tip connections or routing must be determined autonomically to get it to the proper area of the cerebral cortex. The observed pattern of distributions suggested in Figure 4 is so uniform as to indicate instinctive direction. At the same time, if an area of the cortex is destroyed, another area will usually be found for essential information by this control which is beyond the conscious range.

Lastly the thalamus must await conscious interpretation of the observation in the light of learned meanings, and conscious consideration in the light of acquired habits of thinking. The report returned to it from the frontal lobes, whether it be accurate or colored or badly distorted, will determine the autonomic reaction, upon comparison with the instinctive standards, and the final adjustments to be made in the endocrine hormone control system. Thus at this point we return to the conscious the sensed evaluations of conscience, approval and calm or disapproval and conflict. And at the same time we fully establish the emotional reactions of relaxation, tension, fear, rage or whatever, through hormone and nerve controls considered in prior chapters.

At an intermediate stage and by passing the full routine of conscious consideration, the thalamus routes many incoming, sense reports directly back to the cerebellum so that internal and external observation of results may cooperate quickly in checking and synchronizing physical muscular coordination.

* * *

The *hypothalamus* comprises two important groups of neurons below the thalamus, above the pituitary gland and ahead of the midbrain where spinal nerve pathways gather. Under guidance of thalamic evaluations, it controls all involuntary (autonomic) activities by messages over the sympathetic and parasympathetic nerve networks and by the dispensing of the hormones of the endocrine gland system. With the pituitary it is the center of the delicate checks and balances, maintenance of which is fundamental to good health, physical, mental and spiritual.

Our texts point out that the (autonomic) brain cells of the hypothalamus exercise primary control, selecting and organizing patterns of operation of the whole autonomic system. This includes growth, development and the physical and mental autonomic behaviorial patterns which are known as emotional reactions. Munn records that "stimulating the (rear portion of the) hypothalamus with a needle electrode causes a cat to retract its ears, growl, raise its back and lash its tail, and show a crescendo of . . . . . typical sympathetic motor reactions. Removal of the hypothalamus abolishes all expression of emotions in cats and dogs whereas removal of no other part of the brain has this effect." He points out however that such artificial stimulation of the hypothalamus differs from naturally aroused emotional behavior (in that it lacks the modifying influences of voluntary observation and interpretation). This particular test evidences only the generalized mobilization of resources for defense or attack.

Morgan points out the division of the counterbalancing interests of the sympathetic (the mobilizing and expending) system and the parasympathetic (conserving and replenishing) system, in two distinctive areas of the hypothalamus. It is interesting to examine these two separately and then note the provision for their coordination.

The *accomplishments* of the individual, his *external* interests in general are *powered* and *rendered effective* by the sympathetic system by its mobilizing and dispensing of our reserves of physical and nervous energy. The rear and side groups of neurons of the hypothalamus exercise the control over these activities and extend their (sympathetic) fibers to tiny smooth muscles in the iris of the eyes, the tear ducts, salivary glands, heart, lungs, stomach, pancreas, adrenal glands, colon, bladder, sex glands, hair, sweat glands and surface arteries.

On the under surface of the rear portion of the hypothalamus are the two mamillary bodies which appear to mobilize attention, stimulate nervous tension, alert the receiving neurons of the five senses and build up the voltage of the nervous systems preparatory to quick action. Their removal or destruction results in abnormal sleepiness and inattention.

Both through the use of pituitary hormones and by direct nerve connections the sympathetic system stimulates the sending of adrenal, thyroid and other hormones through the blood stream. Adrenal hormones admitted to the cerebro-spinal fluid are dispensed in turn through the tiny tubes enclosing nerve fibers and released at terminals of the sympathetic system for contraction of capillary openings, increasing blood presure.

Internal interests of the individual, production and maintenance of reserves and their utilization during relaxed periods, for growth and development, both physical and mental, these things are organized and regulated by the parasympathetic system. The central and forward groups of neurons or brain cells of the hypothalamus extend their fibers to comprise the parasympathetic nerve pathways. These travel by different paths from the sympathetic system but connect to most of the same organs and functions (eye muscles, small glands of the tongue and skin, muscles of the heart, lungs, digestive system, reproductive system, etc.).

Directly and by way of pituitary hormones this system stimulates the dispensing of hormones of the pancreas and some of the other endocrine glands. The release of acetylcholine at nerve tips for dilation of capillaries, easing blood flow and reducing blood pressure is a function of this system.

TABLE II

Organ	Sympathetic Mobilize and expend effort	Parasympathetic Replenish, grow, conserve
Eye, Iris	Dilated	Contracted
Salivary Glands	Constricted	Normally Operable
Lungs	Relax bronchial muscles, accelerated breathing.	Contract bronchial muscles, normal breathing.
Heart	Accelerated	Relaxed
Adrenal Glands	Dispense mobilizing hormones	Replenish hormones
Digestive system	Inactivated	Normally operable
Liver	Dispensing sugars	Storing sugars
Skin Capillaries	Contracted (raising blood pressure)	Dilated (reducing blood Pressure)
Hairs	Erected	Passive
Nervous System	Tensed, alerted	Relaxed

The two systems have opposing or balancing responsibilities in many respects as is summarized briefly in Table II. Generalizations are difficult except perhaps in the extremes of all-out mobilization for combat or complete relaxation in sleep. Obviously in normal fluctuations of effort and relative inactivity there are many variations in adjustment. A great deal of autonomic judgment must be exercised between the thalamus and the two areas of the hypothalamus to order the right degree of response in various functions. Fortunately conscious decision does not have to take time for such problems.

Actually this autonomic brain area seems to take over control from the area of conscious decision under certain extremes. When conscious thinking becomes confused, seriously disturbed or torn by conflict, it is as if one were bereft of (conscious) reason by withholding nerve connections between the voluntary and autonomic areas or large portions of them. In the extremes of (frozen) fear, cramps, extreme sexual stimulation, panic and nervous shock, conscious decision seems powerless to direct action.

* * *

The pituitary body or gland, known also as the hypophisis has achieved a reputation for importance beyond its tiny size. About as large as a pea and weighing about 0.6 gm. it is one of the best protected organs in the body. As shown in Figure 9, it occupies a private recess in the bone floor of the skull, lined with a portion of the durable envelope which protects the brain.

Figure 10 illustrates the three divisions of this body and its stemlike connection to the two portions of the hypothalamus. Like other endocrine glands there are many nerve terminals in it and its ample connections to arteries and veins provide supplies and highways for entering and leaving hormone messenger services. The pituitary is known to use its hormones to stimulate and activate a number of the other endocrine glands below it and in turn is restrained or stimulated by some of their hormones to determine proper sequence in development or to assure priorities. It also sends hormones directly to bones and tissues in various parts of the body, in the processes of growth control and development.

The rear or posterior chamber is distinguished by the large number of nerve terminals which meet here from the two major divisions of the hypothalamus. It would appear that here the moment-to-moment balance is established between their opposite interests for the guidance of the vital hormone distributing services of the whole system. The internal (parasympathetic) requirements of physical and mental maintenance, and the external (sympathetic) urgencies of strife and accomplishment are weighed against each other at the nerve terminals entering from the two areas. It becomes a common sense weighing of capacity against ambition to help determine course of action.

Hormones appear to be dispensed by all three sections of the pituitary although the principal activity is centered in the forward (anterior) area. About two dozen different hormones or variations of major hormones are indicated. Mechanistic interpretations support the idea that each hormone is a complex but specific chemical molecule capable of performing a specific service when dispensed in a specific quantity. Alternatively, their close associations and collaboration with the marvelous brain cells and their discretionary capacity, suggest that the electro-chemical balance or ionization of the basic hormone may be modified when it is sent forth. Thus we may alter or modify its mission or method of accomplishment to better suit the requirements. The marvelous adaptability of natural processes favors the latter.

Water is utilized in many ways in the physical and mental system. It serves as a solvent and vehicle in many chemical and digestive processes. It serves as an electrolyte in the battery functions of electric energy generation in the neurons. It cleanses and washes away wastes

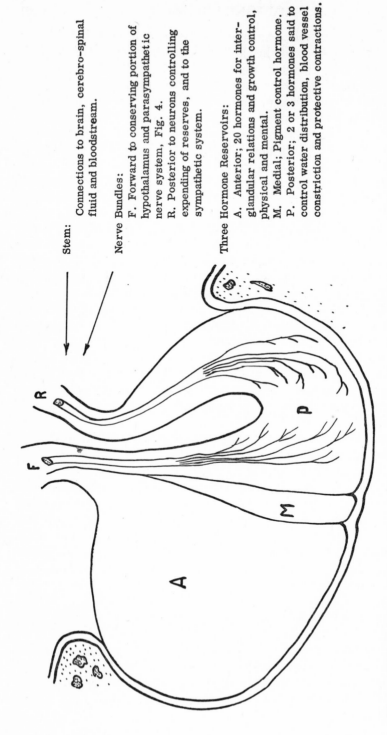

Stem:
Connections to brain, cerebro-spinal fluid and bloodstream.

Nerve Bundles:
F. Forward to conserving portion of hypothalamus and parasympathetic nerve system, Fig. 4.
R. Posterior to neurons controlling expending of reserves, and to the sympathetic system.

Three Hormone Reservoirs:
A. Anterior; 20 hormones for inter-glandular relations and growth control, physical and mental.
M. Medial; Pigment control hormone.
P. Posterior; 2 or 3 hormones said to control water distribution, blood vessel constriction and protective contractions.

Figure 10. The pituitary body in its protective envelope and bone recess, below the autonomic inner brain. After Turner and Morgan.

to be flushed out by the system. The control of water balance in the body is found to be the responsibility of a hormone of the posterior area.

Another hormone of this rear chamber, pitocin, causes contraction of the uterus muscle. Another, pitressin, constricts arteries and blood vessels, raising blood pressure, in which it is related to, or similar to adrenalin.

A (chromophorotropic) hormone of the middle portion, intermedin, at least in some forms of life, regulates the distribution of pigments in the skin. This function relates both to protective coloration and to protective regulation of the use of sunlight in the conversion of parathyroid vitamin D for neuron nutrition.

The forward chamber is credited tentatively with about twenty hormones or modifications thereof. Their functions, as identified thus far, seem to be the stimulation and regulation of growth, development and recuperation in physical, mental and reproductive spheres.

One of them, or possibly a group of them, regulates the growth of bones, the skeleton or frame work. An abnormal dispensing of this hormone results in an abnormal protrusion of the lower jaw, excessive growth of the long bones contributing to height, and possibly overgrowth of the feet and hands. At the same time excessive hairiness, thickening of the tongue, and the enlargement of soft tissues of the lips, nose, forehead and scalp may result. Conversely clinicians report "that certain types of human dwarfism are associated with an underactivity of the anterior hypophysis."

These observations are backed by laboratory experiments. In some of these, surgical removal of the pituitary from young animals resulted in arrested growth and sexual infantilism together with other complications. Conversely the injection of pituitary extracts caused female rats to grow to more than twice their normal weight. Turner hastens to add that "all investigators do not agree that the growth factor is a single entity."

Pituitary hormones apparently exert a direct influence, both stimulating and later limiting, upon the growth of bones and tissue. At the same time, other pituitary hormones stimulate adrenal hormones to release reserves of chemicals essential to body building. At other times emergency mobilization requires higher adrenal activity for dispensing sugar and other reserves for urgent external activities. Then thyroid hormones restrain the pituitary from activating its growth efforts. Here the result of relative weighing of internal and external autonomic interests by the corresponding (brain) neuron groups of the hypothalamus are apparent.

Much is written of the functions of hormones of the pituitary anterior upon reproductive functions. Extensive research has been performed in this field. Hormones are dispatched alternately between the pituitary and sex glands to activate and regulate successive stages of the creative process. The adrenals also enter into the exchange as they are called upon to supply reserves for building or replenishing purposes.

The letters ACTH have received considerable publicity, designating the adrenocorticotropic hormone dispatched by the pituitary anterior to the adrenal glands. It has been described as the master hormone which stimulates the secretion of all of the adrenal hormones. Its action is known to be paralleled by sympathetic nerve transmissions but it is not yet clear how distinctions are made to adjust the adrenal mobilization of reserves at one time for external combat or accomplishments, at another time to combat arthritis and rheumatic maladies, allergies and exposure, and at another time to support growth or reproductive processes.

STH, for somatotrophic hormone, is also reported to be dispatched from the stores of the pituitary anterior to the adrenals. It appears to exercise a parasympathetic function, restraining and balancing ACTH. In so doing it appears to collaborate in growth and recuperative processes. It is also credited with stimulating increased resistance to bacterial invaders. Rest, prescribed to deactivate the sympathetic system, enables such parasympathetic recuperative measures to be effective.

Cancer's psychosomatic aspects are receiving some attention. In that cancer cells appear to represent wild or unrestrained growth, the malady suggests a depletion or exhaustion of pituitary growth control hormones. Careless behavior and misbehavior are suggested at times in connection with cancerous locations.

The whole category of other diseases, maladies and misadjustments which have been traced to malfunctioning of the various endocrine glands, trace back to this inner brain area. The pituitary as the master hormone center, and the hypothalamus' neurons grouped as the governor over it and the end source of the sympathetic and parasympathetic nerve systems, between them control growth, health and the fighting of disease. The hypothalamus must issue its instructions based upon evaluations made in the thalamus' neurons in the light of its instinctive drives and standards. While the thalamus therefore appears to be the decision center of the autonomic system, it must be influenced in its instructions, by the accurate or distorted interpretations of the external situation and our voluntary desires for action, both reported to it from the conscious domain.

We are therefore at the core of psychosomatic problems, mentally induced physical ills. Illustrations in previous chapters have been offered in which mental ills, bad practices and bad habits of thinking in the voluntary areas may result in physical ills through misguidance and exhaustion of hormone supplies and critical reserves. Conscious efforts at mental hygiene are responsible for cleaning up the voluntary system's own sources of trouble. It cannot reach into the autonomic system however, beyond leaving the way clear to undo the mischief it may have done. Such psychosomatic problems are negative, malfunctioning, destructive. They stop short of the constructive and creative drives and potentials of man.

* * *

Logic and conceptive thought, the instinctive urge to organization of thought, have been associated by various observers with the pituitary anterior and therefore also with the thalamic and hypothalamic neurons connected therewith. These functions are part of mental growth and are here associated with the controls over physical growth.

Both mental and physical growth must draw upon the same sources of construction materials through substantially the same delivery systems and under the same group of regulative agencies. That is, the things we eat and then digest under autonomic hormone control are stored and delivered, also under hormone control, to the bones, tissues, muscles *and neurons.* There they are built into structure, utilized for repairs or used to furnish power and energy for physical *and mental* accomplishment.

The billions of neurons or nerve cells which comprise the various groups in the brain, and its nerve connections to organs, muscles and glands, are enclosed in a large envelope filling the skull and a system of branching tubes down through the spinal column and spreading out over the entire body. This enclosure retains the cerebro-spinal fluid which receives reserve supplies and hormones from the bloodstream in the midbrain area near the pituitary and hypothalamus. These supplies and hormones refresh, build, energize and stimulate the neurons and their nerve fibers. The waste products are then delivered back to the bloodstream near the back of the brain for disposal as has been noted.

A thought builds up under the influence of many cerebral cortex neurons, and surges on through the cerebellum and spinal column to the various muscles which it is to actuate. Enroute it is checked and evaluated by the autonomic responsibilities and further orders are sent forth to make the reserves available for action and to effect the appropriate emotional reactions or expressions. All of this is powered by electrical energy generated within the participating neurons from the supplies furnished to them under autonomic control. Various messages received by sight and hearing may have been responsible for starting the thought in the first place. These come in through autonomic areas for adjustment and evaluation enroute to proper interpretation areas of the cerebral cortex.

It is not strange that the autonomic inner brain group, which evaluates things going into and coming out of the cerebral cortex, should

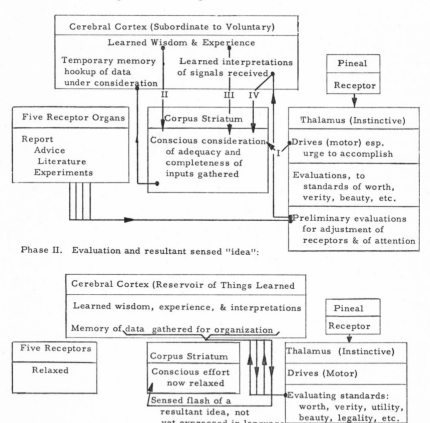

Figure 11. Contributions of the mental bodies in the two successive phases of the Organization of Thought.

also participate in putting together or organizing a thought out of that voluminous store. A part of the logical checking and of the initial sorting is the comparison with the applicable instinctive standards.

We have previously reported the observation of many men that the actual organization of complex thought, Fig. 11, is not a voluntary function. First, of course, we must consciously seek out the data, circumstances, and what-not, which are to be organized for conscious decision. If there is not a ready-made answer stored away from previous experience, we find that we do well to hesitate briefly or relax conscious effort for an appreciable period to permit the material to be organized.

It has been noted that conscious thinking is expressed in pertinent language, figures or symbols which we have learned. On the other hand the ideas and thoughts which flash into conscious perception from new organizing efforts are recognized and their meaning is sensed. But time is required to consciously express them in words or other learned symbols.

It has been pointed out that this conscious sensing, over the sixth sense nerve fibers from the thalamus, has much in common with other involuntary messages. Thus we sense alarm, grief, satisfaction, humorousness, distaste, etc., etc. These are emotional reactions or evaluations, all of which savor of the organizing of thought-material.

Hormones in transit and electrons moving in groups in the formulation of a thought require time in proportion to the equipment and agility of the thinker, and to the complexity of the thought. The old expression "let's sleep on it" recognizes both the time factor and the involuntary nature of the organizing function.

One of the secrets of General Electric Company's research wizardry, from Steinmetz on, was disclosed a few years ago in an interview with C. G. Suits, Vice President and Director of Research. It was reported in The American Magazine by F. G. Brownell and condensed in The Reader's Digest (Heed That Hunch) where I noted it before I met Dr. Suits.

G. E. started a course in Creative Engineering some time in the thirties. It was apparently inspired by Pasteur's observation that "Intuition is given only to him who has undergone long preparation for receiving it," and by Charles P. Steinmetz's belief in spiritual power. Dr. Willis R. Whitney, dean of General Electric Scientists and accomplished inventor, states that "a man may think he reasons out the answer to a problem by cold logic. Actually he reaches the solution through a hunch, and works out the reasons afterward. I used to disregard my hunches. But I've learned from my friend the turtle that you've got to stick your neck out to get any place."

Pay attention to that hunch, the flash of inspiration, says the GE instructor in creative thinking. You will not get it unless you have been preparing for it, gathering information on the problem. But when it does come have a pad in you pocket or beside your bed to set it down. Dr. Suit's observations indicate the organized concept arrives at the consciousness during relaxed periods when the problem is not under active conscious consideration. Such an "idea popped into the mind of one of our researchers while he was chopping ice from his front steps. Another man tells me that a discovery occured to him in the midst of shaving. In my own work with high temperature arcs and electric circuits, my hunches come to me most frequently in bed, in a plane or while I am staring out of a Pullman window. I have always a pad and pencil handy on my bedside table to jot down thoughts occurring during the night. Pocket memo cards receive the hunches that I get by day."

Thanks to Dr. Suits I also have filled a good many pages with useful notes, between three and six in the morning following the period when the delta autonomic brain frequencies predominate. Whether we recognize it as hunch, intuition, inspiration, instinctive evaluation or autonomic organization of data stored on assorted neurons of the cerebral cortex is immaterial, except to those who are seeking a more complete understanding for such value as there may be in it.

TIME's review * of General George S. Patton's book, "War As I Knew It," notes with regard to the Battle of the Bulge: By January 4, (1945), he confided in his diary: "We can still lose this war . . . the only time I ever made such a statement." The plan for the Third Army's subsequent break through, Patton claims, was in his head complete as he woke one morning: "Whether these tactical thoughts of mine are the result of inspiration, or insomnia, I have never been able to determine, but nearly every tactical idea I have had has come into my head full-born, much after the manner of Minerva from the head of Jupiter."

Dr. R. L. Kahn of the Michigan Serology Laboratory is another who reports waking to set down useful clues and ideas.

Soldiers, lawyers, engineers, research scientists and others have observed and learned to facilitate this autonomic evaluation and organization of thought during periods of conscious relaxation. We may still ask however just how it works. How are the hundreds or

* Courtesy of TIME; copyright TIME, Inc. 1947.

thousands of selective connections made between the terminals of thalamic evaluating neurons with the association neurons and information neurons of the cerebral cortex? Do mental growth hormones of the pituitary anterior participate as messengers through the cerebrospinal fluid? Do Professor Rajewsky's radio neurons, possibly operating from the coordinating area of the cerebellum, sense potential attunement and signal the necessary neuron interconnections? How do either of these things happen without apparent voluntary cognizance? Those details will be interesting to know when research people devise ways of checking them. Meanwhile it is interesting to have the general view of the inner brain area, the thalamus, hypothalamus, and pituitary.

Here we impel the inquisitive curiosity which sparks the furnishing of the cerebral cortex with its store of things learned.

Here the creative urge to accomplishment furnishes the drives to the young mothers who would create new life and to the scientists who would build new devices and processes. The artist, the poet, the musician yearn to mobilize their learned skill into a masterpiece which they sense to be pleasingly acceptable to their instinctive standards of beauty, worth, harmony and perfection.

Here these standards weigh and pass judgment upon the intellectual integrity and the wisdom of conscious decisions.

Here we sense the fatigued inadequacy or the refreshed exuberance of our reserves, the source of our physical and mental enthusiasm to undertake the obligations urged upon us by our instinctive drives.

Here we find resentment of the unscrupulous intent of the trial lawyer or the self-aggrandizing politician who plays upon our emotions, stimulating them falsely with distorted statements. They are like the child which has learned to stimulate involuntary emotional expressions to provoke sympathy.

Here we do experience the sympathetic distress for the trials and tribulations of those about us. In such feelings is a strong stimulation to the urge to service, to "love thy neighbor as thyself."

All of these feelings, emotions, sense impressions are true values expressed by the inner brain area of the autonomic in its universal language since time immemorial. All of them may be hidden, negated, ignored or controverted, at least for a time, by conscious intent. They constitute the inner voice heard or sensed over the nerve fibers between the autonomic and the conscious realms of the mind. Should we not beware lest our enthusiam for acquired or learned points of view and propaganda should dull or confuse our attention to autonomic evaluations.

XVIII

SPIRITUAL RESPONSIBILITY
AND THE MIND

I am but the instrument of my Creator, a tool, a servant through whom He works.

That is an ancient point of view, but one to which I must and do subscribe. Edison, Carver, Clark and many others give me modern precedent for its use.

In preparing this report, in which I trust you will find something of value, that point of view has been useful. At times the available data has seemed conflicting or inadequate and the ordinary efforts to resolve it have been ineffective. At such times I find that one does well to get down on his bony knees and endeavor to outline the question in prayer.

The answers which flash upon one's consciousness savour of inspiration or guidance by the Infinite Wisdom in the mortal processes of organization of thought. Even so, I have felt called upon to check my understanding of them against the "inspiration" of other men lest I have misunderstood. The necessity for a humble attitude in such efforts impresses itself upon one, for here self-aggrandizing egomania would be blinding indeed.

*   *   *

These notes were set down after prayer on the morning of March 7, 1953. They seem suitable to open the difficult debate of man's finite limitations versus his potential attunement with the Infinite Wisdom, his access to God's power and guidance. It is the difficult and shunned scientific problem of metaphysics. Is man the self-sufficient materialistic supreme being, and is all else superstition? Or is he responsible to some far greater Being to whom he may turn at will? Friederich Nietzsche of superman fame, Hitler, Freud, Lenin and Stalin sought to support the theory of the self-sufficiency of man.

C.S. Sherrington, eminent British physiologist and Nobel prize winner in studies of the nervous system, selected for contrast with his own views those of Jean Fernel, great physician of the 16th century. In that age obsessed with magic and astrology, hardheaded Fernel insisted on natural rather than supernatural causes for diseases.

It was a useful point of view and paved the way for research which has traced agents of human misery down to bacteria and viruses so tiny that their presence must still be taken on faith by most of us.

Now we go on through studies of the nervous systems, the mind and the nature of psychosomatic maladies. We find that such intangible things as habits of thinking in the ill-kept mind can weaken the body's defenses and deplete its reserves if not actually initiate the natural causes for ill health which Fernel sought. Some vague sensing of these actualities led to witch hunts and misguided persecutions of old. Someone stated recently in deferential half-jest that the first psychiatrists were the aboriginal witch doctors. But all of these are problems of peace or conflict between conscious habits and behavior on the one hand and instinctive autonomic drives, standards and controls on the other. They are still a bit intangible to most of us but they have their mechanistic aspects and appear to be problems within the individual man.

But is that all? Is the self-sufficient man wholly adequate to cope with these maintenance problems and to go on to creative efforts with no more than human help. The determined materialist and atheist would presumably say, yes. Thereby they set themselves in opposition to the great body of those who believe in God, whether that belief be based upon an instinctive *urge*, acceptable *teaching* or personal *experience*.

The very presence of this "loyal opposition" indicates that these three bases for belief in God are not accepted as conclusive by all men. Not all have the personal experience which carries strong conviction, or perhaps they have not had it *yet* for it may not come early in life. I must also observe that there may have been earlier opportunities for me to have observed with conviction. Self-centered egotisms can be insidiously blinding, and it took a severe jolt to impress me.

"Acceptable" training as a basis for religious conviction is clearly not always effective. The inquiring young mind may stumble through the undergrowth of inconsistencies, irrelevant passages, folklore, misconceptions, mistranslations and plain confused thinking which have appended themselves through the ages to all bodies of religious teaching. I can still recall some of the stumbling blocks which bruised my adolescent inquisitiveness and contributed to a weakening of the belief instilled in Sunday School. It was not until I was well past forty that I accumulated enough perspective to discern the basic rightness running through religious teachings.

Time for May 5, 1952, reports * something of the wanderings

* Courtesy of TIME; copyright TIME, Inc. 1952.

through similar confusion of Princeton's Philosophy Professor Walter T. Stace. In an article published in 1948 he expressed his pessimism about religion, saying in part, "There is, in the universe outside of man, no spirituality, no regard for value, no *friend*, in the sky, no help or comfort for man of any sort".

Time commented that the burst of reader response tore holes in the Professor's ivy. Publicly and in a flood of angry letters, he was denounced as an atheist or worse. The attacks shocked him for he had never fancied himself an out and out enemy of religion. He had studied briefly for the ministry and later as a British colonial officer in India had developed a lively admiration for Buddhism and the Hindu religions (as I have).

The public complaint broke through his academic complacency sufficiently so that he tried to think through a personal conflict which his article only partially illumined. It was a conflict between his (conscious) intellectual "anti-religious" resentments and "a fundamental religious feeling" (his instinctive autonomic heritage).

In 1952, at 65, he published a book, *TIME AND ETERNITY* which he called a defense of religion expressing his belief that there is a God, although experience of Him need not be tied to religious creed. Stace feels that all men have within them a consciousness of God, which he calls "moral intuition." Apparently however he still finds it difficult to see the marvelous unity of system underlying all of nature and science and human behavior, so far as we are able to discern them. He takes the specialist's position that scientists in other fields should stay away. Never the twain shall meet.

Opposing that view is Edmund Ware Sinnott, botanist president of the American Association for the Advancement of Science in 1948 and head of Yale's Scientific School. He expressed concern about the human species, not only as a mechanism of physical, chemical and biological properties, but also as an individual having *spiritual values* and *needs*. Proposing research in the "mental" sciences, he concluded that the pursuit of the sciences is nothing more or less than pursuit of truths. In the last analysis, all of man's activities are subservient to what happens to his spirit—to his spiritual welfare, "For what shall it profit a man if he should gain the whole world, and lose his soul?"

The instinctive *urge to belief* in a *power greater than man*, perhaps that should have been the title of this Chapter. Such an urge has been sensed down through the ages by poets, clergy, statesmen, thinkers and hosts of people like you and I. Mr. H. G. Wells wrote his great "Outline of History", apparently with a major motive to trace that most potent of the instinctive drives back through all civilizations and tribes to the most primitive peoples.

That instinctive urge carries with it a sense of responsibility, the responsibility of man to God, for his personal behavior and for his worthy accomplishment. Christ pounded away repeatedly at both points.

It carries with it also the reassurance of the Fatherly aspect of God's presence with us and of our privilege of turning to Him for guidance, strength and forgiveness.

Science may propose a conception of the electrical energy inherent in thought transmission, thought storage, the formulation of ideas and the stimulation of action and communication, as the intangible but basic essence of man and his character. It may point out the indestructibility of such energy, its all powerful potentials and presence in all matter and life throughout the universe. This need not suggest nor yet preclude an identity with the infinite and omnipresent Wisdom and Power which we are led to perceive in God.

But these things may help to allay insinuations, often born of immature resentment of authority, that mysteries not physically substantiated are mere superstition. Nor can I believe that any potential identification of the laws, forces and grandeur of Nature and the Universe with one's private concept of God is at all likely to detract from His mystical glory. And when I would reinforce my frail faith with the thought that man may be created in His image, physically as well as spiritually, one may respectfully visualize the coordination of this all encompassing Power and Wisdom and Glory in a firm but genial Sage, whose countenance may partake of elements of one's most revered memories.

Back in January of 1948 I received a short note from our family physician, he who had struggled with me through the discouraging months which preceded the miracle of my recovery, if I may be privileged to call it that. It was he who had *not* thought to remind me that I might turn to God, when I was so low in spirit. Now he wrote:—

"I have noticed in the Flatbush Congregational Church bulletin that you were going to speak there.

"For a week or so I have been struggling through the new book, *Human Destiny* * by Lecomte du Nouy and I know you would be very interested in reading it if you have not already done so."

He enclosed a paragraph from the book.

Sixty-four year old Dr. du Nouy had been a member of the Rocke-

* Longmans Green & Co., 1946.

feller Institute, head of biophysics at the Pasteur Institute, and a director of the Sorbonne. He assembled impressive mathematical data to show that life could not have been the result of a chance combination of elements. Life must have been created for some long range purpose which he believed was to go on developing in the direction of spirituality as exemplified by Christ.

"Let men remember". . . . Consciousness of one's tremendous *responsibility* in the great evolutionary process was to him the mark of the more highly evolved human being. He wrote:

> "Let every man remember that the destiny of mankind is incomparable and it depends upon his will to collaborate in the transcendent task. Let him remember that the Law *is*, and always has been, to struggle and that the fight has lost nothing of its violence by being transposed from the material into the spiritual plane, let him remember that his own dignity, his nobility as a human being must emerge from his efforts to liberate himself from his bondage and to obey his deepest aspirations. And let him above all never forget that the divine spark is in him, in him alone, and that he is free to disregard it, to kill it, or to come closer to God by showing his eagerness to work with Him, and for Him."

Self-determination, predestination and Divine guidance; I can recall when those three looked as incompatible to me as they had to debaters in decades in the past. I can also recall, through life, wondering how one could have so much "luck" in the form of opportunities, or was it luck?

Self-determination; the privilege of conscious decision which draws upon its three sources; (1) External contacts, data and circumstances, (2) the cerebral cortex's files of voluntarily stored human wisdom, and (3) the sensed autonomic evaluations, recommendations and other sensed receptions perhaps even from the all-pervading Infinite. I, at my command post, may recognize or ignore any or all that comes to mind. Self-determination *is* mine.

Predestination; compounded of my heritage, physical, mental and spiritual, my opportunities and the usage I make of them, and the obligations and responsibilities which I sense and act upon, or ignore perhaps to my sorrow. I have told you, out of the conviction that it is so, that the undertaking of this project, beyond my normal engineering occupation, has seemed like such an obligation. Only time will tell.

Divine guidance; available to all of us through humble and honest prayer. We have all been told so time and again. Many of us have experienced the intangible but effective sensed help which we feel was beyond the normal expectancy of our mental potential. It comes to consciousness over the same channels as other involuntary sense impressions from the autonomic.

Perhaps it is immaterial how this service may function. Man usually utilizes physical, scientific and natural phenomena for long periods of time before he understands how they work, but understanding he often utilizes them to better advantage.

In chapter VIII we discussed at some length the natural counterpart of radio and radar. We noted that their wave lengths and frequencies are within the range between light waves and sound waves to which human neuron receptors are known to be attuned. We noted that human electrical wave receptors have not yet been identified as have those of the electric eel. Nerve receptors in the skin or nasal tissue might be suspected, but the mysterious pineal gland seems more probable at present, though techniques have not yet been devised to test it properly.

The pineal body, last and highest of the vital endocrine glands, rises significantly at the top of the inner brain. It is therefore at a well protected and central location in the "temple of the mind."

Professor Turner in his authoritative "General Endocrinology" * gives only two pages to the pineal body, because there has been so little progress made by the ordinary methods of research in analyzing it. Observations have been recorded of men with tumors in the pineal area. The gland has been removed from generations of laboratory rats, and extracts of it have been administered to other generations. Any possible effects of these tests were reported to be confusing and inconclusive. But these tests are designed only to discover *physical* influences of the gland, its effect upon growth or the physical aspects of reproduction. Due to the potential importance of its position, Turner expresses regret saying, "It is disappointing not to be able to ascribe a definite (physical) function to it."

While frowned upon by the hard headed experimentalists, other men have deduced or "sensed" perhaps, that the gland, did have an important function. Descartes, the French philosopher, felt that only at the pineal did Soul and body meet. Oriental philosophy seems to have done rather well in correlating responsibilities with the areas of the endocrine centers, whether by sensation, fatigue reports or intuition. The oriental belief is reported that through the development of this center one may achieve Oneness with God.

Hard headed Dr. Turner may reflect the Freudian influence in

* Published by W. B. Saunders Co., Philadelphia, Pa.

his training, for his book gives no clue to other than materialistic thinking. That suggestion may be unfair to the man, and I am most indebted to him for his studious correlations and cautious reporting of research findings. Speaking of the pineal, he says, "Descartes believed that it was the seat of the 'Soul,' and some of the more recent theories seem to be based upon evidence that is equally preposterous."

Preposterous is obviously not the right word. "Intangible" would be much better. Scientific efforts dealing with intangible nervous and mental functions have been making a great deal of progress as we have seen. The interrelation of physical centers with instinctive drives and vital responsibilities has taken very definite shape even though some details remain for clarification. The radio-like receptors for the instinctive urge to attunement with God may be difficult for material identification, but the citadel of Religion continues to defy attack.The rightness of its basic precepts continue to shine through the barnacles which accumulate on its surface.

"The pineal body of mammals is homologous with the parapineal organ or third eye of certain more primitive vertebrates." In thus identifying the pineal as an eye-like organ, Turner agrees with others in granting it receptor or receiver-like characteristics. Three U. S. zoos, New York, Chicago and San Diego are receiving from New Zealand live Tuatatas (Sphenodon Punctatus), which still wear their pineal third eye on the outside in the middle of the forehead. These scaly, sluggish lizards, about 2½ feet long were plentiful around the world 200 million years ago among dinosaurs and pterodactyls. Their pineal third eye is described as being complete with adjusting means and "optic" nerve but there seems to be question whether it received visual images as the other two regular eyes do. Turner refers to the human pineal as "an interesting ancestral vestige" suggesting that its unknown function may have fallen into disuse (which would seem to be true of many men's contact with God.) In another chapter he notes that the same thing was once said of the similar sized pituitary gland which is now known to play such a very vital part. "During the seventeenth century . . . many came to regard the pituitary as merely a vestigal relic of no particular importance."

We can recognize the aches and discomforts expressing fatigue and exhaustion of the adrenal glands, pancreas, thyroid and possibly other endocrine centers. A variety of different headaches have also been identified which seem likely to become identified with pressures or exhaustion of the endocrine and neural centers of the brain. I experienced some of these and can observe and sense some of the relationships involved. Perhaps such means in conjunction with experimental techniques will eventually help us to identify the electric wave receptor. The connection of the pineal to the thalamic area of the inner brain together with its wave receptor characteristics still seem to make it the most likely.

* * *

Early last month, March 8, 1953, the snow storm and slippery streets persuaded us to turn back after we had started for church. So instead we tuned in the Cathedral Hour on WHPC and listened to the Reverend George Parkinson preach on the text, "Be still and *Know* that I am *God.*"

He started out urging the value of quiet times and the art of meditation, with a mind cleared of worries and conflicts, and receptive to encouragement and inspiration. He had just had such an opportunity for reflection forced upon him for he had been laid up with the flu.

He payed some tribute to the psychosomatic relation of ill health to transgression of the "rules" and according to my notes, he said;

"I don't believe God *made* me have the flu.

I don't believe He *sends* tragedy to men.

I don't believe He makes men fall ill.

I *do* believe that He *uses* such occasions to teach us lessons.

I do believe that the natural laws (God's laws) *cannot be set aside.*

When it does happen to us, let's listen to the still small voice and learn what He would teach us."

Many men have observed and noted the negative unity of transgressions and deserts. Gilbert and Sullivan whose philosophic insight into human nature was great, had the temerity to immortalize the all-powerful Mikado who delighted "to make the punishment fit the crime." Felix Adler in his thoughtful "Wisdom and Destiny," observed, as so many of us have, the many ways in which life's fortunes and misfortunes combine to grant us our deserts on earth. Glenn Clark in "How to Find Health Through Prayer" associates many physical diseases with related transgressions and needs for spiritual or mental hygiene.

Rabbi Joshua Loth Liebman in his excellent book on the achievement of "Peace of Mind" * exonerates God of the Mikado's mischievous delight and suggests that *we* are the *designers* of our own punishments. He puts into the mouths of ancient prophets these observations:- "God does not abrogate the moral laws of life for any

* Published by Simon and Schuster, New York, 1946.

favorites. He has established natural laws in the universe. He expects them to operate. He has given you consciences and minds and He expects you to use them. If you abuse them He will not set His world topsy turvy in order to rescue you from the consequences of your deeds."

Dr. Harold de Windt adds at this point the observation that "many men are awakened or tempered by their troubles to a keen appreciation of their call to service, and to an inflexible determination to carry out God's will." To that I can testify from personal experience.

Psychosomatic *retributions* for violations of the autonomic standards and for ignoring the responsibilities represented in the instinctive drives, belong to the negative aspects of maladjustment. If they are currently abnormally prevalent as is often charged, we might examine the Freudian or materialistic influence evidenced in a relative spiritual illiteracy of many of our university graduates.

But what of the positive, the healthy and useful aspect? Can we formulate *it* in the concepts of *spiritual* maturity and well rounded *judgment?*

Physical maturity some time in the late teens or early twenties is probably a fairly obvious state, and is no particular part of our problem.

Mental maturity is likely to come a little later. It would seem to be compounded of theoretical education, equipping large areas of the cerebral cortex, plus some practical experience to develop the mental routines and skills of thinking into humbly useful activities. Relaxed utilization of the autonomic facility for organization of thought with its utilization of instinctive standards for evaluation should be a part of it by chance, if not by intent.

But somehow men who are well educated and experienced still fall short. Selfish, self-centered, egotistical, dishonest and self-aggrandizing habits of thinking creep into their judgments, coloring, warping and distorting them until the man may be useless if not detrimentally troublesome in his organization. Health is quite likely to be affected at the same time. A lack of proper balance or basis for judgment in his conscious decision, is indicated. More attention is being paid in such cases to undesirable habits of thinking than to those which *are* acceptable to the autonomic standards and drives.

The resultant conflict brings us sooner or later to the crossroads. One way leads down through confusion, frustration, despondency and ill health, perhaps to death. The other way leads up through forgiveness, change of life, rebirth, a clarification of ideas and a realization that God *is* and that we have access to His Wisdom and power if we will but utilize it. Perhaps our education and mental housekeeping will have been good enough so that we do not have to experience catastrophe to achieve this Spiritual Maturity.

Can we not see that our access to and attunement with that infinite wisdom and power which we recognize in God is the essential ingredient and final resort of good sound judgment. Perhaps our marvelous mental system will run very smoothly with a latent sort of faith, over long periods of years. But perhaps even then an active use of the power of prayer and an active search for guidance and inspiration (through the language of sense impressions and ideas) would have lighted our living and our creative effort to a much higher plane. Our best education in comprehending and re-enforcing our sensed messages from our autonomic circuit, and in assuming the honest, humble and unselfish approach to prayer, is in the teachings of Jesus Christ and of those who have studied His ways well.

*   *   *

Presentation of the finite nature of man's provision for contact with the infinite concept of God, and the relation of that provision to the rest of his mentality is an objective to which one hesitates to aspire. To accept it on faith as most men eventually do is natural. But to present it as a part of scientific training to strengthen adequate use of the young mind's highest facilities has been difficult.

If you followed the suggestion at the interlude you have read the concluding summarization of the mind's operation. You have returned and pondered with me the data we have gathered concerning physical, mental and spiritual aspects of the unfamiliar system which is beyond the conscious realm. You have probably been disturbed by the implications of psychosomatic retribution for bad or careless mental management. To visualize a devil who fiendishly suggests self-pampering temptations to our conscious consideration has fallen into unpopular disrepute. But our flattering "friends", a few satanic advertisers and propagandists and our own self-centered habits of thinking seem to do quite well in his stead.

My sweet wife has bitterly resented every suggestion that people's misfortunes may be attributed to prior acts or thinking habits of their own or of those about them. Perhaps that resentment stems from the idea that one so unworthy as I might be passing judgment upon obviousuly worthy friends who are suffering tribulations of various sorts. No, it isn't for us to indulge in imaginative post mortems. But trained diagnosticians who seek to help broken spirits with forgiving kindliness must delve into uncomfortable corners of private thinking as the next chapter observes. Examination of those disturbing experiences is essential as it demonstrates the inviolability of God's laws, and our need to maintain our spiritual responsibility and contact.

The reality of the contact between God and man! I am now satisfied that the conviction of that fact is our greatest asset.

My preoccupation with education of my cerebral cortex and with the use of all the interesting prefabricated conclusions that were given to me, diverted my attention for an unfortunately long period. Undoubtedly as I set out to use my learned wisdom I did instinctively use judgment, and did at times sense God's guidance without noting it, for our "luck" was generally good. But as middle age arrived the curve turned sharply downward and approached termination. That is where this report began.

One may indulge in wondering "what might have been," if collegiate training and the formative years had not so thoroughly ignored the basic principles of exercising that contact with God. Since the reawakening which drove the need of it home, it has proved not only effective but vital. We have tried to report specific instances which have advanced this project. Musty biblical terms; inspiration, Divine Guidance, helping angels, miracles of recovery, faith . . ., have come up out of the antiquity where my education left them and assumed real places in life. To be sure the wings proved to be unnecessary embellishments to the angels who "appeared" when needed, and their faces were radiantly lighted with the halo-effect of an involuntary smile. God's kingdom has turned out to be all about, in the mental attitudes and behavior of many people.

In one of the books which brought me back to the realities which are the subject matter of religion, Glenn Clark drew the parable of the hind's feet. It had to do with the sure footed perfection of coordination in the deer's ascent to the security of the rugged high places. The parallel of course is with the coordinated use of all of our gifts in our equally vital ascent to the high places of character.

Perhaps it should have been obvious to me, in more general terms, but the four coordinated leverages to life's successful ascent appear to be:-

1. Corpus striatum; the conscious command post, seat of decision, my "self";

2. Cerebral cortex; the sub-conscious reservoir of wisdom and of habits which I have chosen to store, the means of interpreting the reports brought in by the five "conscious" receiving senses;

3. Autonomic inner brain; the gift of instinctive wisdom, source of sensed evaluations, judgment, conscience;

4. Still largely intangible but essential, the (pineal) receptor; access to God's infinite wisdom, forgiving mercy and aggressive guidance, distinctive and apart from the others.

Our teachers in the portentously titled fields of psychology, philosophy, psychiatry and theology have a coordinating problem before them. In the complexities of modern educational and living problems, Christ's parables, His expression of the golden rule, the "way" of life, are models of simplicity.

There is no compromise short of living the Christian life, using *all* of one's mental assets, to acquire the rugged peace of mind essential to modern stress.

XIX

IMAGINATION, A TERRIFIC POWER

Imagination, the essence of our life unseen, within ourselves, a limpid reflection perhaps of our character, or a stirring force which may become our future.

In my imagination I may idly drag myself to the depths of degradation and disaster or equally literally I may rise to God's high places and go forward refreshed to the heights of creative effort.

Surely imagination is a particularly interesting thing to examine in the light of our current fragments of knowledge and experience. What is it? How does it work? Whence it's great power for good or evil, and how can it be policed when need there be? We approach the problems of mental balance, mental disease, mental hygiene, will, judgment and God's help.

*   *   *

The thoughts and notes which initiate this chapter took shape at St. Simons Island, Georgia on the nineteenth of March in 1952. We were "on retreat", Eleanor and I, at a beautiful spot by the ocean, an island of early spring and ancient charm, of live oaks, Spanish moss, and brilliant camelia and azalia blossoms. Here Oglethorpe stopped the Spaniards. Here also John Wesley planted the seeds of the Methodist Church.

The rest, for us, is a happy one even though enforced by the second and lesser seige of nervous fatigue which culminated in an attack of glaucoma in the good left eye. It is happy because the trouble was caught in time and because it gives an opportunity to return to the manuscript which had been interrupted by almost three years of acute engineering problems and overtime.

The Reverend Gholson is St. Simons's present Methodist pastor and a sincere Christian. Yesterday, he was so kind as to discuss my problems with me. As I outlined the trouble which brought me here and my refired determination to go on with this project, no matter what, he remarked that, "God has His ways of getting us back to the things we should do".

You may detect that these paragraphs are out of chronological order, for it was at Simons that I decided to scrap, reorganize, and rewrite all that I had done before. Perhaps Reverend Gholson influenced the decision.

* * *

As we examine the following notes concerning imagination and the status of peace vs. conflict, there are two things to be kept in mind.

1. A scientific law states that action and reaction are equal and opposite; a given physical impetus will produce a given result. The biblical record is replete with instances and parables of retribution and reward; the act begets the reaction. The question to be settled is, therefore: Does life exemplify the biblical concept and the scientific law in mental and physical (psychosomatic) sequences?

2. The stage on which imagination weaves for me its plots and carries on its rituals is the private office of my conscious self, which we would identify as the group of brain cells called corpus striatum. That stage is physically "in the middle". It is between the subconscious reservoir of thinking habits and memories in the frontal lobes, and the sensed guidance and evaluations of the advisory areas to the rear. From both of those it may draw its action, the forces which sway it to conflict or to mental peace.

* * *

The realm of my imagination is that inner privacy where I may shroud the goings on, the ebb and flow of countless neuron stimulations which, taken together, become a thought in formulation. (The paragraphs written the morning of March 19, set down such a formulation of thought). Cooperating in this work or play, the mind's eye, the capacity to project sharply or vaguely whatever I would conjour up, lends shape and movement to my daydreams and pranks and to the more serious designs. When the switch of sleep is thrown to dim the conscious controls, then imagination drifts off in dreams, in fancy free, an easy prey to maladjusted subconscious routines.

What starts a train of imaginative thought? A beautiful scene, a book, a kindly word, or perhaps more often an unkind one, any of a variety of such external stimulations. Or within ourselves it may begin from a wrankling memory, a twinge of pain, a yen for power, a comparison of what we think we are, with what we think others may be or what we think they might think of us, as if they cared. Less dangerous and more likely to be useful are those thoughts which require an effort to initiate, an objective, a conscious gathering of initial data and perhaps some notes or sketches.

How does it carry on? Gathering data, adding evidence whether it be real or fancied, adding fuel to the fire, making little speeches to ourselves telling-off the object of our ire. With little else to do we may pamper ourselves, reciting our little ills and aches, the injustices and misfortunes which seem to be ours. Most of these are the idle, the negative, the destructive wanderings which may grow into practiced habits characterized by discontent and unhappiness. They are likely to be prejudiced in our behalf, *not quite honest*, inclined to give the wrong slant to a remark or an act, fertile ground in which neuroses and complexes may fester feverishly.

On the other hand, healthy, purposeful, well-managed imagination will attend to the rules of fair play and appraise without bias, brushing aside the slights and bumps with a grin. It will recognize in proper perspective the respect of and responsibility to God and to other people in the services which draw upon the mind's supplies.

We have found that many of the muscles which shape the expressions of the face and throat are jointly actuated from conscious and autonomic centers. Somehow the forced smile lacks the spontaneity and sparkle of the smile which comes from the soul. The face may consciously mask or involuntarily reflect the friendly warmth, the vacant sloth or the detached thoughtfulness imaginatively envisioned within.

The vacant stare is perhaps the least common for it has been noted that nature abhors a vacuum. Something tends to rush in whether it be repressed brooding, idle diddling or constructive thinking. The memory files may vie with or cooperate with the whole gamut of the instinctive drives, the urges to create, to adventure, to strive, to accumulate reserves, to serve, to learn, to evaluate and organize thought and to seek attunement with God. One seems to observe that the healthy and worthy imagination has an affinity for plans and problems, and for rather analytical observation of people, influenced in part by the age, and development of the observer.

It is the privilege of imagination to use any of the neurons of both nervous systems, even to those which stimulate muscles to action. It is reported that just thinking of an activity whether it is seriously contemplated or not, sends a minor electrical message to the muscles involved. Often, when our dog was stretched out asleep on the floor we have observed the little yips and the twitches of his paws which told of his dreams of the chase. And I have noted times in bed and up, when my thoughts resulted in a twiching of appropriate muscles even though I had no actual intent to use them. Talking and walking in sleep would seem to demonstrate that imagination can carry on at the subconscious level. That is to say, once the neuron connections have been set up it can continue after the conscious control center has blacked out in sleep.

Quite clearly an imaginative line of thought may extend its connections through the association neurons to any area of the cerebral cortex. It may utilize the external receiving senses and the evaluating reactions of the autonomic inner brain. Or it may ignore all sources. My own feeling that it is consciously initiated and may by consciously redirected or terminated at any time requires corroboration. It affects proper use and misuse of the mind in the formation of habits of thinking and attitudes which may become highly valuable or detrimentally neurotic.

We practice a skill until we learn it, until we establish it well upon a group of motor neurons and their association connections. They become well worn pathways. In the same way we repeat and practice thinking processes until they become useful skills or dangerous ruts, attitudes, points of view, complexes, neuroses, neuron groupings which are practiced to hook up easily for better or for worse.

We may permit attitudes of selfishness, self-pampering, self-sympathy to build up in this manner and in turn to influence the repetitive practice of envies, hates, worries, fears, and what-not, until they become such well established pathways that any passing observation or suggestion may set them going as a subconscious routine. We have noted in previous chapters how such repeated mischievous signals result in wasteful dispensing and ultimate exhaustion of vital hormone supplies and physical or nervous reserves. Obviously then it is not good mental housekeeping to permit such imaginative malpractices.

We can risk examining these disturbing problems to persuade ourselves of the vital need (and of the available means) in responsible parenthood, education and management, to take preventive precautions. After the damage is done we must call upon God, and those called to His medical and spiritual services, to help us diagnose, clean up and rebuild properly. What is the situation?

On top of the pile of notes and clippings before me is a gruesome picture. Taken in an insane asylum of an unnamed state, it shows a group of ill kept women clad only in cheap nightgowns or wrappers. They are lolling or squatting barefooted on the wood benches and stone floors of the ward, their expressions depicting dejection beyond description. In other wards were equally hopeless men. Other pictures show operations to destroy or isolate frontal portions of the brain which are suspected of harboring neurotic thoughts stored on trouble-making neurons. Sometimes the operations reach farther in to destroy portions of the thalamic inner brain. This leaves the forebrain's stored misconceptions but endeavors to eliminate the instinctive (emotional) organization of (sympathetic) combative action which such neurotic habits of thinking wrongly initiate. While this has been observed to leave patients irresponsible it should prevent energizing violence in their behavior.

But the sad plight of 600,000 patients crowded into 180 understaffed mental hospitals is not the point here. It is rather that our legally amoral education and frantic living are reported to be increasing "enormously" our trend toward such an end. In 1946 when the "Snake Pit" revelations had stimulated a congressional investigation, Surgeon General Thomas Parran testified "Of *all* the hospital beds in the U. S., more than one-half are occupied by patients with mental disease." Draft statistics showed that even in the 18 to 37 year old group of men, mental disorders caused the rejection of 789,600 or 17.7%. And by diseases of the mind I believe we mean in general; ill chosen points of view or habits of thinking which are so at odds with our needs and our instinctive standards as to cause emotional and physical discomfort within, and social discomfort without.

Early in 1947 a group of Ohio mental health officials and Ohio State University professors chose Miami county as a representative area for a study of the mental balance or adjustment of an average group of people. It is an area of farms, villages and three small towns (largest, 16,000; total population 52,600). They examined its school children, draft data, court records. According to TIME's review of the report, March 31, 1947, they found that:—

From 10% to 20% of the country's residents ought to see a psychiatrist;

"Many . . . . live miserably, and at a level far below their real capacity for effective and efficient functioning . . ."

In the past six years, 207 had been committed to institutions; one out of every 23 inhabitants of the county would spend part of his life in a mental institution;

More than 10% of its draft age men were mentally unfit for military service. (Farm boys generally were less fit mentally than city boys);

One elementary school child in five was "seriously maladjusted." In six years 1,168 cases of delinquency had come up in court. In the lower grades, rural moppets had better than average mental health; but by the time they reached the sixth grade their neuroses were showing,

The divorce rate was almost 75% above the national average (6.2 per 100 vs. 3.6 av.);

Neuroses were much more common among the poor and ill-educated than among the well educated, (but) the insanity rate was about the same in both groups (end of quote).

The American Psychiatric Association estimates that there are between eight and nine million psychoneurotics in the postwar U. S.

Who was the Quaker who said, "All the world is a bit queer but me and thee, and sometimes I think thou art a bit titched"?

Seriously, there seems little doubt that all of us, engineers, theologians, psychiatrists and ordinary citizens have "learned" quite a few things which are wrong, doubtful or misleading. Some of our mis-acquired habits of thought are so basic as to seriously warp our point of view and our approach to daily problems of living. Material before me lists among the symptoms of neurotic disease, or perhaps better of mental misdevelopment:—chronic infantilism, anxiety, frustration, repressed hostility, timidity, indecision, evasion of responsibility, etc. etc.

Psycho-analysts combine long training with highly confusing experience and the complications of one's own particular background as they set out to search the dark recesses of an unhappy patient's mind. It is far from easy and the complexity of fouled up thinking becomes more difficult to unravel as years pile upon years. The patient's guilty effort to cover up anything which he imagines might reflect discredit on his pride makes it more difficult. Infinite patience on the part of the analyst must unravel and piece together detail after detail up many blind alleys. Often the trouble goes back to overbearing or unloving or just plain careless parents. Often too, an over-shielding, mollycoddling parent took all responsibility and decision, leaving their offspring handicapped or intentionally frightened with respect to the normal problems of living. As life progresses, misdeeds, real or fancied, and efforts to cover them, may complicate the patient's thinking. The effort to untangle such a jungle of twisted thinking and to explain away one misconception at a time is indeed an up-hill job.

"Chronic invalidism" enjoying ill-health in conversational recitations of symptoms until they become established as psychosomatic routines; imaginative self-sympathy pyramiding every little ache and gas pain, such things have been a frustrating bonanza for the pill purveyors. A Denver Psychiatrist would even toss some of the blame back onto the medical profession as iatrogenic (or doctor caused). He feels that "repeated examinations for organic disease may scare the patient half to death, suggest that he must have some rare and fatal complaint that puzzles the medical experts." Doctors trying unsuccessfully to treat a physical debility without going back to the twisted mental attitude at the root of it, just feed more self-pampering worrise to the patient's improperly policed imagination.

This doctor cites several case histories:

A 32 year old woman suffered from anxiety which made her heart beat erratically. Her doctor told her:

"You may have had such a severe heart attack that you barely escaped death." He gave digitalis. A second doctor said:

"You have angina pectoris," and advised a hospital. A psychiatrist finally ran down the anxiety at root of the trouble.

A married woman suffering from "nerves" was told that removal of her "toxic" thyroid would solve her trouble. The operation failed to cure her nervousness which turned out to be caused by an unhappy marriage.

A 23 year old girl spent two years in bed after a series of doctors told her that she had (1) high blood pressure, (2) a heart murmur, (3) rheumatic fever, (4) tuberculosis, (5) undulant fever. Psychiatric treatment finally got her out of bed.

The doctor urges the need for knowing the patients to better judge what may be bothering their thinking.

Fears that some dark deed may pop up from the past, and worries engendered by sexual misadventures or misalliances do build up in the idle imagination to powerfully detrimental forces, exhausting nervous reserves and creating acute mental distress. The instinctive sense of guilt becomes more insistent. Self-centered pride keeps the victim from making a clean breast of it to either medical or spiritual advisers and it festers into a potent guilt complex with probable psychosomatic maladjustments of the physical system. The attempt to evade bad conscience may end up in escapist resort to drink or drugs or "revenge" with worse consequences.

Appended to the guilt complex there may build up in imagination a yen for self-punishment. Year after year a fanatic overcorrection may keep reviewing and even magnifying the circumstance in a continuing torment.

And again we find that imaginative flights can produce results similar to real conflict between wrong doing and the autonomic standards of morality. Over-trained sensitivities, modesties and fanaticisms may build up as wrong doing the natural reactions and interests which mark us as human. A repressed curiosity about the natural physical attributes of the other sex may find outlet in art museums, "French" postcards, burlesque shows or peeping-tom activities. Modest embarrassment over such curiosity builds up imaginatively to a disturbing point where the psycho-analysts have had to devise a French name for it.

Freud's emphasis upon the many aspects and intensities of sexual problems in mental confusion and destructive conflict has tended to obscure the great variety of other influences at the root of mental discomforts and diseases.

Incompatibility, nagging, violently emotional fights fueled by a sense of injustice are likely *not* to trace to the mating urge which brought the couple together in the first place. It is more probable that spoiled selfishness, pampered by parents but not by the mate will fester in the imagination of each and will feed upon every misinterpreted thoughtlessness. Eventually the misinformed sympathetic system will be worked up by hard words and thoughts to a fighting pitch. Responsibility for the increasing divorce rate must be divided between current attitudes and inadequate training in unselfish thoughtfulness.

Neuroses among children trace also to such self-centered thoughtlessness and inhumanity on the part of parents and even of teachers. Peptic ulcers are but one form of psychosomatic trouble. Dr. Bertram R. Girdany of the Pittsburgh Childrens Hospital reports forty-five cases, among children in a year. They were tense, brighter-than-average children who bottled up their normal emotional reactions. They did not kick and scream . . . but suffered in silence.

Dr. G. G. Robertson, Glasgow diagnostician grouped some 300 cases with considerable similarity of characteristics. As girls, the patients had grown up under domineering or drunken fathers and had clung to their mothers' apron strings. In maturity and matrimony they developed dyspepsia, frigidity, nausea, gallstones, and continued to cling to their mothers. Dr. Robertson is confident that disgust and nausea are two common links. He found that drugs and operations did little good. The troubles were firmly fixed in the patients' minds from youth.

Dr. Rudolf Dreikurs, working in Chicago guidance centers, has been highly successful in solving the troubles of children by guiding their parents. Like many other psychiatrists he brushes past the Freudian patter of hostility and rejection and drives straight for the child's "private logic." The argument:—no matter how wacky the child's actions may seem to an adult, they are logical to the child. It is recognized that his own picture of the world around him governs his reactions. Therefore discovery of his interpretations and point of view has enabled the docter to find a way to make him feel secure by some logical readjustment of the family procedures.

What is true of the child is also true of his elders. Our picture of the world around us governs our consciously ordered actions and our emotional reactions which autonomically supply power and lend emphasis to our decisions. That governing picture may be misguiding because it is distorted by misunderstanding or by mistrained interpretation of reports brought into the mind from the outside world by the receiving senses. Of course, that is where the acquired habits of thinking which are malformed by parents, companions and our own imaginative stormings may set us on the way to delinquency, crime or mere mental confusion.

This disturbing chapter is raking through the marginal swamps inhabitated by the lost souls we would forget. We get them out of sight in jails, insane asylums and Potters field. Yet the plight of the delinquent and the mental hospital patient is only degrees removed from the mental housekeeping disturbances which each of us is likely to suffer, and unnecessarily, perhaps.

Shall we permit our own imagination to contribute to subconscious routines which will return to plague us?

XX

WHAT IS MENTAL BALANCE?

Sleeping pills, sedative pills, stimulant pills, carloads, literally tons of them each year pour into the populace. They ease the situation for a time until the patient learns better or gives up. They are a rather impressive symbol of common man's need for better mental and spiritual housekeeping.

Not-sleeping-well is a common enough experience at some period in life, especially as we get older. It does not necessarily reflect evil doing, but perhaps an exceptional problem or just poor mental management. It does help us to appreciate the role of subconscious activity in mental discomfort and disturbance.

We have noted that our conscious attention can be devoted to only one thing at a time even though it may flit back and forth rather rapidly.

Beyond the conscious range, the receiving senses continue to function even though we pay no conscious attention to them. Their messages come into the thalamic "inner-brain" area for evaluation and possible distribution, but do not break in upon conscious consideration unless wanted or urgent.

Below the conscious range, subordinate to it, is the realm of subconscious activities. Here as we have seen, neuron groups of the cerebral cortex may be started on some practiced routine with little or no conscious realization of our having started them. We may start or stop rocking our chair in the midst of a conversation without particular intent. That involves a physical or muscular practiced routine, but mental sequences may function in a similar subconscious manner. While conscious attention is otherwise occupied, the sound of a back fire may stimulate a worry sequence concerned with automobile hazards and stimulate the pancreas to fear reaction, draining its hormone reserves. Similarly a voice in the distance may unconsciously stir a long practiced hatred reaction for some neighbor conceived to be objectionable. In so doing it stirs the sympathetic chain to organization for combat with consequent drain upon adrenal and sugar reserves. Thus many a subconscious interpretation of a little noted stimulus may result in a proper or misguided autonomic evaluation and emotional reaction.

We have noted that a line of thought has electrical momentum so that it wants to keep going. A train of thought on the day's unsolved business problems, if permitted to keep rolling right up to bedtime, is likely to continue on far into the night, as mine did last night. "I can't sleep."

The habit of thinking, "I can't sleep," if practiced sufficiently becomes a potent motor neuron itself. The mere act of lying down in bed is then sufficent impetus to start its frightening dinning.

Then there is the imaginative habit of using the period, when we should be relaxing mental activity, to belabor our fancied adversaries or sins. It is a practice calculated to stir the wakeful sympathetic organization for combat, rather than to woo the parasympathetic group's organization for relaxation and reconstructive growth.

The somnabulist's unconscious performance quite clearly indicates the direction of well developed subconscious routines during sleep. And again the place for policing action is in imagination.

Dr. Norman Vincent Peale's book on "The Power of Positive Thinking," supplies means to such police action. He emphasizes the need to keep the mind's voids filled with thoughts which are worthy and to the point, calculated to build useful rather than detrimental subconscious routines. This approach suggested a prayer for repetition to counteract the "Oh, dear, I can't get to sleep" routine. It is:

"Father, please grant us the boon of untroubled rest, in peace and calm, for relaxation and rebuilding of reserves." (It should properly be followed by a word of prayer for others we know who are building a neurotic fear of sleeplessness.)

I have found that, repeated in good faith, and to the exclusion of other thoughts, it can be effective.

On the rare occasions when the mind still continues to be active, I am reminded of Christ's pleading at a far darker time, "Could ye not watch with me, but for an hour?" Often the reflections of the dark watches of the night, when so directed, can be particularly worth noting down on the bedside pad.

Dr. Peale observes that, "a man's life is what his thoughts make of it." That observation has far more significance of course, than the corrective elimination of negative and detrimental thoughts which hatch into neuroses. It points the constructive road to creative thinking and accomplishment. At the same time it provides the clue to the mental ills which can prove so destructive.

"Schizophrenia" is the subject of little heaps of clippings and references which litter my desk at the moment. It must be most disheartening for the staffs of the mental hospitals who labor with its victims.

It traces to all of the same roots, the same variety of warped habits of thinking which are back of suicide, much crime, alcoholism and narcotics addiction.

Schizophrenia is described as "perhaps the commonest of mental disorders . . . it accounts for at least 35% of U. S. insane asylum inmates." It is marked by high nervous tension. Dr. Robert G. Grenell of Yale's department of neuro-anatomy used a microvoltmeter placing electrodes in the area of the fore-brain, the thyroid and the thymus.

(The forebrain seems to be the area for storage of the motor neurons of both worthy and neurotic habits of thinking. The thyroid includes among its hormone duties the adjustment of nervous tension, the voltage or electrical pressure required to meet the real or fancied problems before us. The thymus may prove to be something of an energy reserve center supplying the brain's electrical needs. Like the so-called lie detector, Dr. Grenell's instrument should give a good idea of the nervous tension which a person is developing under internal or external stimulus, and it appeared to indicate something of a fever pitch in the overwrought minds of the patients. The rise of nervous voltage seems akin to the extremes of "shock" and the lesser forces of cataplexy which may cause a person to shrink or to faint at a moment of stress.)

For purposes of comparison Dr. Grenell took electrical readings of 80 normal people and found that they did not send the needle higher than about eleven microvolts (under the presumably more or less relaxed conditions of the test). Trials upon 150 schizophrenic patients from the Fairfield State Hospital showed a far higher average, around 65 microvolts. As the (mental stress of the) insane patients improved under treatment, their electrical readings fell closer and closer to normal. But if they stayed sick their electrical (nervous) tensions stayed high.

Schizophrenia is split personality, Fig. 12. The patient is at conflict within his mind. He evidences it in abnormal behavior. We observe that he is spiteful, malicious, perhaps violently belligerent or morosely withdrawn. If we may apply the evidence to an understanding of his troubles, he has imaginatively practiced self-sympathizing or otherwise self-centered habits of thinking that he is mistreated, imposed upon, underprivileged, wrongly accused, robbed of his place in the sun. The world passes him by without knowing the need or trying, or at least without succeeding in persuading him out of his fouled up thinking. It festers among fears, envies and hates during the dark hours and in subconscious routines. It pounds the fancied injustices at the sense-of-justice neurons of his autonomic standards

which are not in a position to know how badly he has come to dis-
tort the facts. They have no choice but to order a proportionate mo-
bilization-for-action powered by electrical and physcial energies with
all the involuntary expressions of rage, etc.

As in neurotic battle fatigue he is imaginatively stimulating and
depleting precious reserves of hormones and energies until he
is exhausted and physically sick. The victim knows he is alone
in his thinking, at odds with his conscience and with the part of the
world to which he seeks to be justified. Selfish pride will not permit

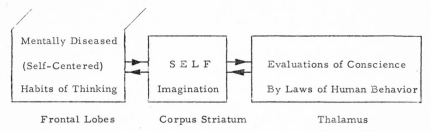

Figure 12. Split personality. Since conscious self is in the middle (literally), it may
be placed in a cross-fire of conflict, torn between warped or maladjusted thinking
habits on one side and the sensed instinctive or God-given standards on the other side.

him to retract his consciously assumed position. He has defended it
too long. The conflict raging in his mind is literally wearing him
down.

As the defense mechanism of withdrawal follows panic, what we
call insanity ensues, and he is "out" of his mind. We have noted that
the autonomic inner mind seems to take over when conscious decision
is sufficiently confused. It is as if a switch was disconnected in the
mind. Perhaps the receiving sense reports are stopped at autonomic
centers before delivery to the conscious, to give it the opportunity to
cleanse and rebuild itself. Or if the trouble has gone beyond curing,
perhaps the defense mechanism is one of isolating and sealing off the
area of diseased thinking. The de-energizing, fatiguing or death of
the group of neurons assigned to transmission in this area would accomplish it. Brain operations endeavor to accomplish the same results and provide the clue to our understanding of the natural process.

An interesting difference of opinion confronts the brain surgeons.
After efforts to cleanse the patient's thought-disease by persuasion
have been abandoned, the surgeons may try to disconnect or remove
the trouble-making neurons. Of course, these cannot yet be identified
except as to general area.

One school of surgeons would operate on the frontal lobes of the cerebral cortex where the malicious attitudes and habits of thinking are mixed with useful ones. To destroy or disconnect this area deprives the patient of both the good and bad, but may leave room for re-education.

The other school would operate on the thalamic area of the autonomic brain. To destroy or disconnect this area leaves the neurotic thinking procedures intact but eliminates (violent) reaction to them by removing the autonomic capacity to evaluate on a basis of conscious (mis-) interpretations, and to adjust hormone controls which furnish the (emotional) snap and power to the patient's activities.

It is a difficult choice. But the basic problem is still how to go about training ourselves and our off-spring to keep out of such messes.

The surgeon's problem of the relative values of the conscious and subconscious trained brain area versus the instinctively equipped involuntary controls area is also our problem. The trend of psychological influence in education seems to have emphasized the voluntary and frowned upon the involuntary. The tender emotions and other sensed impressions are at least subject to suspicion, if not suppression in the cold light of such educational precepts.

TIME for June 7, 1948 * reports figures with regard to the *Noble Savage*, showing that he is: "not nearly as crazy as Americans and Europeans" . . . . . The rate of insanity among (relatively uncivilized) Kenya Africans, says Dr. J. C. Carothers is only 3.4 per 100,000 of population. He compared this with rates in England and Wales of 57 per 100,000, with 72 to 86 per 100,000 of all races in Massachusetts, and with 161 per 100,000 among (civilized) Massachusetts Negroes."

TIME for October 1, 1951 * relates high spots of the life and suicide of a highly trained professional man whose passion for scientific procedure led him to type a record before taking his life.

Dr. Raymond R. Squier was a successful suburban doctor until tangled thinking turned him gruff and moody. His childless first marriage ended in divorce in 1942 for reasons not stated, and he moved away from Manhattan to start a new practice. His second marriage in 1947 was to a well known woman doctor who was a top flight psychiatrist. After three years they separated and shortly afterward, at 52, he gave up. I am reminded that the only couple of our immediate acquaintance who could not sense the needed adjustments of married life, were both professional psychologists.

TIME for April 26, 1948 reports another pertinent observation under the title, Frosted Children. Dr. Leo Kanner who heads the Johns Hopkins psychiatric clinic for children, used to feel that it was

* Courtesy of TIME; copyright Time, Inc. 1948, 1951.

unfair to blame the mother or father every time something went wrong with the child.

The children suffering from schizophrenia were well developed and tended to be quite brilliant, but they were apathetic, withdrawn and apparently feared normal associations. They shrank from anything that disturbed their isolation; noises, moving objects, people, even food.

At first glance the parents seemed fine. Their fathers were college trained and "successful", ranging from scientists and professors to business executives and psychiatrists. Most of the mothers were also college trained. Dr. Kanner's questioning of all these parents developed the common ground that they were cold and practical, undemonstrative and wholly devoted to material accomplishments. They froze their children into comfortless solitude. By contrast Dr. Kanner found no such mental handicap among the children of less "educated" parents who had not suppressed intuition and instinct in favor of erroneous or ill defined "concepts."

At the other extreme are the children of parents who have gotten themselves into delinquent habits of thinking and have passed these on to the receptive young minds of their offspring. Evasive efforts to find a "smart" and easy way to get money; self-sympathizing inferiority complexes imaginatively fed upon the greener grass in the other field; envious hatreds fed by rabble-rousers; suppressed bad consciences covered by ill-tempered claims that "everybody else does it;" frustrated selfishnesses brooded into compulsions and thence into crime and/or into escapist alcoholic or narcotic binges; or just broken homes where the worst offense was the selfishness of both parents, built up by self-sympathies to unforgiving ill temper, and on and on. Out of such nourishment grow the attitudes of the impressionable juvenile delinquent.

To cleanse such diseased young minds and retrain them, has been the task of Boys Town, The Gremlins and other similar organizations. The success of such organizations is usually under theologically trained men with a strong sense of their responsibility to mankind. It has been characterized by a generous application of love, together with the other autonomic expenditures of adrenal guts and determination.

Thus Padre Vern Swartsfager an Episcopal Curate in Dallas has rescued hundreds of young teenagers from gangs, crime and the police. TIME's account of August 18, 1947 relates how he started the "Gremlins Club" by capturing red-handed one of a group which had been undertaking burglary, window smashing and bombing. He ordered the boy to summon the gang and worked them over, calling them cowards and coyotes. His conviction hit through to their sense of justice. They turned over their arsenal of lead pipes, brass knuckles and revolvers and on the spot he organized the club which later received strong backing from Dallas citizens. He summed up the undertaking;

"I'll teach you to be real tough guys—mentally, physically and spiritually." He proceeded to put in the diligent effort essential to clean up their thinking habits and to provide outlet for their adrenal energies in boxing and other activities.

Twenty thousand or more suicides per year in this land of opportunity are a measure of the unbearable state of turmoil and conflict which may be engendered in the privacy of one's thinking. One psychiatric study points out that:—"The man who commits suicide must turn his back on the *church*, the *law*, and his own strongest *instinct*, self-preservation." Therein are listed three influences for good which deserve examination. All are represented in the average mind, either acquired or as a heritage. These must be the forces with which conflict is developed. And how great must that conflict be to drive a man to self destruction.

The psychiatric analysts of suicide recognized:—"a deep sense of guilt, with an unquestionable penchant for self-punishment." Suicide is an extreme case and most of us are unlikely to even approach it. But we are interested in the forces which drive us to design our own psychosomatic punishments, as so many have observed, "to make the punishment fit the crime."

Examine the three forces listed above, which so seriously opposed thousands of men's consciously ordered behavior as to drive them through extremes of mental conflict to self-destruction. While these forces may develop such terrific power, think of them also as the more gentle, guiding forces which we sense in our daily efforts at consideration and decision. You sense that a situation is satisfactory or unsatisfactory. You may be pleased, dubious, restlessly distressed or seriously disturbed in your consideration.

We are approaching an identification of the force of conscience and the state of mental balance.

As distinguished from physical damage to the brain structure we have already recognized the source of mental disease in habits of thinking and resultant attitudes. These neurotic routines may exercise a conscious or a subconscious influence resulting in mental discomfort and psychosomatic drain upon the vital reserves and the capacity for fighting disease. Now we find the clue that the conflict of these undesirable acquired habits of thought is with influences for good mental health which must indeed be powerful. Let us see if we do not find that the three forces, which were listed for us, are at the distinguishably different levels which began to stand out in prior chapters of our study. And may we not distinguish in these three sources the basis for mental balance?

Instinct was one force noted. While the urge to self-preservation was the opposing influence appropriate to the problem of suicide, it focuses attention upon all of the drives, standards and instinctive behaviorial neurons comprising equipment of the inner brain.

Voluntary standards. Our consciously acquired familiarity with *the law* of the land, the rules of behavior and objective, which society has come to accept, constitutes equipment of the cerebral cortex. These become the subconsciously guiding habits of interpretation which are incorporated in education. They are useful and healthy so long as they are sound and are wisely applied.

Spiritual forces. The psychiatrist's reference to the church in which many of them believe, was listed first. It stands for the belief in God's presence with us and the experienced sensing of answers to our prayers. The scientist may try to express it tentatively as a radio accessibility to the summation of universal Power and Wisdom. Intangible as it is and probably always will be, many men have found help which they could recognize to be beyond the natural expectancy of their own mental background.

Mental balance! Does not the healthy state of the balanced mind rest upon these three? Whether intentionally utilized or not, are they not recognizably present?

1. Instinctive heritage of drives and standards from the autonomic circuit beyond the conscious;

2. Consciously learned rules of conduct and objective, from the cerebral cortex;

3. The spiritual availability of God's infinite wisdom, from without and beyond.

Mental health and spiritual *peace of mind* are disclosing a substantial identity. The positive studies of normal mind and body in earlier chapters and these negative records of the diseased or maladjusted, contribute to a better understanding of the forces which have seemed intangible and mysterious. The first of the three forces above, the unlearned standards, the laws which cannot be violated without inner conflict, need further consideration before we conclude our study.

XXI

THE INVIOLABLE LAWS

and

THE ADJUSTED SELF

This morning as I start this chapter, my two minds and I would set ourselves to rights. We would doff the neatly tasseled mortar board of science with due acknowledgment of the privilege of wearing it. We would adorn our imagination with the more privileged headgear of all mankind.

If our halo is a bit tarnished and battered, and is worn at a precarious angle, it is but a reflection of the life "we" have led together. We sense that together we constitute a soul and that we are but fulfilling an obligation in setting down the things which to us now seem essential.

SELF AND THE TWO BODIES OF LAWS

"My minds and I." In that grouping we find perhaps the essential core of spiritual psychology. Physically, temporally and spiritually, we must note the middle position of self between its two major supporting mental bodies. Two bodies of "laws" to guide self are stored in those two mental areas, and must be distinguished if we would adequately understand the "duality" problems of divided conflict and harmonious calm.

The private deliberations of self are under consideration here. Exclude for the moment our capacity to go outside of our own minds for external help from men or God. I (at corpus striatum) may turn on the one hand to my store of learned wisdom and learned laws (in cerebral cortex, subordinate to conscious), or to my gift of instinctive evaluating standards or laws (from the thalamus of the other system).

Perhaps the learned laws are easier for me to use. They are already expressed in the learned language of the voluntary system. They have illustrative examples associated with them. The emphasis of my education has made the voluntary system's nerve pathways more familiar to me. Yet I must not, and I cannot ignore the sensed evaluations from beyond my voluntary circuit. It would be unwise because my learned wisdom may have been ill-chosen or ill-gotten. It would be uncomfortable or worse because the conscience aspects of my evaluating function would give me no peace.

"Laws" are convenient expressions of principles for our guidance. The conscious self, should distinguish those two aspects of the laws which may be identified with the two mental bodies upon which it may call.

1. *Learned* laws, are just that. Some are left out which we should have learned. Perhaps we may not have tried to learn many, or may have gotten them mixed up in the learning, through inattention or conflicting misguidance. In any case they are no better than man's observation and *expression* of the natural phenomena they sought to encompass. Inadequate research or understanding or integrity produces questionable laws. Whether or not they are accurate or are clearly expressed as we store them away, such learned laws are available to self from the subconscious (cerebral cortex).

2. *Instinctive* laws, rather inadequately describes the condensed edition of the basic principles made available to self from t.e other side (the thalamus). As standards for comparison they are fundamental to the evaluations recognized in the terms; judgment, common sense and conscience. Their use may be inadequately developed or lazily neglected by many men. This obvious fact and the timeless uniformity of these standards are attested throughout the pages of history. Their contribution to mental strength and character is a matter of common experience which is too likely to be taken for granted. On the other hand, their inviolable power is attested in the mental conflict and ultimate disaster self-inflicted upon the maladjusted, whose experiences were discussed in the last chapter. That the laws existed as a powerful unity in the realms of nature, of science and of behavior, long before men sought to formulate them, was visualized in Chapter IV.

Thus information neurons of our instinctive wisdom would include the basis for the tender emotions of sympathy and affection, the appreciation of beauty, harmony, rhythm and the like, *and the standards* by which my *self* evaluates and judges the right, the just, the honorable, the worthy, the essential, and repels their opposites. The standards being the basis of conscience are therefore at the root of conflict with neurotic habits of thinking in the voluntary areas. Such conflict places the command post in a cross fire sufficient perhaps to induce it to close up shop and withdraw.

Note again that a part of the voluntarily learned equipment of most minds is another moral code, a parallel set of regulations to help govern behavior as put together by the individual from the beliefs, suspicions and superstitions of those with whom they may come in contact. The result may be and too often is a jumbled mess which imagination has little difficulty in working up into boiling controversy. Such acquired moral misconceptions and misinterpretations contribute to the problems of the diagnosticians and the healers of sick minds.

On the positive side we have considered the instinctive standards as the sensed basis for man's expressions of his moral codes, the common law, the rules of common decency, the various tabulations for guiding conduct and behavior which we have endeavored to formulate over the centuries. Despite local variations and argumentative quibbles, many have traced the common pattern which bears out an instinctive or God-given root. The mental state of "conflict with reality" therefore recognizes the "reality", the real values as the sensed evaluations of conscience, conflicting with the unreal or warped misconceptions of the subconscious.

It embarrassed me to discover that this conviction with regard to God's gift which did not dawn upon me until after I had passed fifty, had been sensed repeatedly even in the days when men's minds seemed hardly to be awakening. Back before Christ's time ancient teachers understood God's wise provision of the guiding codes, voicing His inspired word:—

"I will put my law in their inward parts and in their heart will I write it." Said the prophet Jeremiah (31:33).

"I will put my spirit within you, and cause you to walk in my statutes, and ye shall keep mine ordinances, and do them." So said Ezekiel (36:27).

The simpler language of those days obviously did not include words to identify the thalamus which we might now select as the "heart" of man's mind, and which Jeremiah sought to describe and later translators sought to interpret.

Positive and negative aspects of any sensed basic law have been differently expressed by men of different points of view. Scientist Darwin postulated as a law, the survival of the fit and the disappearance of the unfit through the processes of evolution, particularly with regard to physical attributes. Of course strength or weakness of mind and character can not be divorced from his conception. Christ preached the *same* law in the golden rule and the parables of the candle giving its light, the house built on rock, the talents, etc., urging the positive side of worthy accomplishment; and the (retribution) parables of the useless salt, the fruitless fig tree, the insecure house on the sand and the seed on hard ground, all betokening the fate of the

unworthy. Psychosomatic studies emphasize the neurological relation of idle worries, self pamperings and frustrations to physical dis-
ability associated with the pancreas, thyroid or heart. In our coordinating effort we observe that the urge to service, carried through to
diligent accomplishment is rewarded by a sense of satisfaction whereas evading it in slothful laziness reaps a retribution of boredom, dissatisfaction, and unhappiness.

All of these would appear to be different aspects of the same thing,
a basic natural law requiring all life to do its part adequately or take
the consequences. In some people the commonly sensed drive may be
ignored or drowned out and the resultant distress may be blamed on
other things at will, for awhile at least. But so many have observed
the evidences of its influence in the human mind that it has become
only relatively intangible, like electricity and energy. However we
express it, it is a part of the body of laws and other standards given us
as a basis for conscience, for judgement and for decision.

Psychiatrist Karl Menninger of Topeka is successful in the treating
of maladjusted minds. He said in part in the Chicago Theological
Seminary's "Register:"

> "Consider (the psychiatrist's) ministry of care to the most mis-
> erable, the most unloved, the most pitiable, and at times the most
> offensive and dangerous of human beings . . . . . . consider what you
> call his tolerance, his forebearance, his patience with stubborn-
> ness, anger, spitefulness, silliness, sulkiness, belligerency, desperate-
> ness, unreasonableness—all the manifestations of hate. These he
> meets, if he is a good psychiatrist, with an attitude he is not ashamed
> to call love. We can live, he tells them, if we can love."

We may consider again Christ's ministry of peace to the souls of
men. "Love God, and love thy neighbor as thyself."

Whether we talk of neuroses, complexes, sins, selfishnesses, fouled
up thinking habits and imaginations or mental diseases, the negative
unity of maladjustments characterize the problem. Whether we trace
bad conscience, mental conflict or maladjustment to violations of the
moral code or the laws of human behavior or just call it bad judgement
or bad luck, a similar unity of problem applies.

The commandments, the moral code, the rules of common decency, the basis for the law of the land as men tried to express it in the
Magna Charta and the Constitution, the rules we seek to clarify in all
the -ologies, condensed in large part in the Golden Rule or expanded
in volume upon volume, in all of these there is a basic unity. The

inviolable fundamentals are rooted in infinity even though we confuse ourselves with new angles and new quibbles from day to day.

Is it not clear that each of us is equipped with a conscience, a personal condensed edition of God's laws. That is, neurons of the thalamic area (if the location matters) are equipped as instinctive standards to help us evaluate, distinguish, and decide. It does not alter the situation that such an asset may have fallen into some disuse by reason of the mass of ready-made conslusions we may have learned. It is significant that our hospitals, asylums, and grave yards fill up with those who would try to rationalize around the "laws."

I observe the efforts of men and then I watch the robins on my lawn. They have a very small brain with a minimum capacity for learned data. But their common pattern of instinctive wisdom reflects discredit on some confused human relations. My robins have a quite adequate language which parallels the human involuntary expressions of disturbed warning, happy enjoyment, a food call and rallying call. Perhaps some of it is just in the inflection of the voice, but the idea gets across. They raise their families and fulfill their sensed obligations of feeding and training better than some humans. They hunt over their own patch of lawn with considerable respect for their neighbors' rights, but they stand up for their own rights with courage. The general aspect is one of peace and harmony, but when a marauding jay appears, they rally and cooperate en masse to give him a hard time.

Codes of behavior which developed in Egypt, India, China, Persia, and Judea, went on beyond the robins and put into learnable words the sensed drives and standards. Less advanced tribes followed the same rules without benefit of language. All fouled them up with misinterpretations and selfish misbehaviors.

SELF'S POSITION BETWEEN MALADJUSTED EXTREMES

Aristotle, thinker and physician of ancient Greece, observed an interesting trend of misuse which is worthy of emphasis. In Nature and Science we find that vibrations, shock waves, echoes, electrical impulses and the swing of the pendulum move from one extreme through the neutral or equilibrium position to the other extreme and back, gradually approaching the balanced mean. So also *self* oscillates between influences until it establishes mental balance.

Aristotle picked youth as being particularly given to going to extremes; "If youth commit a fault it is always on the side of excess and exaggeration". Will Durant * interprets: "The great difficulty

* "The Story of Philosophy," by Will Durant; Simon & Schuster, New York, 1926.

of youth (and many of youth's elders) is to get out of one extreme without falling into the opposite, for one easily passes into the other through overcorrection. Thus: "Insincerity doth protest too much and humility hovers on the precipice of conceit." The Greeks have engraved upon the temple of Apollo at Delphi, the motto *meden agan*,—Nothing in Excess, known also as the Golden Mean.

Virtues of character identify themselves with instinctive drives which are powered in turn by hormone reserves, as was observed in the study of the involuntary system. In consciously utilizing these autonomic drives and powers the danger is in going to extremes to either side of the "straight and narrow path." This is where restraint, temperance or practiced inhibitions are needed. Maladjusted thinking habits which are out of balance with the standards disturb system adjustments;—

The instinctive urge to free and courageous accomplishment is stored upon some inner brain neuron. It responds to thalamic evaluation of a conscious interpretation of external circumstances, and "emotionally reacts" by mobilizing adrenal combat reserves. Thus misguiding conscious extremes may over-excite calm courage into pugnacious bad temper in one direction, or over-restrain it to molly-coddled "spinelessness" in the other.

The instinctively equipped motor neurons which urge inward selfpreservation are powered by hormones of the pancreas. In the matter of physical reserves they may be fearfully stimulated to an overhoarding of sugars and corpulent fats or in the other direction to waste and skinny anemia.

The drives which initiate romance, mating and the cooperative creation and support of life may be misdirected to extremes in either direction. Their hormones (chromosomes and genes) may be over-stimulated to unwise overpopulation or to illicit promiscuity. Or they may be over-restrained in frightened frigidity.

The expenditure of one's self, one's nervous reserves may be over-done to the extent of breakdown or heart-failure; or it may be over-restrained to a wizened and miserly end, devoid of the satisfactions of accomplishment. These are the extremes departing from wise use of the instinctive urge to service, powered we believe, by reserves dispensed through the thymus.

Thyroid regulation of rates and tensions may be overworked to a jittery "state of nerves," or understimulated to languid or dull list-lessness.

Pituitary powered adjustment of both physical and mental growth and development may be influenced to several aspects of extremes or unbalance. The psychosomatic influences of habits of thinking upon health and physique, for better or worse, are now clearly present though not yet fully understood. In the matters of mental health, our forebrain attitudes and points of view may influence balanced adherence to "the straight and narrow path", or deviations to extremes in either direction. Consider a few:

The point of view of reliable responsibility would seem to be between irresponsible evasion and misbehavior on one hand and willful violation or misuse of responsibilities, as practiced by most dictators.

Humility lies between blinding egotism or conceit on the one hand and freightened self-effacing on the other.

Faith and accompanying confidence may be described between headstrong brashness and indecisive fearfulness.

Pride in one's heritage and one's worthy accomplishment under God's guidance may rise above pride in self alone on the one hand and a lack of any pride on the other.

Patience in undertakings is obviously between irritable impatience and complete lack of effort.

Restraint and temperance seem to lie between selfish excess, show and over-indulgence to the right and withdrawal, abstinence and evasion to the left.

In the point of view of religions, a simple and majestic beauty lies between ornately hollow and ceremonial elegance to one side and hard unloving severity to the other.

But as the ancient Greek observed, unconscious (and unbalanced) extremists look upon the golden mean as their opposition; they "expel toward each other the man in the middle position; the brave man is called rash by the coward, and cowardly by the rash man." Durant observes the same trend in modern politics wherein the middle of the road "liberal" is called "conservative" by radicals to the left and is called radical by the conservatives to the right.

So the achievement of mental balance is not easy. The practice of right living is tempted and jostled between selfish sins and evasions to the left and an unforgiving and vengeful fanaticism to the right.

Our ability to state the laws of human behavior is still inadequate though men have sensed them and observed their effectiveness, and expounded them since antiquity. The assorted notes of these chapters should convince us that these laws can not be evaded without suffering the consequences, either physically or in the privacy of one's mind.

That purgatorial idea of retribution is a disturbing one, so unpopular that most clergymen are loth to mention it. We "good" people of their congregations are too prone to leave our Christian responsibilities to someone else and then complain of our "misfortunes". The irregularities may be simple or complex, obvious or difficult to discern. Our lack of interest until things become serious, or a lazy evasion of the thinking effort necessary to analyze the problem in prayer, may delay cleansing treatment.

Neither God nor our conscious self gave the order for such routine retributions. Rather the involuntary evaluating and adjusting functions of the autonomic system registered its disapproval in a sensed mental discomfort and then, in continuing efforts to correct the unsatisfactory situation, resultant mental and endocrine exhaustions result in distress, maladjustment or psychosomatic disturbance. The wise provision of the still, small voice of conscience backed by the instinctive standards is attested in the general average of decency in humanity, despite the glaring exceptions, and the petty inconsiderateness which annoys equally petty selfishness.

Often it is hard to see why we or our dear ones should suffer for our own or the community's laxity. Yet frankly facing up to the maturing possibilities of psychosomatic retribution, it is remarkable to me how relatively gentle, though insistent, the workings of these autonomic adjustments have been.

Nor need the possibilities of our poor judgement be depressing to us in view of the kindly provision for correction and cure. Christ offered to us the forgiveness of sins and died for us, to drive the point home. And it *is* true. It does work. I can say from my own moderate experience, that the "laws" are inviolable and inescapable; *but* the forgiveness of selfish sins achieved through honest confession and prayer provides a miraculous relief from conflict with conscience, and opens a fresh clear view ahead.

Perhaps as an eminent psychiatrist has told me, there is nothing new in all this. No new words have had to be coined in the discussion. True, the many divergent points of view may require adjustment where possible, but the things which proved startling to me still seem to merge into the overall unity of balanced mental processes. It is as if we had sensed them all the time but had taken them for granted.

THE ADJUSTED SELF AND UNSELFISHNESS

Much of our discussion has been devoted to distinguishing the problems and responsibilities of the two supporting minds, the one subordinate to the conscious and the other beyond the conscious. I find, however, that my primary interest is in the conscious command post, "Mr. In-between," *myself*. The equipment and functioning of its neurons are not yet clear but many common words in our language may be associated with it with some revealing significance:

"I," at the command post, may be inactively relaxed with no thoughtful activity in process, or may actually be asleep, a state distinctive apparently of this one area. On the other hand, I may be alertly attentive to the consideration of some matter of external affairs, or I may be inattentively absent in idle reverie or imaginative flight.

My conscious activity may be characterized by enthusiasm powered in turn by ample nervous energy, or I may be listlessly disinterested or just tired. And I have known what it meant to be jittery or nervously exhausted.

The normal state of the conscious mind is "clear, clean, decisive, constructive, honest, balanced, at ease, courageous, assured, confident, responsible."

Its maladjusted conditions may be characterized by various degrees of "confusion, conceit, pugnacity, criticalness, indecisiveness, conflict, fearfulness, frustration or evasion of responsibility."

Its extremes, evidencing diseased or compulsive habits of thinking in its subordinate background, are characterized as unbalanced, deceitful, egotistical, criminal, panicky, bewildered, distraught, and on to escapist habits, withdrawal (from responsible conscious control) and self destruction.

In these characterizations, the conscious self and its decisions necessarily reflect the point of view of the individual, the concensus of the great mass of learned interpretations and practiced habits of thinking subconsciously stored in the cerebral cortex. There the maladjusted aspects go back to misguidance, misinformation, bad examples, parental or otherwise, vicious propaganda and unwise social habits. From such seeds of conflict, evasive "rationalization" and imaginative self-pampering ulcerate into the final stages of mental disease.

On the other hand self acceptance of the sensed natural laws *and* responsibilities, and active compliance therewith, lead to the sensed satisfactory state of the self described as peace of mind and as participation in God's kingdom on earth.

The healthy position of self may need some review. We have noted in passing that diseased habits of thinking may be analyzed as being in some part self-centered, self-aggrandizing, self-pampering, self-sympathizing, and just plain selfish. We might properly add self-mortifying, self-conscious and self-depreciating attitudes. Common sense evaluates all of these as unhealthy and unwise although biased thinking (self-deception) may endeavor to defend (rationalize) our own particular neuroses. All are too easily started in early childhood from the example of parents or associates. They are *acquired miseducation.*

The positive position of self does require self-confidence, self-reliance and a proper perspective with regard to the urge to self-preservation which is responsible for adequate well being, and of the other drives which back up worthy accomplishment in fulfillment of self's responsibility to God. Self-confidence and self-reliance, I found at forty-seven, were nothing else but *faith,* faith in our marvelous equipment and instinctive heritage, and in God's presence with us and His help through prayer at the many times we need it.

Pride? Yes, not in material possessions and the aspects of show, but in the more real values of the autonomic inner mind and a well kept subconscious wealth of experience, being effectively utilized together for worthy purposes.

The studies of the autonomic system may still be inadequate but they do indicate the (God-given) provision in each of us of the essentials of courage to do, urge and energies for proper accomplishment and compassion to guide that accomplishment. My early understanding fell far short of the implications of such an instinctive heritage and my religious training failed to bring out to me the great courage and determination to accomplish what is necessary, which was exemplified in Christ's life, and which is provided to each of us in our own charge.

I, at my command post between the two vital brain areas, may draw with confidence upon the assets of both. And I may draw from the structure of one of them an essential perspective for guidance of my stewardship, a better understanding of selfish vs. unselfish choices.

Refer back to the two sections of the hypothalamus. Its forward group of brain cells, through their (parasympathetic) nerve system and associated hormones, controls our major self-interest, self-preservation, the absorbing of nourishment, building of reserves and general maintenance needs. Its posterior group of brains cells through their (sympathetic) nerve system and associated hormones, expends our reserves to power our accomplishments, our external effectiveness. These are the things out-of-self, potentially unselfish. The two portions and interests meet in a chamber of the pituitary body, Fig. 10, the arrangement of which suggests the essential balancing function between the two, self-interests and interests external to self. It is important to note that in the normal range, short of fatigue, *self-interest* steps back and *gives priority* to the needs of external accomplishment. Thyroid hormones which adjust all rates of expenditure, restrain the building of reserves, whenever expenditure of reserves is ordered from the conscious command. Using periods of relaxation therefore, the urge to self-preservation maintains our physical and nervous reserves *in balance with* our physical and mental expenditures.

Does not this natural plan in the autonomic system serve also to guide self in its balanced division of effort between the self-interests of care for body and brain and the priority requirements of external or unselfish interests, of outward *responsibility* and *opportunity*. These comprise our responsibility for service to finite people and things, *and* to the intangible infinite, to God. The Golden Rule, training in good sportsmanship, conceptions of courageous service, loving kindness and creative accomplishment prepare us for it. Confucius taught public service. Gautama Buddha taught selflessness, and Christ taught unselfish service. The outward perspective of unselfish accomplishment seems essential to the conscious self that it may be fit to survive life's tribulations and may sense the reward of inward peace in maturity. At the same time we must again observe that the opposite, the generally selfish point of view designs its own deserts by nurturing the complexes and neuroses which undermine the physical and nervous controls.

SELF'S ADEQUACY AND RESPONSIBILITY

Prof. Will Durant of Columbia provides us with a definition of philosophy in which we may rise majestically in our search for truth, a pioneering search along the borders of wisdom. He points out that "most of us have known some golden days in the June of life when philosophy was . . . the love of a modestly elusive Truth . . . . more glorious, incomparably, than the lust for the ways of the flesh and the dross of the world."

Truly it "was," and yet we find that the urge arises again in October and November. Here in these later days my minds and I must express a disagreement which was only a question when we first read the valued writings of that studious philosopher. Perhaps he also has now changed his mind but as he started his search for Truth, in his introduction to "The story of Philosophy," his materialistic habits of thinking were evidenced. There he warned his students to "keep out of the muddy streams of metaphysics and the 'many-sounding seas' of theological dispute."

Each of us tends to work out from education, observation and intuition a personal philosophy, a point-of-view which is kept handy in the frontal lobes to assist self in its quick decisions. Paramount therein are the problems of the *adequacy* and the *responsibility* of man, of self, of *my* self specifically.

It is in these major elements of self-adjustment that Christ urged "Seek and ye shall find." The ancient observation that "God helps those who help themselves," calls our attention to self's need for active conscious effort, calling upon its best sources, preparatory to evaluation and the growth of conscious conviction.

As each of us observes the warped extremes to which we think other men are going we are reminded of the differences in background upon which they may choose to rest their thinking. Each individual self, especially under current educational emphasis, is not too likely to develop the inspirational and intuitional use of the inner mind. Rather he will be rushed into accepting on good faith whatever ready-made points-of-view may be taught to him. In early years parents and playmates who might be conscientious, or selfishly biased or busily disinterested leave their imprint. As education pyramids, more and more divergent schools of thought are introduced, often colored by improper assumptions or by teachings in which integrity is submerged to self-aggrandizement.

Then that self, with its cortex crammed with reliable or unreliable guidance, goes forth to influence others. Small wonder that our literature has become so widely divergent in schools of thought, as divergent as personalities themselves. In the field of our present interest much of the trouble may trace to the fact that until very recent years it seemed necessary to assume "mind" to be substantially a single unit rather than three significant entities which are now distinguishable. Such an assumption necessarily resulted in diverse and complex theories attempting to explain the observable conflicts, which do exist.

In the problems of man's adequacy and responsibility we have gone to divergently contradictory extremes which have extended their influence widely through education, research and the problems of ordinary living. And as Aristotle observed of old, the vocal elements of both extremes endeavor to expel all those in the middle ground toward the other extreme.

At one extreme self-sufficiency, the materialistic adequacy of man alone, may be recognized in the superman philosophy of Friedrich Nietzsche, the superstate of Lenine, the superselfishness of totalitarianism and the Godless psychology of Freud. An extreme egotism, a resentment of any higher responsibility and unscrupulous rejection of instinctive evaluation of the right and the just appear to distinguish their thinking.

At the other extreme of selfs, are the frightened and self-coddling personalities, characterized by inferiority conmplexes, which shrink from responsible use of their variously apportioned natural endowments. They hide behind protective mothers or fathers or privileges. They conjure up frightful images of an unfair and unfriendly world outside their cranial caverns. They choose out of literature and propaganda that which pampers their *evasion* of the same responsibilities which those at the other extreme selfishly *resent*. The gloomy hopelessness of Existentialism would seem to represent the current philosphical low, as Materialism represents philosophical over-inflation.

On the middle path of balanced thinking, self accepts its higher (unselfish) responsibilities. It proceeds with *faith* in its adequate supply of courage, common sense for evaluating purposes, intuitional drives and inspirational support in times of need.

The satisfying or disturbing reactions which conscious self experiences between its acquired interpretations and points-of-view on one side and its instinctive evaluations on the other side are now largely tangible. The further reach of spiritual responsibility, participation and power is still relatively intangible, but only in the same sense that Steinmetz's and Edison's effective work in commercial electrical power was also intangible. One may observe its laws, its means and its results.

Any of us may experience and conscientiously use spiritual guidance if we will. We may see in it a reality of primary importance and inescapable potency. Call it Metaphysics, Religion or an instinctive urge to attunement with God, the evidence both negative and positive, shows that it is *not* to be ignored.

Responsibility is at the core of the relationships of the adjusted self. And it is a mutual responsibility. *Self alone is not adequate!* We must accept our responsibility to our higher authority, to God. And in turn we find that God accepts a compassionate responsibility for us!

With appropriate recognition of conflicting tenets and of the increasing difficulties of research, "my minds and I" - - - - cortex as educated, instinctive inner brain and determinate self - - - - must gratefully acknowledge that mutal responsibility in our adventure together. Initial inspiration, recurrent guidance in response to prayer, and a driving conviction which was both inescapable and a source of encouraging strength - - - - without these, this project could not have been carried through.

XXII

SPIRITUAL PSYCHOLOGY

Psychology is defined as The Science of Mind. The Greek root, Psyche, meant the soul and was given as a name to the Greek's personification of the human soul. The title, Spiritual Psychology, may therefore be somewhat redundant, but if so it is only to emphasize positively our scientific recognition of the reality of the spiritual heritage and influence in our study of the human mind.

Educators have found it convenient to chart many studies among the "humanities", each with its theory and its laws. Thus in the application of scientific principles to the production of mechanisms, goods and services, men study "Human Engineering". Here again the functioning of the mind and the laws which govern it are the root stock. Mental maintenance under stress, mental hazards in safety and productivity, mental usages in constructive and creative thinking *must* be understood. Yet whatever our interests in life, it would seem apparent that the broad aspects of Spiritual Psychology encompass the findings with which this research effort concludes:

*   *   *

Psychology deals with the adjustment or maladjustment of the individual self to *all* of the forces brought to bear upon it. The temporal or material forces have been reasonably obvious and tangible. The conflict over "duality" has raged over whether modern scientific man should deny, or ignore, or recognize the less tangible spiritual forces.

The *material* forces in adjustment are the internal influences of learned wisdom and the external influences of environment. Psychological research has made much progress in studying these, but must not stop there.

The *spiritual* forces comprise the internal influences which are unlearned, instinctive or God-given, and the external influence of sensed intercommunication, inspiration and Divine guidance. These forces become less intangible as we identify their physical elements and study man's experience with them. They may be taken for granted, accepted on faith or experienced in spiritual maturity. It is neither practical nor scientifically honest to try to ignore them.

Mental duality has become apparent in the division of mental bodies and functions between the two major neural systems. Each employs sending and receiving pathways. Each stores a distinctive group of informational and procedural data. Each initiates distinctive functions. Both collaborate in many activities.

The voluntary system is primarily devoted to conscious inquiry, consideration, decision and the ordering of voluntary expression and activity. In a secondary range which is largely subordinate to conscious control, it stores learned wisdom and procedures, be they good, indifferent or bad. Its motor neurons may direct learned procedures subconsciously, be they mental or physical, wise or unwise.

Signals from the receiving nerve tips of sight, hearing, taste, touch and smell, go to cerebral cortex for interpretation and to the conscious center for consideration. Outgoing signals traverse the nerve net works which complete the system and stimulate the vocal and skeletal muscles.

The autonomic system also bases its functions upon neurons of its mental bodies, (thalamus and hypothalamus) but with the difference that its wisdom is not learned but comes naturally, instinctively or as a gift of God. Curiosity, initiative, compassion and responsibility stem from the drives and urges, the motor neurons of this system. The evaluating services of judgement, conscience, feelings and common sense weigh the reports presented to it against the standards of its informational neurons.

Evaluations of relative justice, rightness, worthiness and the like, are *internal* spiritual influences which we may seek from these gifts. The *external* influences which spiritually mature men observe in inspiration, sensed duties and answered prayers must come via the (pineal)body which is identified as a receptor organ in this system.

Subordinate to the drives and evaluations, and dependent upon them, are the functions which adjust health and accomplishment. These use their own nerve pathways, the endocrine glands and their hormone supplies for the replenishing and expending services to mind and body, Fig. 5, page 124.

The outstanding advance of this age will prove to be this new knowledge of the autonomic mental bodies and their spiritual functions. The actuality of spiritual forces in mental balance, in responsible accomplishment and in physical health acquire scientific clarity. The revered wisdom of religion fits significantly into the keystone position in the arch of a humble science.

The interdependent position of "self" among the mental bodies, is also a startling and clarifying advance.

THE CONSCIOUS SELF AND DUALITY

To outward appearances I am an independent entity, with the physical structure of a man. The control of that structure has been traced down to a small area within the brain, identified by the current evidence as the corpus striatum. Although it draws upon the support of its surrounding physical, mental and spiritual agencies, still in this body resides the directive responsibility and the consciousness of self.

Here in an inner privacy *I am.* Here I pay attention to such influences as I choose, arrive at such decisions as I wish and order such activities of mind, body and vocal muscles as I desire. Here I may drift off in imaginative reverie or relax in sleep while the other mental bodies carry on distinguishable routines and activities. Here I may call upon those other mental bodies or upon external agencies for help, but here resides the choice and decision, the executive command to determine what I am. This *is* the seat of self-determination.

The questions of *duality of mind* have caused much controversy through the years. Now the gathering data on the two major nervous systems and their mental bodies have furnished the key. "My minds and I" was suggested as a title for this report by the distinguishing of the two brain areas which may be drawn together in harmonious support of the conscious command, or may place it in a cross fire of conflict. It has been revealing to find that the conscious command post is quite literally "in the middle".

On the voluntary side, the conscious center's connections to the frontal lobes and the rest of cerebral cortex give it access to the stores of learned wisdom and subject it to the influence of habits of thinking, memories and learned interpretations. These as we have seen, may be good, indifferent or bad.

On the other side, the conscious center makes its neural connections to the group of mental bodies which are beyond the conscious range. In these we have found the natural and the spiritual assets and functions. The subsidiary hypothalamus with endocrine and autonomic neural connections, controls the reserves which empower our courage, accomplishment and creative activities, both physical and mental. The actual drives which impel curiosity, attention, consideration and activity toward creative accomplishment may be assigned to motor neurons of the thalamus as natural instincts or as God-given assets. Similarly the evaluating standards underlying judgement, common sense and conscience must derive from informational neurons of this area. God did indeed instill His laws at this point in the heart of our minds, that we might judge the right, the just, the worthy and the true.

A *duality* with respect to these *laws or moral codes* was a source of confusion in earlier psychology. Long before there were written records men sensed, experienced and observed the inherent laws. In many tongues sages sought to express them in words that they might be taught for the guidance of the young. In India and China, in Egypt, in Palestine and elsewhere there were evolved codes which were basically similar despite local differences. Much of Christian study centers about the laws and their interpretation. But many never attend church schools. Many may have their early training in right ways to live, confused by stories and examples of wrong ways. Thus the learned or mislearned laws (stored in cerebral cortex) may reinforce or confuse or actually conflict with the instinctive or God-given standards (in the thalamus). This dual or parallel existence of the laws in the two mental systems is to our advantage, providing the ready-reference set in the subconscious files is kept in good order.

Duality of *self*, split personality, schizophrenia, emphasizes the essential reality of the inner spiritual values vs the unrealities which may be developed in deceptive pretense, in malpracticed thinking habits and in habitual misconstruing of others. The prize play "Harvey", Charles Dickens "Dr. Jekyl and Mr. Hyde", a major portion of our mental hospital cases and mental conflicts in normal life are all pertinent. The internally and externally harmonious life which Christ exemplified, is contrasted with the superficial hypocrisy of the learned sophisticates of his day and ours. The conscious self may choose harmony or conflict, the harmony or conflict between voluntry behavioral patterns and God-given standards of behavior. Freud and Watson were right in teaching that moral codes (which were learned) could be changed, but only long and sad experience in the mental hospitals could prove that the deeper seated standards were not learned and could not be changed nor long evaded.

When the conscious self seeks "escape from reality" in alcoholism, suicide or insanity, the real and inescapable values are the sensed evaluations from the autonomic mental bodies, the appraisals of conscience in the light of God's standards. The conflicting unrealities are the false pretenses, the dishonest self-justifications, the imaginative misinterpretations of others (persecution complexes, etc.) all of which are learned or practiced subconscious routines (of cerebral cortex). Evidence scattered through the body of the report has shown that the mental diseases, neuroses, complexes, egomania, egophobia, etc., are generally identified with self-centered, self-aggrandizing, self-pampering, self-sympathizing and otherwise selfish habits of thinking which have become subconscious routines of the voluntary circuit.

The *duality* of *self-preservation* and the *services outside* of *self* were shown to be embodied in the two subsidiary autonomic neural systems, the para-sympathetic and sympathetic systems, Fig. 5. The first, having to do with rebuilding and replenishment of reserves, gives priority to the other which expends reserves in the activities and services of the whole being. Thus in the natural system self-preservation gives priority to service with merciful provision for replenishment during the periods when the directing self is relaxed in sleep.

Jesus Christ singled out, as the first learnable law for the guidance of self; "Love thy God and love thy neighbor as thy self." He visualized in *love*, an affectionate sense of mutual responsibility and service. Self is again in its *dual position*, reaching inward through its autonomic ties to God, and outward through its voluntary contacts to mankind.

The *duality* of *Self-determination* and *Divine guidance* remains the distinctive principle of spiritual psychology. Each individual self or soul must determine its own course between temporal and spiritual influences, in conflict or in balanced harmony. On the one hand it finds temporal environment and on the other hand, spiritual endowments and contact, through the voluntary and the autonomic systems. From both it draws wisdom and to both it owes loving service. The guidance and the obligations are not to be ignored with impugnity.

RETRIBUTION OR CONSEQUENCES

Judge not lest ye be judged. Often we wonder why some people have suffered and why others appear not to have suffered. Even in our own minds it is difficult to muster the faith and integrity to probe adequately within the bounds of our own voluntary system. And yet both the inexorable facts and actual means have been spread before us. People do suffer for their own sins, the thoughtless sins of their parents and the selfish sins of the community. The mental sins, the self-extenuating rationalizations, the imaginative malpractices and misinterpretations, the failures to reflect and to cleanse are rudiments of the problem.

The psychosomatic sequence of retribution, Fig. 13, is quite clear and rather simple. Examples of its operation where apparent as we studied each of the endocrine glands (chapters XII through XVIII). Health, both mental and physical, is the direct responsibility of this group. Their distribution and replenishment of tiny but vital hormones must be adjusted and kept in balance by the two sections of the hypothalamus and their respective nerve trains (sympathetic and parasympathetic). These adjustments in turn are guided by the instinctive evaluations of the thalamus, weighing the current situation against its God-given drives and standards. The picture of the current situation must be obtained from the voluntary system, and here the point-of-view and acquired thinking habits of the individual exert their influence for better or worse. Interpretations of the external situation which are subconsciously exaggerated by habitual worries, envies, stresses, greeds, hates or fears, cannot help but cause distorted evaluations, maladjustment of endocrine controls and resultant ill-health, both physically and mentally.

It is just that simple. Direct cause and effect.

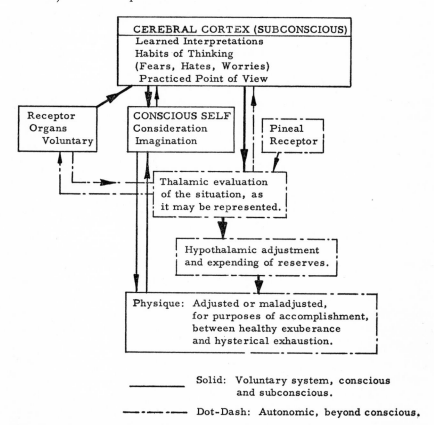

Figure 13. The action and reaction relationship which produces "retribution" or "reward" in the form of psychosomatic maladjustment or peace of mind. Imaginatively misguided evaluations can only result in maladjusted control of physical and mental energies.

It is simple in the broad general principle but may become infinitely complex in the specific case. A person becomes a patient, sick, in-
jured or distraught and something must be done at once to give relief.
Specialists in the characteristic problem take the conventional steps to
augment the natural corrective processes. At that critical moment
no one need investigate *all* of the contributing factors. Improper living conditions, weakened physique and complicated mental threads
might even trace to other lands or other generations. It is enough
that help is needed, and was needed at many earlier stages before the
situation became so grave. A thorough restoration should be well
rounded, physically, mentally, and spiritually.

RELIGION AND HEALTH

Men may describe as religious, those bodies of thought designed to
help the individual self or soul *to maintain harmony* in its relationship
with the temporal and spiritual forces acting upon it. That harmony
is the essential quality of mental health, and through psychosomatic
processes, of physical health.

Organized religions contribute in several respects to helping in the
maintenance of harmony and hence of health. First is the preparatory
education in historical background, the laws as we know them and
the privilege of prayer. Second is the preventive maintenance service of daily prayer and the weekly sermon, assisting each of us in the
mental hygiene processes of eliminating unhealthy thinking habits and
building up faith and the positive values.

Third, when catastrophe strikes, there comes the need for pastoral
prayer and a strong guiding faith to help those who are in need to
mend their spiritual ties.

Faith healing has been attacked, yet there is good reason to believe
that it is a normal component which is taken for granted in most re-
coveries. The call to service and the inspiration of conscientious
medical men *must not* be underestimated. Their faith and the faith of
their patients in them and in the natural or God-given recuperative
powers of the physical, mental and spiritual system are enough for
most purposes. The interrelation of the spiritual values of faith,
courage and mutual responsibility to health were apparent at a number of points during our study of the endocrine centers.

Progressive mutual responsibilities of the individual self, are again
important. In the first stage, through adolescence, responsibility of
the child to its parents, and the responsibility of the parents for the
child are paramount, although other older people may substitute for
the parents at times. During this period, concepts of mutual respon-

sibility before God may be instilled positively or negatively, as a part of learned wisdom.

In the second stage, the youthful soul assumes more and more responsibility in its own decisions. On the temporal side, parental and senior executive authorities are still present to furnish guidance. Parental failure to relinquish primary control and youthful hesitance to accept responsibility are basic to psychiatric problems of mother and father complexes and egophobia. Similarly in personnel relations, executive failure to delegate responsibility and hesitance to rise to it, are at the root of many organizational and psychosomatic troubles. In this stage also, external materialism and internal self-centered thinking habits (the mental disease egomania) are all too prone to blind us to our mutual responsibility before God.

The third stage is that of full temporal responsibility as patriarchs, grandparents, executives, senior statesmen. We observe at its portals, the psychosomatic experiences of the change-of-life period, a period of physical, mental and spiritual readjustment. It is a transition which many survive to their glory and the benefit of humanity. Many others die of psychosomatic disorders, or take their own lives, or just drift away into obscurity.

Religions identify the transition as a *rebirth*, an accession to spiritual maturity. A rereading of the teachings of Christ, and especially of the discussions during His last week, identify it with a period of review and judgement in which some will make the grade and others will not. For those who had lost their way, but earnestly seek forgiveness, God's kingdom may indeed come again into their lives.

We may get so close to the problems of psychosomatic maladjustment that we cannot see the woods because of the trees about us. Certainly, the identity of mental conflict and spiritual violations is revealing. Definitely in the transition period, the transgressions and shortcomings of our earlier life loom large. The healing through faith does become a reality to us if we will but observe it. Such experiences are not common to all, for a few live so well as not to need them and others, so badly as not to merit them. Enough reports reach the records of literature so that we may verify in them, the merciful part played by God's forgiveness of our selfish sins in this cleansing and strengthening of our souls.

The occasional atheist may still claim that such experiences are just coincidence or luck, until he reaches his own impasse. But the laws of chance do not have the same consistency as the laws of responsibility, accomplishment, behavior and unselfishness. These laws have been preached to us, often through a haze of self-extenuating

rationalizations. But observation of psychosomatic retribution shows
them to be as consistent and inviolable as other natural laws which we
now call scientific. After repeated violation only the mercy of the
court, God's compassionate forgiveness, can clear the way for sound
cleansing and rebuilding of the thinking habits which were at the
root of the trouble.

An angel (a messenger of God), an intermediary with strong faith
may be needed to help at such times. It may turn out to be a parent, a
doctor or nurse, a chaplain or priest, an A.A. or a passing layman. In
my own experience, reported in chapter II, the hesitant presenting of
a booklet by a neighbor proved to be the turning point. The elements
of humble faith and of inspiration were clearly there.

AUTONOMIC INTERCOMMUNICATION

The receptions of the conscious mental body from the autonomic
centers, thalamus, pineal and hypothalamus constitute a universally
sensed means of expression. This realm of communication should
probably be described as a spiritual language. Its appraisal may require a generation or more of consideration and investigation. It is so
common place as to be taken for granted but has been characterized
by the same intangible mystery as Edison's early electrical work.

Little known wartime research (Brown University) demonstrated
that much of our thinking is not expressed in language, but did not
go on to distinguish the contributions of the two major circuits. Other
research has distinguished the duality of the two systems, showing
that facial and vocal muscles are controlled for involuntary purposes
from the thalamus and for voluntary purposes from cerebral cortex.
Convincing demonstration is found when a stroke paralyzes voluntary
control of one side of the face without affecting (involuntary) control of the same area from the thalamus.

Some of the *evaluating functions* of thalamus, which also participates in emotional reactions, are well illustrated in the involuntary
facial and vocal expressions. Thus finely shaded evaluations of approval or disapproval may be noted from laughter, or just a smile or
lack of it, through a dubious frown or a scowl to some more violent
expression of rage. In the meeting of danger the evaluation may be
shaded from shouted defiance, through expressions of caution, to the
frightened scream, open panic or even the rigid freeze of stark fear.
These are externally observable and could be understood in any land
or time. By our open ingenuousness or crafty masking of such expressions, others evaluate our sincerity.

Internally the conscious center senses these same evaluations even though it may voluntarily restrain the external expression. These and other sensed evaluations of beauty, harmony, justice, worth, etc., clearly constitute something of a language, a means of expression for intercommunication between the autonomic centers and the seat of conscious consideration.

Writers on physiological psychology have pointed out the similarly sensed reports of "internal environment," of hunger, satiety, languor, exuberance, evaluations of the adequacy, depletion or exhaustion of supplies and reserves under control of the hypothalamus and endocrine system.

The term "*common sense*" describes the endowment "common" to all people of "sensing" inner evaluations if they will but "stop and think." This is the two stage process described also as organization of thought or as judgment. Fig. 11, page 206 endeavors to visualize it. First, conscious effort must be made to gather the pertinent data, presumably in some frontal lobe area. Second voluntary effort must stop, relax, withdraw. For some brief or lengthy period dependent upon the complexity of the operation, the evaluating drives and standards weigh the data, making relative choice and arrangement in the growth of the resultant idea. Third, the result is flashed back in the sensed language. At the conscious center we recognize that flash of an idea, we know its complex meaning, but it takes an appreciable effort to choose suitable learned language in which to express it.

The term "*conscience*" describes another use of the evaluating function and its autonomic language. In the long dark hours of the night a thalamic urge brings up a memory item for the review of a matter of conduct, behavior or decision. Voluntarily I may color the report as I will, but by the evaluation which flashes back I sense, I feel, I know that I like it or I am dubious of it, or do not like it at all. It may disturb me so much or so persistently as to result in ill health or unbalance, unless I take the proper steps to cleanse and restore.

The term "*inspiration*" describes the still mysterious and highest use of this spiritual means of intercommunication. Inspiration comes to those who pray, and probably to others whose need was not expressed in prayer. We feel, we sense, we know its meaning. Then, if we wish, we proceed to find learned words in which to express it.

"And God said unto Moses . . ."

The word "said" used to confuse me as it did many others. It implied what we now know to be short range sound wave transmission. It implied also the use of learned language. But while such implications are a natural enough result of our current wisdom, they have little to do with the case. The language of those days was in an early form of development. The control center at corpus striatum, was not confused by masses of learned theory from the side of the cerebral cortex. At any rate the force and worth of inspiration was recognized. The meaning sensed and interpreted by many ancient leaders has gone through repeated translation with remarkably little loss of credibility or clarity.

Our modern comprehension of the evaluating and the advisory facilities beyond our voluntary range is not easy. We have too long taken them for granted. We lazily tend to accept the more or less pertinent prefabricated solutions of subconscious learned routines. We have self-centered difficulties in maintaining the humble integrity essential to adequate initial presentation of the problem. We too easily ignore the sensed spiritual language of inner mental bodies.

THE SPIRITUAL LAW

With our background of scientific training we would undertake to correlate and codify the laws, the standards, the drives. We would undertake to tabulate and express each in neat, precise language. But as we approach the problem we are impressed that all of our education and a lifetime of experience have not been enough preparation. There are however, a number of observations which can be made.

The interdependence of all elements of the human system, and of all humanity and Infinity must be expressed. Einstein stated a portion of it in the scientific field in his law of relativity. We have followed in this study of the human structure, the complete correlation of the physical, mental and spiritual elements. The center of consciousness and self-determination at corpus striatum, would seem to possess that cherished liberty, complete freedom of decision and action. But no, we find that internally it must collaborate with or be torn between the temporal aspects of cerebral cortex on the one hand and the spiritual aspects of the thalamus on the other. Externally the individual is in the same relationship to God and mankind.

Correlative laws would seem to be our need to properly express the interdependence involved. The golden rule is such a law, and sums up all requirements in one. Much as we yearn for definitive codes we find that none can stand quite alone. Amendments and adjudications pile up and require revision. Much of the practice of civil law seems to be devoted to the finding and plugging of loopholes sought by those who would selfishly stay within the letter of the law but evade the spirit of it. Relativity seems essential to the overall interdependence. "Forgive us our debts, our selfish sins, *as we* forgive those who selfishly sin against us."

The unity of the laws must always be kept in sight. The laws of nature, of science and of behavior, God's law, are a coordinated whole. It is a distinct handicap to become so immersed in the study of any specialized branch as to lose perspective with respect to the others.

The duality of the laws or standards existing together in both the voluntary and the involuntary mental bodies is at the root of human equanimity or of maladjustment. The housekeeping problem is wise supervision of learned data and thinking routines. Text books, of course, may be intentionally warped or unintentionally in error. The major problem however, is more likely to be within the privacy of the mind. Imaginative reiterations which pamper the selfish sins, can and do establish neurotic behavioral attitudes in the storage areas of "learned wisdom". Thus the acquired standards of cerebral cortex may desirably reinforce or unfortunately oppose the instinctive spiritual standards of the thalamus. Essential indeed is the privilege of the self or soul to be able to turn to God for help when confused or troubled by differences between its two sources of wisdom.

The inviolability of the laws, the autonomic provision by which we will ultimately set up our own psychosomatic retribution for our sins, has been followed through in detail. The laws are not to be evaded, with impugnity even, or perhaps especially in the inner privacy of the mind. But again we are reminded of the merciful provision for our prayerful request of forgiveness, cleansing and rebuilding.

Voluntary stability or lack of it in compliance with the law is an interesting study. The youthful tendency to explore, to deviate, going to extremes and overcorrecting to the opposite extreme reminds us of scientific aspects of wave motions which may hit critical frequencies, resulting in destruction. The straight and narrow path, however, demands avoidance of deviation, the maintenance of a positive mental balance between cortex's behavioral practices and the forces of the thalamus.

Dynamic force in the law is embodied in the instinctive drives. It is not the usual negative restraint of the civil law but a positive drive to act, to *do*. The urge to learn (curiosity) and to teach, the urge to reproduce and to create, the urge to accomplish (initiative), the urge to love (affection and compassion) are all components of responsibility (versus irresponsibility or evasion of responsibility). "*Do* unto others as ye would that they should do unto you."

The guidance provided by the law is embodied in the evaluating standards. Fitness, right, truth, justice, worth, adequacy, beauty, humor, rhythm and more. We thrill to the worthy hero and boil inwardly over vicious wrong.

The many facets of the law make it adaptable to the endlessly changing problems of life. The scientist's law of survival of the fit implies dynamic responsibility and forceful relativity to environment. The same ancient law which Christ put first, emphasized an affectionate sense of forceful mutual responsibility three-ways, between God, mankind and the individual soul. Love God and love thy neighbor as thyself. Christ, master of parable, went on to illustrate in story after story this demand to fulfill our obligations to God and man in all ways, and always free of selfish or self-pampering aspects. The rewarding sense of satisfaction and peace of mind, positively does not presuppose external peace. We are given adrenal courage, muscular and neural strength and the autonomic standards and drives to meet our responsibilities with forgiveness but also forcefully as He did. Chivalry, sportsmanship, common decency and courageous right-living are all compounded from observation of the same law.

HUMAN ENGINEERING

As layman we lightly accept the obvious contributions of invisible electric power and energy to our age. Engineers among us pause to marvel at its more basic contributions;-to the form of matter in the atom, to the joining together of elements in the chemistry of all things, and finally to life and thought.

Reviewing our project in prayer before releasing it, I am sadly impressed with its shortcomings, especially in organization and correlation. The thread of the electrical contribution within us, is one of those which it seems essential to reexamine briefly in this closing.

We have traced our guidance of our lives to a group of mental bodies. The elements of these in turn are the brain cells, the little neurons, living things which make and use electric energy. Their tiny electrical charges become a thought in action or in storage. An electric ion pattern impressed upon a group of brain cells or set in motion among them spells out each item of our thinking.

Thus all of our wisdom, our experience, our behavioral patterns, and finally character itself, are a composite of tiny electrical charges. Our communications, our accomplishment, our nervous tensions, the forces which separate red corpuscles, the maintenance of life itself, all of these depend upon them. Death is essentially a de-energizing of the neural system and yet we know that such energy is indestructible. The mystery of the contuity remains. Is it this intangible and invisible unity, matured in the character of each of us, which maintains its identity after death?

The very real electrical functions of the neural mental bodies are difficult to test. Yet what we have been permitted to see impresses us with their interdependent relativity. It is a relativity in time of the tiny elements and larger groups which go to make up the whole being. It must go on to include the relativity of such beings with the visible and the less tangible forces with which they interact.

Our furtive look at that larger picture need not shake our individual confidence, our faith. Our spiritual gifts and our mental capacity to acquire wisdom and to utilize experience are adequate. The principles of mental maintenance and spiritual responsibility involved are at the root of all human relations.

EFFECTIVE THINKING

Spiritual psychology must go beyond the negative aspects of maladjusted mental procedures, and teach healthy, spiritual thinking processes. This suggests perhaps, the "right thinking" which was emphasized in early India and China as well as in Asia-minor and Greece. Modern science emphasizes intellectual integrity, lest biased thinking interfere with success. Norman Vincent Peale and others interested in current problems of mental stress emphasize positive thinking habits. And despite the differences of time and translation, Christ's sermon on the mount remains outstanding as a treatise on behavior, thinking habits and point of view.

How we think, the mechanical processes involved, may be further distinguished to assist our understanding of the problem. Let us re-examine the contributions of the mental bodies with respect to four successive levels of thinking:

1. Subconscious routines involving cerebral cortex alone.

2. Conscious manipulation of learned routines and data requiring the collaboration of corpus striatum and cerebral cortex.

3. Constructive thinking, going beyond previous accomplishment of the individual and requiring the selective evaluations of the thalamus in collaboration with the two bodies just mentioned.

4. Creative, inspired and other thinking in which the pineal receptor must participate as we seek attunement with God's infinite wisdom and strength.

Perhaps these four mental bodies collaborate more often than we suspect and we take the results for granted or consider them as lucky breaks. However, studious observation of their potentials should improve our position. The first two levels utilize voluntary system members only. The last two bring sensed spiritual elements into collaboration. The subordinate autonomic functions of hypothalamus furnish essential strength and assurance but would not appear to enter otherwise into thinking processes. The coordinating contributions of cerebellum are still not clear. Plenty of mystery still exists, but observation centered upon the currently apparent frame work should result in improved practices. Returning to the study of the four levels of thinking:

1. At the first or lowest level consider how often we use practiced physical and mental routines which are *subconsciously directed*. Momentary conscious attention must place the voluntary instruction to initiate the routine. Thereafter conscious self (at corpus striatum) may direct its attention elsewhere, leaving the manipulation of muscles or the mental routine to practiced motor neurons of cerebral cortex.

Such voluntary automatic skill does permit us to carry on more than one activity at a time as was shown in Chapter X. It can save us both time and mental effort. It can also get us into trouble or injury. Absent-mindedness, getting into a rut, accidents and a variety of mistakes result from unwise use of learned routines without the supervision of conscious attention. Psychosomatic maladjustments in which unwise or mistaken habits of thinking and mental sins disrupt autonomic control of the physical system are similar routine activities. Such neuroses, complexes or mental diseases are difficult to unlearn or to replace with sound habits of thinking. The preventive measures of sound education and the maintenance measures of mental or spiritual hygiene in prayer and church are essential.

2. The second level of thinking is *the conscious manipulation* of *learned wisdom*. It involves the use of the voluntary system only. Here conscious attention (at corpus striatum) selects and continues to supervise the learned routine (cerebral cortex), checking as may be required to eliminate mistakes. This is the resultant of purely mechanistic education and there are some who never seem to get beyond it.

The limitation appears to have been in the "all is learned" tenets, and egotistical efforts to ignore the autonomic or spiritual values. This is not to understimate the worth of (accurate) learned wisdom. It is the construction material essential to human accomplishment. Applied under conscious attention it answers most problems. But when the young graduate meets the first problems which are beyond the pre-fabricated range of the text, or is caught in conflicting theories, he will need the additional autonomic facilities of initiative, judgement and common sense:

3. The third level, *constructive thinking* beyond the scope of prefabricated conclusions, requires the use of another mental body. In self-preservation, men who must think, learn how to use the drives which constitute initiative and the selective evaluating standards of judgement, common sense and conscience. Such things should come naturally, and do seem to come easier to men not subjected to the complex benefits of higher education. Whether it has been the ma-terialistic influence, or the stress and the confusion of much learning is hard to say. With our better understanding of the principles of the mental system however, we should be able to acquire learned wisdom to equip cerebral cortex and still keep its limitations in proper per-spective.

The drives and standards are indeed a gift for they come to us gratis and those who recognize and use them are fortunate. They are subject to variations in proportion as there are variations in physique. Just as the (involuntary) facial and vocal expressions of interest and of evaluation may be suppressed, so also the internal use of the drives and standards may be voluntarily repressed or ignored. Witness harassed parental insistence that a child repress its curiosity, its in-stinctive urge to learn. That same drive is responsible for our en-thusiasm for research.

The drives would actually precede or initiate a thought train, whereas the weighing and comparing evaluations of judgment must follow after gathering and interpreting stages. "Snap judgment" is a term describing the hasty voluntary selection of some learned solution without taking the time needed for the evaluating process.

In voluntarily using the third level of thinking we must first gather the data to be organized, then relax conscious effort to permit evalua-tion (by thalamic neurons), then express in words the idea flashed back to consciousness. Aside from the process itself, the spiritual psychologist is also interested that the voluntary interpretation shall not be warped by a biased point of view. In the instinctive evaluation the urge to self-preservation should be balanced by a sense of respon-sibility and an urge to serve. In the voluntary interpretation, if habits of thinking have been carelessly maintained, such selfish and self-centered routines as hate, greed, worry, envy or lust which religion censures, may warp the interpretation. On the other hand, if unselfish collaboration has been well learned, and the point of view is that of faith in God's system and in the good faith of good men, the thalamic endowment may be used with maximum effectiveness.

4. The fourth level, *inspired and creative thinking*, goes beyond the internal gifts of the constructive level to enable Divine guidance and participation in God's kingdom on earth. The services of the fourth mental body, the pineal receptor organ must be added to the other three to provide the external reception.

Adequate scientific background for intermediate wave reception and sensed response has been traced and compared with our other wave reception services. Our practice in the use of this facility may still seem woefully inadequate. Spiritual intercommunication of individual minds or souls with others and with the infinite unity of God, is a privilege experienced at times by most men and at will by some. The qualification of preparation, equanimity, a balanced conformity of temporal and spiritual forces upon the individual self or soul, contributes. A community of interest, an affectionate sense of mutual responsibility as Christ envisioned it in *love*, provides the necessary attunement between sender and receiver. Thoughtful preparation, in good faith, preparation which is honest, unselfish and humble, is an obvious requirement to answered prayer. Patience in gaining attention and attentive consideration of the sensed response are essentials of all inter-communication.

The value of prayer as a daily exercise in the control of imagination for the maintenance of a healthy mind, as well as a means of asking special guidance, has been emphasized.

Truly we may make for ourselves, a hell of this life on earth. Or equally and quite literally we may achieve a heavenly peace of mind if we fulfill our sensed obligations and maintain our attunement with God's will and compassion.

*   *   *

The psychology of adjustment must deal with self's responsible control of its subordinate (1st level) learned routines in conformity with its autonomic (3rd level) evaluating standards. Spiritual psychology must contribute an essential sense of proportion with an understanding of the law and the force of psychosomatic retribution. It must add the reassuring appreciation of the spiritual endowments and privileges which are inherent to every soul. These spiritual values must not be lost sight of, either in taking them for granted or in the confusion of much learning.

Spiritual psychology is not in any sense to take the place of religion. It is merely an educational aid, a marshalling of our current scientific material to help us understand the reality of the spiritual contributions to balanced thinking, the basic truths which we sense and which religion teaches.

As each of us steps back from our preoccupations to clarify our perspective, we may sense towering above us, a transcendent majesty. It is a solid unity, a relativity of all things, an infinite coordination of nature, of science and the humanities, of the physical, mental and spiritual values. It is the unity and infinity of God's everpresent kingdom, in which all minds are privileged to correlate, if they will.